Devoted to God

Devoted to God

Blueprints for Sanctification

Sinclair B. Ferguson

THE BANNER OF TRUTH TRUST

THE BANNER OF TRUTH TRUST
3 Murrayfield Road, Edinburgh EH12 6EL, UK
P.O. Box 621, Carlisle, PA 17013, USA

*

© Sinclair B. Ferguson 2016
Reprinted 2016
Reprinted 2017

ISBN:
Print: 978 1 84871 690 2
EPUB: 978 1 84871 691 9
Kindle: 978 1 84871 692 6

*

Typeset in 11/15 pt Adobe Garamond Pro at
The Banner of Truth Trust, Edinburgh

Printed in the USA by
Versa Press, Inc.,
East Peoria, IL

To

David and Adèle Ellis

Servants of Christ
Devoted to God

Contents

Introduction

T here are already books on this subject. Why add to their number? Is there anything different about *Devoted to God*? It contains no novel teaching. But it sets out with a distinctive goal: to provide a manual of biblical teaching on holiness developed on the basis of extended expositions of foundational passages in the New Testament. By the end of the book we will have worked our way together through some of the most important biblical blueprints for building an entire life of holiness.

There is a wise adage that 'it takes the whole Bible to make a whole Christian'. That, of course, is true. For another way of describing sanctification might be: learning how 'to glorify God and enjoy him for ever', to use the famous words from the Shorter Catechism. Spiritual growth certainly requires everything between Genesis 1:1 and Revelation 22:21.

It takes a long time to read the Bible, longer to know it well, and even a lifetime is too short to master it. But what if we were to take one of the central themes of the Bible—like holiness, or sanctification—select important passages on that theme, and then try to gain some mastery of them? Of course we would not cover every conceivable passage; we would not learn everything we need to know. But we would have built a foundation that otherwise might not have been there. We would be able to build on it securely. Or, to change the metaphor, we would have attached some Velcro®[1]

[1] Velcro® is a registered trade mark of Velcro Industries and refers to the fabric hook and loop fastener invented by the Swiss engineer George de Mestral and first patented in 1955.

strips into our minds that would help us to organize all of our future learning and enable it to stick in the proper places.

Or, think of it another way. If a group of young Christians were to ask you to do a Bible study with them on the New Testament's teaching on sanctification and holiness—would five or six passages immediately come to mind almost without you having to stop to think? You will probably find them in this book.

If there is a specific design and goal then in *Devoted to God* it is to fasten into our minds and hearts a number of these central passages that will create the possibility for exponential growth in our understanding of what sanctification is and how it is nurtured. Think of it as a box of Velcro® strips, each fashioned out of a single passage in the New Testament central to the subject.

In the main these passages focus on teaching that is given in the indicative rather than the imperative mood—passages that *describe* sanctification rather than passages that *command* it. This is not so much a 'how to' book as it is a 'how God does it' one. It is not dominated by techniques for growing in holiness.

In fact the New Testament has—at least compared with contemporary expectations—very little to say directly about the 'how-to' of the Christian life, although it is anything but lacking in the 'what to'. It is far more concerned with shaping our understanding, so that a new life style emerges organically, than it is with techniques—although, as we shall see, it certainly includes instruction on the way to a holy life, motives for living it, and, yes, indications of how this can be accomplished.

So the pages that follow invite you to give attention to the content and shape of some key passages in the New Testament. These passages are quoted throughout the book, but to facilitate reflection on them, they will be found in Appendix 5. They are not all equally easy to understand or to put into practice. But they have been selected out of the conviction that will be repeated again and again, that transformed lives require renewed minds—a clear understanding of what the gospel is and how it works leads in turn to the development of new affections and a new lifestyle. Thus each chapter focuses on one of these passages.

I would like to encourage readers to give close attention to these passages, meditating on them, and even memorising their contents. Since all Scripture is 'profitable for teaching, for reproof, for correction, and for training in righteousness'[1] we should expect illumination, challenge, and restoration along the way. But perhaps the most important fruit of our journey will be the cumulative effect of gaining a working knowledge of these central passages.

This approach reflects another conviction. We need to be able to retrace the biblical foundations of holiness for ourselves. Otherwise, to one degree or another, we end up creating our own personal brand of Christianity. We will then tend to fall into the trap of being guided by our own thoughts and feelings when what we most need is to be anchored to the basic foundation stones that Scripture sets in place.

A visitor to the contemporary church materialising from an earlier century would probably be struck by how enormously privileged we are. Many of us receive education until we are in our early twenties, while most of them left school by the time they were young teenagers. We each own a Bible (some with helpful study notes built in); if they owned a Bible it was in small print Elizabethan English. We carry entire theological libraries on our eReaders, have access to vast resources via the worldwide web; they perhaps owned one or two Christian books. And yet, if the truth be told, what might surprise them most is that their familiarity with God's word, their knowledge of the key passages in the New Testament, the degree to which they had thought long and hard about what Scripture means and how it applies, would leave us feeling

[1] 2 Timothy 3:16.

ashamed. They would be surprised how hard we find meditation on the word of God, how little we actually know of it and how poorly we have nourished ourselves from it. They might marvel at the extent to which evangelical Christianity has been infected by our age of narcissism and how subjective so many Christians have become. They might notice that many modern Christians are often too interested in the development of the self but little interested in the development of their understanding of the triune God—that we are, to use Luther's expressive Latin phrasing, *incurvatus in se*, turned in upon ourselves.

Scripture can deliver us from this, and heal the spiritual curvature of the spine from which we suffer and enable us to walk tall in the world for God's glory. If only we would learn as Christians to think more biblically, surely our lives, our churches, our work and our witness would be moved on to a new plane; and a new quality of Christian life and fellowship would become evident. We are keenly aware, surely, that while we share Paul's conviction that the gospel is God's saving power,[1] as individuals, families and churches we give all too little evidence to the world that we are being 'saved', that is to say, that we are in the process of being sanctified and made more like Christ.

So *Devoted to God* is a manual written to encourage those who read it to 'strive … for the holiness without which no one will see the Lord'.[2]

Writing is a solitary discipline. But no author is 'an island, entire of itself'. Once again therefore I would like to express my gratitude to the publishers and their staff for their encouragement and for their commitment to these pages. And behind the scenes, my wife Dorothy and our extended family in different ways have provided the 'back-story' within which I have learned what I know about

[1] Romans 1:16-17.
[2] Hebrews 13:14.

sanctification—even if it is all too little. I am grateful to them and for them, more than words can express.

I pray that reading these pages will do spiritual good; working on them has done me good and I am grateful for that blessing.

SINCLAIR B. FERGUSON

June 2016

I

The Ground-Plan

The very mention of the word 'sanctification' can send a shiver down the spine; its Anglo-Saxon equivalent, 'holiness' even more so. After all, most of us feel we have failed frequently and badly just here.

But we need to begin further back than ourselves and our failures by asking two questions. The first: What does 'holiness' mean? And the second: What hope is there for me to grow in holiness and to make progress in sanctification?

What's in a word?

Probably the most common explanation of the term 'holiness' is that to be 'holy' means 'to be separate from', 'to be cut off from', 'to be placed at a distance from'. And so we often say that God's holiness means that he is separate from sin and therefore separate from us.

There is a good measure of truth in this. But in my own view it starts from the wrong place. It describes the Creator's attribute of holiness from the viewpoint of the creature; it describes his purity from the standpoint of the sinner. And ultimately that is to do our thinking the wrong way round. It may give us a partial perspective but not the entire picture.

Why is that true?

Any description we give of what God is like in himself—in technical terms, describing his 'attributes'—must meet a simple test. For anything to be true of God as he is in himself it must be true quite apart from his work of creation, quite apart from our existence or even the existence of angels, archangels, cherubim and seraphim. It must be true of God simply as he always existed as the eternal Trinity. But in that case, the Father, the Son, and the Holy Spirit had no 'attribute' that involved separation.

This is not to say that God the Trinity cannot be described as 'holy'. But it is to say that holiness cannot be *defined* as separation. Yes, there were personal *distinctions* within the fellowship of the Trinity (Father, Son, Holy Spirit), but there was no *separation*, no *being placed at a distance from* each other. In fact it would be nearer the mark to say that the reverse was true.

What then is God's holiness? What do we mean when we say '*Holy* Father' and '*Holy* Son' and '*Holy* Spirit' and '*Holy* Trinity'?

We mean the perfectly pure devotion of each of these three persons to the other two. We mean the attribute in the Trinity that corresponds to the ancient words that describe marriage: 'forsaking all other, and cleaving only unto thee'—absolute, permanent, exclusive, pure, irreversible, and fully expressed *devotion*.

When we grasp that this is true in the Trinitarian fellowship of God's being it will help us understand several things about holiness.

First, that it is not something mechanical, or formal, or legal, or even performance-based. It is personal. In a sense 'holiness' is a way of describing love. To say that 'God is love' and that 'God is holy' ultimately is to point to the same reality. Holiness is the intensity of the love that flows within the very being of God, among and between each of the three persons of the Father, Son, and Holy Spirit. It is the sheer intensity of that devotion that causes seraphim (whose holiness is perfect but creaturely) to veil their faces.[1]

---

[1] Isaiah 6:2.

Ministers of the gospel often have the privilege of occupying 'the best seat in the house'. You see the whole congregation when you preach (it is interesting to discover that people sitting listening to you do not always realise that if they can see you then you can see them!). You stand looking out on the people you love when the church gathers round the Lord's table.

You also get a better view of a couple taking their marriage vows than any of the groomsmen or bridesmaids or even the parents do. You stand only a few feet away. You orchestrate the event close up and personal. And then the moment comes (even in traditions where it never used to!) when you say: 'You may now kiss your bride.' People always love that moment. Personally, at this point in the service, I usually experience a deep instinct to look down, to unfocus my gaze. This is a moment for two people who love each other. It is not the time for an outsider to their unique relationship to be watching. Yes, perhaps at a distance. But not from up close and personal; you do not belong there.

Perhaps the seraphim that surrounded the throne in Isaiah's vision of God in his majestic holiness felt the same way. To gaze on the sheer intensity of this flow of triune holy love would be to endanger themselves. They must distance themselves, cover their faces, and be separate. In that sense holiness does involve separation; but the separation is not in God the Trinity so much as in the sense his creatures have of what his holiness means.

We have other analogies in our human experience. In western society there remains a kind of unwritten etiquette that the act of a woman setting her lingering gaze on the eyes of a man and vice versa should be reserved for a relationship and commitment of the deepest intimacy. To attempt it outside of the bond of devotion that makes it appropriate is to sully it. If we may stretch the analogy: the Father, the Son, and the Holy Spirit may 'lock eyes' with one another, and do so eternally. We however cannot bear that intensity. We can only see the face of God in a way that is accommodated to our creaturely capacity—in the man Christ Jesus.

If this is what holiness means *in God*, then *in us* it must also be a corresponding deeply personal, intense, loving *devotion* to him—a belonging to him that is irreversible, unconditional, without any reserve on our part. Simply put, it means being entirely his, so that all we do and possess are his. We come to think all of our thoughts and build our lives on this foundation.

If we ask, 'But how can this definition of "holiness" apply to inanimate objects, such as the liturgical vessels of the Old Testament?' the answer is at hand. They too were wholly devoted to the Lord; they were to be used for no other purpose because they existed for no other end than to be employed in his service for his glory. What is true of the 'saint' is true of everything the saints use.

To be holy, to be sanctified, therefore, to be a 'saint', is in simple terms to be *devoted to God*.

Can this be true for us? Robert Murray M'Cheyne often prayed 'Lord make me as holy as a pardoned sinner can be made.'[1] If we are Christians then we too will have shared such desires. But we have failed so often. And the more clearly we understand what holiness is the more keenly we feel that failure. Is there any hope for us?

Can I hope for holiness?

When it comes to failure in sanctification, Simon Peter is probably the disciple with whom most of us can readily identify. John and Paul seem stable by comparison. Peter seemed to stumble more frequently, more seriously, and also more publicly—or at least we know more about his ups and downs.

Like Peter, most of us begin the Christian life with great hopes. We will be out-and-out for Christ; nothing will ever be allowed to dilute

[1] Andrew A. Bonar, *Memoirs and Remains of R. M. M'Cheyne* (1842; enlarged 1892; repr. Edinburgh: Banner of Truth Trust, 2009), 159.

our faith and commitment. But then, like Peter, we falter; sometimes we botch things up. Instead of being wholly yielded to Christ we discover instead that a stubborn and sinful resistance movement retains a foothold in our lives.

Again, we thought we would become fruitful, if not exactly famous, evangelists. But then our failures began. We had a God-given opportunity to say something about the Lord Jesus Christ but we felt it would be too embarrassing if we spoke. It wasn't quite as bad as Simon Peter. We didn't curse; we didn't actually *deny* that we belonged to Jesus. But when we escaped from the situation, we knew his eyes were watching us just as certainly as they watched Simon Peter the night he denied him. We may not have gone out and wept bitterly but we knew we had let Christ down badly.[1] And, at least momentarily, we shivered to remember his words: 'Whoever is ashamed of me and of my words ... of him will the Son of Man also be ashamed when he comes in the glory of his Father with the holy angels.'[2] And perhaps we wondered why he specifically mentioned being ashamed of his *words*.

Yet Peter, with whose failures we so easily identify, was restored. More than that, he made progress. Even more than that, he became an outstanding leader in the early Christian church. If anyone in the New Testament can teach us that even we can be devoted to God and make progress in holiness despite our past failings, it is Simon Peter.

Peter learned the hard way. This much is obvious from the words with which his first letter begins:

> Peter, an apostle of Jesus Christ, To those who are elect exiles of the dispersion in Pontus, Galatia, Cappadocia, Asia, and Bithynia, according to the foreknowledge of God the Father, in the sanctification of the Spirit, for obedience to Jesus Christ and for sprinkling with his blood: May grace and peace be multiplied to you.
>
> Blessed be the God and Father of our Lord Jesus Christ! According to his great mercy, he has caused us to be born again to a living hope

[1] Luke 22:54-62.
[2] Mark 8:38.

through the resurrection of Jesus Christ from the dead, to an inheritance that is imperishable, undefiled, and unfading, kept in heaven for you, who by God's power are being guarded through faith for a salvation ready to be revealed in the last time. In this you rejoice, though now for a little while, if necessary, you have been grieved by various trials, so that the tested genuineness of your faith—more precious than gold that perishes though it is tested by fire—may be found to result in praise and glory and honour at the revelation of Jesus Christ.[1]

What is Peter saying?

Who am I, and what am I for?

When Peter wrote this first letter to churches located in modern-day Turkey, his readers were facing antagonism and persecution.

How would you begin such a letter? Perhaps with words of sympathy, saying how sorry you were that things had become so difficult? Not Simon Peter. He began first by reminding them of their identity in Christ and then by breaking into a doxology as he reflected on its implications.

Peter had perhaps learned from experience that when faced with challenges the most important issue is not the size of the challenge but the identity and character of the person who is facing them. He was all too keenly aware that he had stood only yards away from Jesus as he was facing crucifixion within a matter of hours, when he himself crumbled disastrously under the questioning of a young servant girl. Without explaining his approach to his first readers he addresses them in terms of their new identity in Christ. They are:

Elect exiles of the dispersion in Pontus, Galatia, Cappadocia, Asia, and Bithynia, according to the foreknowledge of God the Father, in the sanctification of the Spirit, for obedience to Jesus Christ and for sprinkling with his blood.[2]

[1] 1 Peter 1:1-7.
[2] 1 Peter 1:1-2.

They have been chosen (elect) through the love God had set upon them (foreknowledge) in order to be reserved by the Spirit (sanctification) with a view to their devotion to Christ (obedience) and the enjoyment of a life of covenant fellowship with him (sprinkled with his blood).

Peter's subliminal logic is: As you face life with all its trials do not lose sight of who you are and what you are for. Be clear about this and you will make progress. Forget this and you will flounder and fall. The reason? *Knowing (i) whose you are, (ii) who you are, and (iii) what you are for, settles basic issues about how you live.*

In the course of these pages we will see this principle expressed and applied in a variety of ways. It is foundational.

There is a great interchange in the Old Testament narrative of Moses' meeting with God at the burning bush. During his encounter with the Lord two questions arise: (1) in response to the Lord's words to him Moses asks, 'Who are you?' (2) In response to the Lord's calling he asks 'Who am I?' Everything that follows is dependent on the answers to these questions.

In our lives too, albeit in the lower case letters in which our biographies are usually written, the same questions are paramount. I need to be clear about who and whose I am, and what I am for in Christ. And Peter is teaching us how to answer them here. If you are a believer you are someone who has been chosen in grace, loved by the Father before you were born, and in your experience sanctified by the Spirit in order that you might become obedient to the Saviour who shed his blood to bring you into covenant fellowship with God. Using a completely different vocabulary Peter says to believers in Turkey exactly what Paul said to believers in Corinth: You are not your own; you have been bought with a price—the sacrifice of Christ; you are his, so live for his glory because it is for this that you have been purchased.[1]

[1] 1 Corinthians 6:1-20.

The biblical teaching on holiness, of life devoted to God, is simply an extended exposition of this basic statement.

But then, following this description of our identity Peter breaks into a doxology: 'Blessed be the God and Father of our Lord Jesus Christ!'[1] What is the connection? It is that in Christ God has made all the provision that is necessary to develop our awareness of our new identity and to turn our destiny into a reality. Peter the stumbler had become Peter the encourager.

Encouragement

Peter's doxology, although by definition God-directed ('Blessed be the God and Father of our Lord Jesus Christ') encapsulates the reasons why we bless him. In that sense it opens out into a whole series of reasons for these young Christians to be encouraged. Their lives were built on an overflow of God's grace. They were the recipients of an entire catalogue of divine blessings. They had many more reasons to be encouraged than to be discouraged. So do we.

The first thing Peter wanted to clarify was the secure foundations on which the Christian life is built. What he says is so rich and health-giving it merits a book all of its own. As Martin Luther once wrote, this little letter contains virtually everything a Christian needs to know. The German reformer had a fine line in hyperbole. Nevertheless, Peter's opening words constitute one of the New Testament's most comprehensive descriptions of what it means to be a Christian. Here he lays the basic foundations for wholehearted devotion to God.

Why is holiness in this sense such an important topic?

(1) It is obviously important as a Christian *doctrine* because so much of the New Testament is taken up with expounding it.

(2) It is also important as an aspect of Christian *living* because the New Testament emphasizes that salvation is impossible without

[1] 1 Peter 1:3.

it. Thus the anonymous author of Hebrews urges us to 'Strive ... for the holiness *without which no one will see the Lord*.'[1]

The necessity of a new life style

Justification (God counting us as righteous in Christ) and sanctification (God making us more and more righteous in ourselves) should never be confused. Nor is the former dependent on the latter.

We are justified in Christ by grace through faith. We are not justified on the basis of what we have accomplished, either before or after we become Christians. Nor are we justified on the basis of anything that has been done in us—not even what God has done in us by his grace. By contrast sanctification is something that is worked into us. We actually become holy.

Despite these important distinctions, the New Testament also stresses that justification and sanctification are both ours through faith in Jesus Christ. It is therefore not possible to be justified without being sanctified and then growing in holiness. This is why Hebrews says sanctification is essential, since without it none of us will ever see the Lord. In order to experience final salvation, sanctification is as necessary as justification.

Why is this? Simply because there is no justification without sanctification. Both are given in Christ—our new status is always accompanied by our new condition. Justification *never* takes place apart from regeneration which is the inauguration of sanctification. Put differently, if Christ is not Lord of our lives, sanctifying us, how can he have become our Saviour? Indeed unless we are *actually being saved* Christ has not become our Saviour. If he is our Saviour, the evidence of that will be—*being saved*; saved from the old life style into a new life style.

Here then is one of the most important basic principles of the gospel. We are not justified on the basis of our sanctification; yet

[1] Hebrews 12:14.

justification never takes place without sanctification beginning. As John Calvin so well put it, they belong together because Christ was given to us for both. To separate them would be 'to rend Him asunder'.[1]

The dying thief—justification without sanctification?

But what about the dying thief—the criminal who turned to Jesus at the end of his life and asked for a place in his kingdom?[2] Surely he is the illustration *par excellence* of a man who was justified without being sanctified? He had no time to be sanctified.

In fact, this anonymous penitent turns out to be a powerful proof of the principle: no sanctification, no justification—no changed life, no changed status. For his justification was demonstrated by an immediate transformation. How so? He confessed his own sinfulness; he recognized Jesus' lordship; his attitude towards him changed from despising him to respecting him; he prayed. Even more than this, he defended Jesus and rebuked his companion for the vitriol he heaped on his new-found Master. In the last moments of his life he demonstrated that he was a justified believer who was already in the process of being sanctified and prepared to see the Lord in Paradise. He was not justified on the basis of his sanctification but on the basis of God's free grace. But neither was he justified without being sanctified.

But what exactly do we mean by 'sanctification'?

---

[1] John Calvin, *Epistle of Paul to the Romans and to the Thessalonians*, tr. Ross Mackenzie, ed. D. W. and T. F. Torrance (Edinburgh: Oliver and Boyd, 1960), 167.
[2] Luke 23:39-43.

The meaning of sanctification

In both the Old and New Testaments, the language used for sanctification contains the idea of being devoted to a special purpose, 'withheld from ordinary use, treated with special care'.[1]

As you walk through a department store you may notice a piece of furniture with a one-word sign on it, 'Reserved'. You may see a similar sign on a table in a restaurant. Even if the piece of furniture is the only one left of the item you need, you may not have it! Even if there are no other tables free in the restaurant you may not sit at the table marked 'Reserved'. They are being kept for someone else (however frustrating that is for you). This is what 'sanctification' means: God has put his 'reserved' sign on something—temple vessels for example—or on someone who thereby becomes a 'saint', a person reserved for the Lord. He marks us out for his personal possession and use. We belong to him—and to nobody else, not even to ourselves. We become devoted to God.

It is sometimes suggested that there may be another idea hidden in the Bible's concept of holiness—that of brightness and shining, of intensity of light.

Holiness and light are often associated together in Scripture. Whatever is holy communicates a sense of light that shows up our darkness; it creates a sense of awe and unapproachability. Isaiah noticed this in his vision of the God of Holy-Love—the perfectly holy creatures who praised God for his holiness 'veiled their faces' as they did so.[2] There was a blinding brightness about God's *uncreated* holiness that was simply too intense for *created* holiness to gaze upon or bear.

Of course, whatever the precise nuance of meaning of 'holy', it involves not only belonging to God but being influenced by

---

[1] *Dictionary of Old Testament Theology and Exegesis*, ed. W. A. VanGemeren (Grand Rapids: Zondervan, 1977), 3, 877.
[2] Isaiah 6:2-3.

him—being claimed by him in order to be possessed by him and to become increasingly like him. In that sense holiness involves being separated off from whatever is sinful. The effect of this will be a new shining in our lives, a new brightness beginning to emerge. We may not detect it in ourselves; but we can observe it in others, and trust that the same is true of ourselves—as expressions of God's grace and glory begin to appear in our lives.

This is why in the Old Testament holiness and beauty belong together.

Holiness is often seen as a rather metallic idea, perhaps tinged with hypocrisy or a 'holier than thou' atmosphere. By contrast Scripture teaches that holiness puts back into our lives the attractiveness of personal character for which humans were originally created but which has been so badly marred. Thus the Bible speaks about the *beauty* of holiness.[1] Since there is an infinite beauty in God,[2] when he makes us his personal possession reflections of the beauty of his holiness begin to appear in us too.

If this is what holiness means, then sanctification—making someone holy—is the work which God does:

(1) To separate his people from what they were by nature in sin, and

(2) To transform them so that their lives reflect his own being and character.

This is why sanctification is so central to the New Testament's teaching. God is restoring in our lives the image which we were created to reflect.[3]

Knowing this produces in us both awe and praise.

There is *awe* because this work of God is so amazing but also so arduous. If you ever wonder why the Christian life turns out to be so

[1] 1 Chronicles 16:29; 2 Chronicles 20:21; Psalm 29:2; 96:9; 110:3.
[2] Psalm 27:4; 90:17.
[3] Genesis 1:26-28; Ephesians 4:24; Colossians 3:9-10.

hard, and why many Christians find themselves saying, 'I thought I had difficulties before I became a Christian, but I seem to have even more since becoming one', then here is the answer: God is doing nothing less than changing you from what you were to what he means you to be—making you more and more like himself.

But there is also *praise*. For if God is changing you in this way to reflect the purity and glory of his Son, Jesus Christ, then surely you will want to sing his praises for such a privilege!

Peter's teaching

All this is involved in what Peter says about the basic foundations of sanctification.[1] That is why he begins his letter with such enthusiastic words: 'Blessed be the God and Father of our Lord Jesus Christ!'[2] You can sense his personality bursting through his words and hear him breaking into praise, so amazed and grateful is he for the work of God in his life.

We sometimes fear that the New Testament's teaching on being devoted to God, and on growing in holiness, will place unbearable demands on us. Remember therefore that it is to the apostle Peter we are listening here. Few disciples of the Lord Jesus can have made more of a public mess of their early Christian life than he did. But the very fact that it is *this disciple* writing about holiness ought to reassure us that Christ does not command what he will not provide. There is no need to be permanently disabled by past failure or paralysed by the fear that we are doomed to repeat it.

In summary

Sanctification, then, is God setting us apart for himself. Thus as saints we have already been sanctified by him.[3] Then he gradually

---

[1] Holiness is a basic theme throughout the letter. See 1 Peter 1:15, 16; 2:5, 9; 3:5.

[2] 1 Peter 1:3.

[3] Cf. John Murray, *Collected Writings* (Edinburgh: Banner of Truth Trust, 1976), 2, 277-278: 'It is a fact too frequently overlooked that in the New Testament the

transforms us so that we begin to reflect his attributes and attractiveness. Jesus Christ's life begins to be mirrored in our lives and personalities. The Peter of 'First Peter' is still very obviously the Peter of Caesarea Philippi, and of the Mount of Transfiguration, and of the Garden of Gethsemane, and of the courtyard of the high priest's house, as well as of the dinner tables of Antioch—all scenes of his failure.[1] Yet he is not what he once was. He has grown. Grace has begun to show that it is reigning in his life.[2]

Here, against that background, the apostle's words to his Christian friends provide them with the foundations on which a life devoted to God can be built and sustained.

Foundation 1: The purpose of God the Trinity

The first foundational principle is this: Our sanctification is the purpose of God the Trinity.

Peter addresses Christians as '*elect* exiles ... in sanctification of the Spirit'.[3] He develops this further by explaining that this status of being 'elect' is rooted in the Father's foreknowledge of them.

God's foreknowledge of us is the love which he set upon us long before we responded to him. He chose us in love. In this sense Peter states that Jesus himself was 'foreknown'.[4] Here Peter and Paul are at one in stressing that holiness finds its ultimate source in God's loving election.[5]

Peter does not mean that God chose to save those he knew would want to be saved. For one thing that would make our

---

most characteristic terms that refer to sanctification are used, not of a process, but of a once-for-all definitive act.'

[1] For these moments of failure on Peter's part: Matthew 16:21-23; 17:1-5; 26:30-35, 36-46, 56b; 69-75; Galatians 2:11-14.

[2] Romans 5:21.

[3] 1 Peter 1:1-2.

[4] Acts 2:23. Cf. 1 Peter 1:20.

[5] See Ephesians 1:4; 2 Thessalonians 2:13-14.

salvation dependent on something in us, when Scripture tells us there is nothing in us that would constrain God's choice. Such a view also operates with an inadequate understanding of sin. We are spiritually bankrupt; we are also God's enemies. There is nothing in us that could qualify us for the loving election of the Father. We are 'by nature children of wrath, like the rest of mankind'.[1] Neither our good living nor our ability to make good choices causes divine election. They are the result of it. In fact, says Peter, this divine choice had in view the sanctifying work of the Spirit which in turn would lead to our obedience to Jesus Christ. God chose us *in order to* sanctify us.[2] Divine election is the foundation of sanctification— not the other way round. Everything depends upon God taking the initiative.

Notice the way Peter spells this out. The Father, the Son, and the Holy Spirit are all involved in transforming us ('elect … according to the foreknowledge of *God the Father*, in sanctification of *the Spirit*, for obedience to *Jesus Christ*'.[3] It is not only that God takes the initiative, but that he specifically does so as God *the Trinity.*

It is staggering to think that these are the words of a Galilean fisherman—even if, as seems likely, he had the ability to run a prosperous family business. Peter has discovered that his Christian experience, beginning in a remote seaside town in Galilee—and indeed every Christian's experience, wherever it begins—has its ultimate origin before the dawn of time in the heart, mind, and heavenly love and purpose of God the Father, the Son, and the Holy Spirit!

---

[1] Ephesians 2:3.

[2] This of course is the reason why when rightly understood the doctrine of election *never* leads to moral carelessness, although that accusation has often been levelled against it. The logic of election is not: 'I have been chosen for salvation and so I can live any way I please' but 'I have been chosen for salvation and therefore I will live in a way that pleases God'.

[3] 1 Peter 1:2.

Once we notice the reference to the Father, Son, and Holy Spirit here, it alerts us to the way similar references to their joint activity are frequently to be found in the New Testament.[1]

This discovery may astonish us. For today there is a tendency to think that the Trinity is no more than an obscure, almost speculative Christian doctrine, of little practical importance in the Christian life. But see its significance here and we will begin to notice that throughout the New Testament every aspect of our salvation, not least our transformation into the likeness of Christ, is explained in terms of what the Father, the Son and the Holy Spirit all do, always in harmony and unity with one another.

The Father, Son and Spirit are always working. Occasionally one person is mentioned, often two, sometimes all three. The New Testament is all about the activity of our Triune Lord. The entire being of God in the fellowship of the Trinity—in what we might think of as an inner-Trinitarian planning meeting—had this great purpose in mind for us: chosen by the Father, we will be saved by the Son, and sanctified by the Spirit. God set his heart on accomplishing all this for us even before the foundation of the world. He chose us; we experience sprinkling by [Jesus'] blood to cleanse our consciences from the guilt of sin. The Holy Spirit comes to sanctify us. The Triune God has devoted himself to bringing about our devotion to him. This is, as it were, priority number two on the divine agenda. It is superseded only by God's over-arching goal of bringing glory to himself and simultaneously giving enjoyment to us.

Priorities

This biblical perspective gives rise to a challenging implication. If sanctification is not my priority then it should not surprise me if I find my Christian life being dogged with frustration. For in this case I am seeking, consciously or not, to withstand the eternal purposes

[1] See Appendix 1.

16

of God. I am missing out on the central privileges of the Christian life, namely glorifying and enjoying him.[1]

So we need to settle the issue of our priorities. If God has committed himself to changing our lives, to sanctifying us, then wisdom—not to mention amazed gratitude—dictates that we should be committed to that too. Otherwise God's will and my will are in competition with each other. But if by God's grace I commit myself to his purposes, Peter's teaching provides me with all the encouragement I need: the whole Trinity co-operates in bringing me to the goal. The Father, the Son and the Spirit co-operate *with one another*, but they also co-operate *with me* in order to make me more like Christ.

We do not know exactly how or when all this became clear to Simon Peter. Slowly but surely he realised the importance of what Jesus had taught him, perhaps especially in his farewell discourse,[2] and then in the six-week seminar between his resurrection and ascension.[3] Now Peter wanted others to know that in the struggle for holiness in an unholy world, God is with us; God is behind us; God is not only at our side but on our side. Whatever opposition there may be from the world, the flesh, and the devil, God the Trinity has determined to pour his energy into making us like Jesus Christ. It is his settled purpose. In this sense T. S. Eliot was right when he wrote that 'Time present and time past are both perhaps present in time future.'[4] In fact there is no 'perhaps' about it. For God has in the past destined us, and in the present is transforming us, so that in the future we will 'be conformed to the image of his Son'.[5]

---

[1] As we are reminded by the opening question and answer in the *Shorter Catechism*.

[2] John 13-17.

[3] Acts 1:3.

[4] The opening lines of 'Burnt Norton' the first of T. S. Eliot's *Four Quartets*.

[5] Romans 8:29.

Foundation 2: The commandment of God to be holy

Holiness is not only the desire of the Trinity; it is a specific command (and therefore a *commandment*) of God the Father: 'as he who called you is holy, you also must be holy in all your conduct, since it is written "be holy, for I am holy"'.[1]

One of the places where the words 'Be holy, for I am holy' appear is in Leviticus 19, a chapter which expounds in some detail the principles of the Ten Commandments recorded in Exodus 20. It is as though God were saying: 'All of these commandments may be summed up in this single principle: "You are to be holy, because I am holy."' In other words, 'Be like me!' Later we learn that the fulfilment of the commandments is love for God and for others.[2] This suggests that holiness and love do not exist a diameter apart from each other (as is sometimes imagined). In fact they have a symbiotic relationship. Sanctification is growing in holy-love; love is growing in holiness.

As with much else, this is a biblical principle that God explained progressively and cumulatively to his people.

The Lord unfolded it at first through liturgical rites and ceremonies prescribed in the law given to and expounded by Moses. Think of these as being like the pop-up picture books we give to and read with small children. They learn not only from words but also from pictures. The appeal is made to their senses: they hear the words; but they can also see and touch what these words express. In the same way the Lord built physical ceremonies and objects into old covenant life, which the people could hear, see, touch, and even smell. They experienced a multi-media expression of their sin and of

---

[1] 1 Peter 1:15-16. Peter is quoting Leviticus 11:44; 19:2. In this way he indicates that God's basic desire is the same throughout Scripture, even although there was a distinctively Mosaic 'shape' to holiness in the days of the old covenant. Now, after Pentecost, holiness has an 'internationalizable' quality and takes its shape from Jesus Christ.

[2] Deuteronomy 6:5; Luke 10:27.

God's grace and way of salvation. They also learned that they were to be separated from the world, different from others, and devoted exclusively to the Lord. Their lives had a distinct rhythm outwardly (they had a unique calendar), their daily existence was governed by personal and community laws that made them different from other nations. It was all meant to express the basic principle that the Lord had claimed them for himself. They were his. Therefore they were different from those who were not his. That was what being holy meant. The Lord had chosen them, redeemed them from Egypt, and claimed them for himself. Now in turn they were to reserve themselves exclusively for him. There was to be no unrequited love.

As the narrative of the Old Testament progressively unfolded, God explained what being devoted to him meant at a personal and moral level. This process reached something of a climax in the ministry of the prophet Isaiah, especially in the way he spoke about God as 'the holy one of Israel'. In his own experience and prophetic ministry it became crystal clear that holiness was never intended to be merely a matter of keeping the Old Testament rituals, nor simply of outward obedience to the Ten Commandments. Holiness meant knowing God, the Holy One, and reflecting and expressing his character—having fellowship with him in such a way that, as his bride, his people became like their Husband, the One with whom they lived.

In the throne room

This is why Isaiah's experience of access to the heavenly throne-room sanctuary was so significant for him and is so instructive for us.[1] He seemed to have gone through a fold in the curtain that separates earth from heaven. He found himself at a worship service in the heavenly temple.[2] During it a new consciousness of the inner

[1] Isaiah 6:1-13.
[2] The New Testament parallel is found in the experience of John recorded in

nature of God's holiness broke through; he realized that, for all his reputation as a holy servant and prophet of God, he was profoundly unclean.

Nor was this merely a ritual matter. It was not about whether he had kept the food laws, or observed the Jewish calendar, or attended the feasts. It was about the very nature of God and his own contrasting sinfulness.

Isaiah now realized that he was a sinner, not just someone who had committed various sinful acts contrary to the divine standards. Here this prince among prophets, this preacher whose eloquence soared to the loftiest heights, whose words tore down the self-justification and self-defences of his contemporaries, discovered that sin infected his own lips and came to expression whenever he preached. It had woven its way into the very words he spoke for God. It was not merely at his lowest and poorest, but in fulfilling the most sacred tasks that he was sinful. No wonder he fell to pieces.

Any consciousness Isaiah might have had of his own ability to conform to the inner standards of God's law was shattered. The sheer bright intensity of God's holiness made him—of all men in Jerusalem—feel unclean, unfit for God's presence. He felt undone. Here one of the greatest prophets or preachers of his (or of any) generation discovered that it was precisely in the area of his strengths and gifts that he was deeply sinful. And so, following the six woes he had uttered against sinners,[1] the climactic, consummating *seventh woe*—the ultimate woe—was reserved for himself: 'Woe is me! For I am lost; for I am a man of unclean lips, and I dwell in the midst of a people of unclean lips.' How did he know that? Not because of his or anyone else's powers of self-analysis, but because his eyes

---

Revelation 4-5. Exiled in Patmos, unable to gather on the Lord's day with his people, he finds himself 'in the Spirit on the Lord's day' (Revelation 1:10) and brought into the presence of God.

[1] Isaiah 5: 8, 11, 18, 20, 21, 22.

had 'seen the King, the LORD of hosts'.[1] His ears had heard the perfect praise of holy creatures who had never sinned. He realized how impoverished his own praise had been. But more, he saw that these perfectly holy creatures also had to cover their faces in the presence of the uncreated holiness of the Lord.

This was clearly the beginning of new things for Isaiah. He encountered God himself in his holiness. This was not now only in the liturgy, or in a series of moral commands, but in the sheer undiluted holy-love that is God's very nature. From that hour he could never be the same again or use his gifts in the same way. For now he had seen what God meant when he said: 'Be holy for *I am holy.*'

Isaiah presumably never imagined that holiness meant mere external conformity. Yet only now, in the light of God's beauty, did the nature of true holiness dawn on him. The words of the divine commandment to be holy were unchanged. Now he sensed what they meant. In the presence of holy-love he realized his unholiness, his unloveliness and his unlovingness. But now too, from holy-love came holy-pardon in the form of a coal from the altar of sacrifice, too fierce in its searing heat for even a seraphim to hold except with tongs. It touched his lips. He tasted the exquisite refining pain of 'the double cure' of justification ('your guilt is taken away and your sin atoned for'[2]) and the cleansing fire that purified and sanctified his speech. Now his lips were cleansed. Now he could speak—as he would forever after—of God as the 'Holy One'.[3]

This helps to explain why those who are becoming holy will always have a two-fold impact on those around them.

On the one hand there will be the irresistible attraction of the beauty of holy-love showing what life in the presence of God really is—life as it was meant to be lived. This cannot but attract the

[1] Isaiah 6:5.
[2] Isaiah 6:7.
[3] Following Isaiah 6 there are more than two dozen references in his prophecy to the Lord as 'the Holy One'.

human heart since a deep desire remains in us to be all we were meant to be.

But on the other hand, this holy-love, so attractive in itself, also involves loving-holiness that will offend those who are repelled by God's holiness and live in rebellion against him. It cannot be otherwise. The holiness of the Christian comes from another world-order for which non-Christians have no taste.

By the time Simon Peter was writing his letter to the Christians in Turkey he clearly understood this. Much earlier he had gone through his own Isaiah-experience; indeed more than once. First he had fallen down before Jesus and said 'Depart from me, for I am a sinful man, O Lord.'[1] But then he had gone on to discover more subtle layers to his sinfulness. He had collapsed spiritually in the presence of a servant girl. He had wept because his sin had been exposed in full gaze of his Saviour. But then he began to learn. In the early days in the Jerusalem church he had seen this. People felt they dare not seek to join the new community, such was the sense of God's holy presence among them. Yet at the same time many were crowding into its fellowship, as if by an irresistible attraction:

> None of the rest dared join them, but the people held them in high esteem. And more than ever believers were added to the Lord, multitudes of both men and women.[2]

No wonder then that Peter quoted Old Testament words about holiness when he exhorted the young Christians in Turkey to be holy. He knew there was all the weight of grace in the commandment of God: 'Be holy, for I am holy.'

Two of the foundations of holiness are now in place: (1) It is God's eternal purpose that his children be holy. That is why (2) Since God himself is holy, his children should be holy too.

---

[1] Luke 5:8.
[2] Acts 5:13-14.

Foundation 3: Exiles with a Saviour

'Exile' is another word Peter uses to help us understand what is involved in our sanctification: 'If you call on him as Father who judges impartially according to each one's deeds, conduct yourselves with fear *during the time of your exile.*'[1]

An exile is someone who is separated from his native geographical and cultural sphere and is now living in another place altogether.[2] That is exactly what the holy Christian is—someone who once belonged to the world but now belongs to a new and 'holy nation'.[3] During the second century early Christians were described as a 'third race' of men.[4] To the rest of the world, whether Jews or Gentiles, they seemed to be outsiders, aliens, exiles in this world—different, seen as both strange and as strangers.

What is it that causes this? And what sustains us in it? Peter answers that it is

> knowing that you were ransomed from the futile ways inherited from your forefathers, not with perishable things such as silver or gold, but with the precious blood of Christ, like that of a lamb without blemish or spot. He was foreknown before the foundation of the world but was made manifest in the last times for your sake, who through him are believers in God, who raised him from the dead and gave him glory, so that your faith and hope are in God.[5]

Holiness means being reserved for God. Understanding this involves coming to appreciate the price he has paid in order to possess us. But it also means that we realize we have been set apart for him; he has claimed us for himself. We therefore no longer 'belong'

---

[1] I Peter 1:17. Cf. 1:1; 2:11.

[2] Some scholars have thought that Peter's first readers may have been literal exiles, but it is more likely that he is using this language metaphorically of those whose 'citizenship is in heaven' (Philippians 1:20).

[3] I Peter 2:9.

[4] According to the early Christian author Tertullian (155–240), *Ad Nationes* I, viii.

[5] I Peter 1:18-21.

to this world. Yet this same realization—that Jesus Christ shed his precious blood for us—is precisely the encouragement we need to cope with the cost of no longer 'belonging'.

The magnitude of the cost of our holiness is spelled out in three ways, each of which emphasizes the greatness of Christ and his work on our behalf.

In one sense this costliness takes the whole of the Old Testament to explain. If you want to understand Jesus, then you need to know:

(1) Jesus was a lamb without blemish or defect who was slain for us. We need to understand the Old Testament sacrificial system to see what this means.

(2) Jesus was chosen for this before the creation of the world. His sacrifice goes right back into the heart of God.

(3) Jesus redeems us not with silver and gold, but with his own blood. There is no cheap grace. What is free to us was costly to him.

This helps to explain Peter's statement that even the angels are in awe of the dying love of their King.[1]

You can almost imagine these angelic beings watching in silence, holding their breath as they witnessed the crucifixion of God's Son. How could this be? How could he love sinners like that? If Christ is so much admired by those angels for whom he did not die, then Peter's point is surely well taken. How much more valuable should he be to those whom he died to save and sanctify? He is worth living in exile for. He is worth living the life of holy-love for. If such a Saviour suffered such a death in order to make us holy, how else should we respond but by giving ourselves entirely to him?

---

[1] 1 Peter 1:12.

Peter has now emphasised the choice of the Father and the sacrifice of the Son. But in this discussion of our sanctification he does not neglect the third person of the Trinity.

Foundation 4: *The ministry of the Holy Spirit*

Sanctification is the fruit of the Spirit's ministry. We have been chosen 'according to the foreknowledge of God the Father, *in the sanctification of the Spirit*'.[1]

The Spirit brings us to new life and into the family of God. Whereas Paul seems to think more in terms of the Father's act of *adopting* us into the family of God, Peter and John think in terms of the Spirit's work of regeneration, or new birth. He brings about a rebirth in us that creates new dispositions. We thus become 'partakers of the divine nature'.[2] We experience not only a change of status (as in adoption) so that we belong to God's family, but also a real transformation of our lives so that we begin to develop the characteristics of our adoptive family. As John puts it, we are born of God; we are now the children of God; we have the seed of God abiding in us.[3]

The implication then, for both Peter and John, is that like new babies we all resemble our Father. We manifest the family likeness, and this means growing in holiness because he is our 'Holy Father'.[4]

As we have seen, justification is a declaration made about our status, not based on anything in ourselves. But the Holy Spirit who unites us to Christ for justification, in that very act of union also sanctifies us, transforming our dispositions and desires. Now we love what we once despised, and despise much that we once loved. Now, while the Christian life remains a battle to the end, we find that there is all the difference in the world between seeking to be holy

[1] 1 Peter 1:2.
[2] 2 Peter 1:4.
[3] 1 John 3:1-2, 9.
[4] John 17:11.

when that is a burden, and seeking to be holy because we belong to the family of God and have the new family nature.

But Peter is not yet finished in outlining the ground-plan of sanctification. He has much to say in his letter about—

Foundation 5: The function of trials

Peter must now teach us what for him was an unexpected, and at first a very unwelcome lesson: if necessary we will be 'grieved by various trials'.[1]

This often comes as a shock to new Christians, especially when we discover that our personal holiness is one of the reasons for the trials we experience. Yet painful as they are, we can rejoice in the midst of them because of the purpose God has through them:

> so that the tested genuineness of your faith—more precious than gold that perishes though it is tested by fire—may be found to result in praise and glory and honour at the appearing of Jesus Christ.[2]

God knows what he is doing in our lives. We are his workmanship.[3] And he knows he can rely on and test his own work. A skilled workman always has that confidence.

Most of us do not like tests—especially if they involve pain. Nor do we enjoy suffering. But growth requires it. The point that Peter is making is that difficulties, trials, opposition, suffering, together constitute one of the chief instruments that God uses in the process of refining, sanctifying, and strengthening his people. He throws them into the fire of affliction, like gold in a refiner's furnace, in order to bring impurities to the surface, and to draw them off.

Why does he do this? To build Christian character, making us more like Christ. For it was through affliction that the Father moulded his life. If his Son's obedience was developed through

[1] 1 Peter 1:6.
[2] 1 Peter 1:6-7.
[3] Ephesians 2:10.

suffering, we should not be surprised if he continues to use the same method with us.[1]

Think of it this way. You may know somebody who becomes impatient and irritated but then apologizes: 'I am sorry. I am *usually* a very *patient* person.' But the truth is he or she is really an *impatient* person whose patience has never been fully tested! For patience develops only in contexts that can stimulate impatience and irritation. Certainly it is only in such an environment that it undergoes testing and proving. A fundamental way in which Christian character is strengthened is by stress.

The friction God builds into the Christian life is, therefore, not accidental. It is deliberate, strategic, and intended to produce growth in holiness.

This leads us to a final element in Peter's teaching. It appears last but it is by no means least:

Foundation 6: *The glory to come*

Our growth in holiness is intimately related to how we view the future, and to how firm a grip we have on the reality of the world to come and our destiny in it.

This is a dominant note in the New Testament. But it is often overlooked, perhaps because people confuse it with 'pie in the sky when you die'—allow yourself to be deprived of pleasure here in order to have treasure hereafter; live a disciplined life for God's glory here in exchange for a reward then.

But Simon Peter's perspective is very different. For him—as for all of the New Testament writers—it is the certainty and the reality of the grace and the glory that are yet to be revealed that together transform the way we live here and now.[2] Far from being an exhortation to sacrifice the visible, tangible and real for an uncertain future,

---

[1] Hebrews 2:10; 5:8.
[2] 1 Peter 1:3-7; 4:12-15.

the New Testament teaches us to live in the light of a future reality that is far more substantial than the present. This is why Paul can call the afflictions we go through 'light' while the glory to come possesses 'weight'.[1]

In addition, both Peter and Paul relate these two things—suffering and glory—not only *chronologically* but *causally*. Afflictions *produce* glory.[2] They are the raw materials out of which God will shape us for eternity. And therefore knowing what we are destined to be in the future determines, transforms, and energizes the way we live now.

Christians therefore live their lives back from the future as it were. Knowing what will be true for us then makes an impact on how we live now. And because we 'are being guarded through faith for a salvation ready to be revealed in the last time' we can rejoice now as well as then.[3]

This final salvation will be holiness completed. We will see the face of Jesus Christ and be transformed into his likeness.[4] This is simply the consummation of the sanctification that God has already begun. We are already being changed 'from one degree of glory to another' by the Lord who is the Spirit.[5]

If holiness is our heavenly happiness, and true happiness is, ultimately, holiness, then the prospect of the future will influence and shape our lives here and now. How strange it is that people think (as many seem to do) that they will be happy pursuing holiness there and then in heaven, if they are singularly unhappy about the calling to pursue it here and now on earth! No, there is a continuity. Love holiness now, because we love the Holy One and we will love it all the more then, in the presence of the Holy One when we see him

[1] 2 Corinthians 4:17-18.
[2] Romans 5:2-5; 2 Corinthians 4:17-18; 1 Peter 4:13.
[3] 1 Peter 1:5-6.
[4] 1 John 3:1-3.
[5] 2 Corinthians 3:18.

face to face. Despise it now and we will despise it then too. Or, to put this the other way round: if we do not desire heaven as a world of holiness and freedom from the presence of sin, a world of delight in Jesus Christ *here and now*, what possesses us to think we will love it and enjoy it—or him—*then*? There could surely be no greater self-delusion. For then, as John's interpreting angel in the vision of the Book of Revelation says to him, it will be true:

> Let the evildoer still do evil, and the filthy still be filthy,
> and the righteous still do right, and the holy still be holy.[1]

Those who will enjoy holiness there and then are those who want to pursue holiness here and now.

With these different building blocks then Simon Peter lays down the foundations on which sanctification is built. We need to fix them into the foundations of our own thinking and living, and make holiness a priority. For—

(1) God the Holy Trinity, is devoted to it;

(2) God the Holy Father has commanded us to pursue it;

(3) Christ the Holy Son has died to effect it;

(4) The Holy Spirit works in us to bring forth the fruit of it;

(5) God sends trials into our experience in order to produce it;

(6) Heaven itself is a world that is full of it.

With these foundations built into our lives we have every encouragement we need to be *devoted to God.*

---

[1] Revelation 22:11.

2

All of Me

———

God has made provision for our sanctification in the gospel. His ultimate goal is the development of family likeness— our becoming like our elder brother, Jesus Christ, and expressing the character traits of our heavenly Father. This we can do only as the Holy Spirit works in our lives. In the New Testament the basic command of old covenant life, 'Be holy as I am holy', now means, 'Become like Jesus.'

God involves himself in this work as the triune Lord: the Father commands it; the Son has died to provide the resources for it; the Spirit indwells us in order to effect it in our lives. As Augustine famously prayed, God commands what he wills and gives what he commands.[1]

Transformation

We must now turn to consider this sanctification in terms of the transformation it produces in us. Paul provides us with the classic statement:

> I appeal to you therefore, brothers, by the mercies of God, to present your bodies as a living sacrifice, holy and acceptable to God, which is your spiritual worship. Do not be conformed to this world, but be transformed by the renewal of your mind, that by testing you

[1] Augustine (354–430), *Confessions*, 10.29, words that irritated Pelagius!

may discern what is the will of God, what is good and acceptable and perfect.[1]

These words form the hinge on which Paul's extended exposition of what he calls 'my gospel'[2] turns into his detailed practical application of this gospel to personal, social, church and civic life. In each sphere Paul urges the Christians in Rome to pursue holiness. But first they are to present themselves to the Lord as sacrifices that are 'holy and pleasing to God'. This is not a lecture on self-improvement. Rather Paul brings to the surface four important gospel-centred principles.

Principle 1: Sanctification flows from the gospel

Notice the similarity between Paul's mind-set in Romans and the mindset we saw in Peter. It is too superficial to think of one (Peter) as a marginally-educated Galilean fisherman and the other (Paul) as a university-trained theological scholar. In fact they were not only united as brothers in Christ,[3] but also in their profound way of thinking about the gospel. In particular, they both grasped its inherent logic. Peter, we saw, emphasized that the exhortation to be holy is rooted in God's character and grace. Paul does exactly the same.

What we saw in Peter could be summarized like this. When God urges us to be holy he is not throwing us back on our own resources to pull ourselves up by our boot strings and to do better. Rather he encourages us to swim into the sea of God's love, to immerse our lives in his grace, and to live on the basis of the resources he has provided for us in Christ. To change the metaphor, growing in holiness and sanctification requires that we put down deep roots into the soil of gospel.

[1] Romans 12:1-2.
[2] Romans 2:16; 16:25.
[3] 2 Peter 3:15.

One way of describing this pattern of thinking is in grammatical terms—because there is a kind of grammar we need to learn in order to live out (as well as to articulate) the gospel coherently. This gospel grammar, employed in the New Testament, and coming to expression in our lives, always operates according to a basic rule:

> *Divine indicatives* (statements about what God has done, is doing, or will do)

logically precede and ground

> *Divine imperatives* (statements about what we are to do in response).

This is true no matter the actual order in which the indicative and imperative statements appear in any given passage. Thus:

> Who God is, what God has done, is doing, and will do for us (*indicative*)

provides the foundation for

> Our response of faith and obedience (*imperative*).

Thus his grace effects our faithfulness. This is the logic that explains the power of the gospel.

Reversing the grammar

A recurring difficulty we face in explaining the gospel to people who are not yet Christians is that they often hear what we say but then turn the grammar and logic of the gospel on its head. Their way of thinking about the gospel is:

> If I do this then God will do that,

Or

> If I do my part then God will respond to me and do his part.

This is the way many people think about salvation. Ask them why they believe that they are acceptable to God, or will be 'saved', or go to heaven. They will answer largely in terms of what they themselves are or have done. Because they have lived in a satisfactory (but not perfect) way, God will be gracious, make up the deficit, and they will be safe. But this stands the gospel on its head. It reverses its logic and its grammar. It no more expresses the gospel than someone who reverses English grammar is speaking English properly.

Christians often seem to fall back into bad spiritual grammar.

Think of a situation in which a child picks up the habit of saying 'Me and John played football.' You gently correct him: 'In English we say "John and I".' He says 'John and I'. But three days later he has relapsed. As believers we can also relapse into a misuse of gospel grammar, falling back into this native tendency to turn the gospel on its head—as though justification is by grace but the Christian life is essentially a biblical form of 'self-help'. It is therefore vital to see that in Paul's gospel both justification and sanctification are rooted in 'the mercies of God'.[1]

One illustration of this must suffice. Here is the gist of his thinking in Romans 8:3-4:

> Although the law commands me to be holy, it does not have the inherent power to make me holy.
>
> *Question:* How is it possible then for me to become holy and obedient, a person who fulfils God's commands?
>
> *Answer:* It is possible only because of
>
> (1) What God has done for me in Christ: By sending his Son in the likeness of sinful flesh and as a sin offering on the cross, he condemned sin in the flesh.
>
> (2) What the Spirit is now doing in me: He did this in order that the righteous requirements of the law might now be fulfilled in us who walk, not according to the flesh, but according to the Spirit.

[1] When Paul appeals to the Christians in Rome on the basis of 'the mercies of God' he is probably referring not only to his immediately preceding discussion of God's purposes in history in relation to Jews and Gentiles, but to his entire exposition of the gospel from Romans 1:16-11:36. The whole letter thus far is about 'the mercies of God.' Throughout he has been using gospel logic, both in his explanation of the way of justification and in his exploration of the implications of our union with Christ. Then he continues to do so in his practical applications.

If we are to understand the nature of sanctification and success-fully pursue it, we must immerse ourselves in appreciating the grace of God expressed to us in Jesus Christ and applied in us by the Holy Spirit. Our response is dependent on it and motivated by it. This alone empowers us to grow in the kind of holiness of which Paul is here speaking. Justification, forgiveness, acceptance, and union with Christ are the logical and actual grounds for sanctification and obedience—not the other way round.

Almost any page of the New Testament letters provides further illustrations of this pattern of thinking. An outstanding example is 2 Thessalonians 2:13-15:

> We ought always to give thanks to God for you, brothers beloved by the Lord,
>
> *Why?* Because God chose you as the first fruits
>
> *For what purpose?* To be saved,
>
> *How?* Through sanctification of the Spirit and belief in the truth.
>
> *By what means?* To this he called you through our gospel
>
> *What was God's final goal?* So that you may obtain the glory of our Lord Jesus Christ.
>
> *What are the implications?* So then, brothers, stand firm and hold to the traditions that you were taught by us, either by our spoken word or by our letter.

Paul's thinking is always: God has done this for you in Christ, therefore you should respond in the following ways. Sanctifica-tion—being devoted to God—is always the fruit of his setting us apart in and through Christ.

Again, when Paul describes commitment to Jesus Christ he says it means that we should no longer live for ourselves but for Christ.[1] This lies at the heart of sanctification: not living for myself but living

---

[1] 2 Corinthians 5:15

for Christ. But where is the dynamic for this? Answer: Christ died and rose for us, and the love of Christ thus manifested constrains us to live for him. It is because we understand the *significance* of his death and resurrection that we are devoted to him. In Isaac Watts's words, it is

> When I survey the wondrous cross,
> On which the Prince of Glory died

that I am overwhelmed by his devotion to me and I respond:

> My richest gain I count but loss,
> And pour contempt on all my pride.[1]

Thus the motivation, energy and drive for holiness are all found in the reality and power of God's grace in Christ. And so if I am to make any progress in sanctification, the place where I must always begin is the gospel of the mercy of God to me in Jesus Christ.

This has an important practical implication; for one of the snares that can entrap serious Christians is that our pursuit of holiness becomes metallic.

Heavy metal?

Metallic holiness was the problem with the Pharisees, certainly the ones Jesus encountered. They began life as a holiness movement within Judaism and slowly became a distinct sect.[2] God had graciously given his people *torah*, his law. It included a raft of

---

[1] From the hymn by Isaac Watts (1674–1748) 'When I survey the wondrous cross'. This much-loved hymn could be taken to express the so-called 'Moral Influence' understanding of the atonement associated with the medieval theologian Peter Abelard (1079–1142), rather than 'Substitutionary Atonement'. But it should be remembered that the cross is multivalent. Christ died for our sins, in our place. His death is substitutionary. But at the same time the New Testament makes clear that such love does call forth a response from us. Paul makes both clear in 2 Corinthians 5:14-15, 21. In fact the 'influence' of the atonement on us arises from its substitutionary character.

[2] The historian Josephus (AD 37–100) suggests that there were only around 6,000 of them at the time of Jesus. *Jewish Antiquities*, 17.42.

commandments and ordinances. But over time the focus of the Pharisees became fixated on the details of the law itself rather than on the gracious God who gave it. Implications that flowed from his grace ('I brought you out of Egypt, *therefore live like this ...*'[1]) were turned into qualifications for standing in grace, and for all practical purposes qualifications for grace itself.

The second law of spiritual dynamics?

There seems to be a kind of law of spiritual dynamics akin to Newton's Second Law of Motion—a body in motion tends to remain in motion. If we reverse the order of gospel logic it will not be long before we are smuggling our sanctification into the foundations of our justification. Our ongoing status before God will then be seen to be dependent on our performance. Gradually our eyes will become fixed on our performance and we will begin to lose sight of our relationship to God in Christ. The result? Mercy and grace are squeezed out of sight. Then holiness begins to take on a metallic character, an external correctness that is lacking in graciousness; an obedience that is its own end. Then accomplishment begins to obscure need. It is not that we have no theology of grace; but it now remains in our theology when it has ceased to be a reality in our hearts and lives.

Jesus illustrated this in his parable of the Pharisee and the tax collector who prayed in the temple. The former *thanked God* that he was superior to the tax collector. In doing so he acknowledged God's grace but distorted it (he gave thanks to God for his superiority!). He now anchored his present acceptance with God in what he perceived as his degree of consecration and sanctification.[2]

---

[1] See Exodus 20:1ff.

[2] Some readers will note that this represents a different view of the Pharisees from the one that tends to be held by exponents of 'The New Perspective on Paul' who have often stressed that pharisaic religion was one of grace, not of works, and also that traditionally the Pharisees have been read backwards through the lenses of the Protestant Reformation (thus for some Paul was not converted from a religion of

Christians can fall into the same mistake. This is why the hinge-point in Romans (12:1) begins with the connective 'therefore'. Consecration and sanctification are rooted in the reality of our justification by grace alone through faith-union to Christ alone. The gospel logic falls to pieces if we reverse this order. The Christian life begins, develops, and ends with grace—with the mercy of God. We never grow out of it or beyond it; we never cease to need it; it is never superfluous.

The indicative medicine

There is a prescription readily available to help us here. It may take an hour or so to administer it. And once administered it will be worth taking further doses. But the value of the medicine is out of all proportion to the sacrifice of time involved in administering it.

Here are the instructions for taking the medicine:

(1) *Take an old Bible.* or download the text of Paul's letter to the Romans.

---

works to a religion of grace on the Damascus Road but simply recognised Jesus as the Messiah). At least in its earlier formulations this 'school of thought' lacked both pastoral and psychological insight and also historical perspective. A measure of these would have prevented much confusion. As Jesus' parable strikingly illustrates it is possible for someone to use the language of grace (the Pharisee attributed his 'goodness' to God, not to himself) while resting subtly on his or her own actions. Had we been able to ask the Pharisee as he left the temple: 'Do you believe that Yahweh is a God of grace', he would surely have responded, 'Of course, I have just been thanking him for the fact that I fast twice a week and tithe everything I have—quite different from that tax collector who left a moment ago and refused to be interviewed by you!' But we would be deceived if we thought this meant he had really tasted God's grace. These were the Pharisees whom Jesus had in his cross-hairs during his ministry. Similarly the Reformers knew well that the late medieval theology they contested was punctuated by the language of grace and how it works. After all the Church taught that salvation was by grace. Only when the meaning of 'grace' was analysed did it become clear that the Church taught that sinners are justified on the basis of the righteousness which sacramental grace produces in us as we cooperate with it. For the Reformers this is not justification by grace entirely on the basis of what Christ has done for us, but on the basis of a transformed life that renders us justifiable. At the end of the day this dis-graces true grace. Cf. Romans 11:6.

(2) *Have a pen or marker to hand.* For the medicine to work properly it is essential for you to note the occurrence of a single feature in Paul's letter to the Romans.

(3) *Read slowly through the text of Romans chapters 1 to 11.* As you do, have one object in view—it is very important not to lose your focus here: *Mark every statement that occurs in the imperative mood*—that is, every statement that is in the form of a command, telling the reader to do something.

(4) *Note that Romans chapters 1-11 contain 315 verses.*

(5) *Write down the number of verses containing an imperative in these chapters.* (Again, remember that imperatives are verbs telling the reader to *do something*, i.e. they contain commands.)

(6) *Check your answer.*

Of course we can draw all kinds of implications for and applications to our lives from these eleven chapters. But in terms of actual imperatives? You will find them in an English translation such as the ESV only in Romans 6:12, 13, 19; 10:4; and 11:18, 20, 22.[1]

In essence Paul devotes 308 out of 315 verses to a sustained exposition of what God has done, and only then does he open the sluice-gates and let loose a flood of imperatives.[2]

Clearly Paul believed in the necessity of exhortations, commands, and imperatives. And his are all-embracing and all-demanding. But the rigorous nature of his imperatives is rooted in his profound exposition of God's grace. He expects the fruit of obedience because he has dug down deeply to plant its roots in the rich soil of grace. The weightier the indicatives the more demanding the imperatives they are able to support. The more powerful the proclamation of

---

[1] Sometimes the ESV (rightly) renders as imperatives words that are not in the imperative form in the Greek text.

[2] There are more than 20 of them in chapter 12 alone.

grace the more rigorous the commands it can sustain. This is the principle that destroys both legalism and antinomianism.[1] For this is how the gospel works:

> I am not ashamed of the gospel, *for* it is the power of God for salvation.[2]

> I appeal to you *therefore*, brothers, by the mercies of God, to present your bodies as a living sacrifice, holy and acceptable to God, which is your spiritual worship.[3]

Get this right and we have a strong foundation for growth in sanctification. Go wrong here and we may go wrong everywhere. Remember Newton's Second Law of Motion!

Principle 2: Sanctification is expressed physically

If you were asked: '*Where* does Christian holiness express itself?' how would you answer? Paul's answer? *The body*. His over-arching exhortation is, 'present *your bodies* as a living sacrifice'.[4]

Why so much emphasis on the body? The noun Paul uses (*sōma*, body) could be taken to mean 'self' (i.e. offer yourselves), but he is probably speaking here specifically about the Christian's physical body.[5]

Why should he be so specific about this? Because we not only have a body; our body is part and parcel of what we are. True, we have more than a physical dimension; but we live with and through our bodies. We do not exist in our present condition apart from the body. We express ourselves only by means of our body. In that sense we are our bodies!

---

[1] Strictly speaking 'antinomianism' is the view that there is no place for the law of God within the gospel of Christ. But this bleeds into the view that grace means that any commandment (moral imperative) is a form of legalism. The point made here states the reverse: the proclamation of grace to sinners leads to moral imperatives.

[2] Romans 1:16.

[3] Romans 12:1.

[4] Paul is here developing the first imperatives in the Letter in 6:12-13.

[5] As in ESV and NIV.

Since this is so any real sanctification by necessity takes place in and through the body. There is no such thing as sanctification that does not involve us physically. That is why it is so important for us to 'present'[1] our bodies to the Lord.

There is, of course, another reason Paul insists on this. It is in our bodies that sin, and sinful tendencies, addictions, and habits have exercised their spiritually destructive influence on us. The effect of sin is felt in bodily ways, and manifests itself in what we do with our bodies—with our eyes, hands, ears, lips, feet, and every other part of us. They are the instruments of either sin or holiness.[2] Through them we express what is in our heart. By them the core of our thinking, feeling, desiring, and willing comes to expression.

Jesus taught the same truths. The tongue serves as the index of the heart. It is out of the heart that the mouth speaks.[3] Jesus speaks about our right eye or hand causing us to sin.[4] Sin in the heart thus manifests itself in our bodies. Therefore the radical change the gospel brings into our lives will also manifest Christ's saving power precisely there—in the body.

Paul's concern here is by no means unique to Romans. It reappears in other places. He writes to the Corinthians, 'Don't you understand that the body is for the Lord and the Lord is for the body?'[5]

We need to remember this every morning when we wake from sleep. As we become conscious of ourselves at the beginning of a new day we would do well to say: 'Today this body is for the Lord, and the Lord is for this body.' Therefore—

> I offer my eyes to Christ;
> I offer my ears to Christ;

[1] Paul's verb (*paristēmi*) is also used elsewhere by him in sanctification contexts: 2 Corinthians 11:2; Colossians 1:22, 28.

[2] Romans 6:13.

[3] Matthew 12:34.

[4] Matthew 5:29-30.

[5] See 1 Corinthians 6:12-20.

I offer my feet to Christ;
I offer my hands to Christ;
I offer my mouth to Christ
I present myself,
    deliberately,
    consciously,
    sacrificially
        to him.

You can see immediately why this is a key to living the Christian life. For each day, through what our forefathers called eye-gate or ear-gate, mouth-gate, hand-gate, or foot-gate, we are confronted by temptation. But we can face it well-armed if the eye, or ear, or mouth, or hand, or foot has already been devoted as a living sacrifice to the Lord Jesus Christ. We are his and it is his. Indeed it is no longer ours but Christ's. Therefore it will not be sin's or Satan's. In this way we can say both to Satan and to temptation, 'Do not dare take my hand away from Jesus Christ and cause it to wander from doing his will and purposes. Do not try to prize away from Christ my eyes or my ears or my feet or my mouth. They are his, because I am his.'

Sacrifice

Paul chose his words carefully. It is not accidental that here he employs sacrificial language. Our bodies are to be living sacrifices.

Sacrifices were common occurrences in the first century. They were deliberate and costly, even bloody. Jesus himself employed similarly graphic language to describe what is involved in consecration to him: 'take up the cross', 'pluck out', 'cut off', 'die'. There are no gains without pains. This consecration is also volitional—our bodily functions, tainted by sin as they continue to be, do not automatically give themselves in devotion to the Lord. Holiness requires deliberate action on our part, and the exercise of our will.

This is our 'rational service'.[1] If we are Christ's, body and soul, then yielding our body to him is, quite simply, 'reasonable'.

For one thing, it involves imitating Christ. The New Testament picks up the words of Psalm 40:6-8 and puts them into the mouth of Jesus: 'A *body* have you prepared for me; ... I have come to do your will, O God.'[2] Since the Son of God took a body in which to do the will of God, believers also yield their bodies to do the will of God in Christ's strength and by imitating his example.

For another, it is the only appropriate response to what Jesus has done for us:

> But drops of grief can ne'er repay
> The debt of love I owe;
> Here, Lord, I give myself away,
> 'Tis all that I can do.[3]

This emphasis on the body is particularly significant for Christians in the twenty-first century.

We live in a generation that has smothered God-consciousness and rejected the worship of the Creator. But Scripture emphasizes that since we were created as the image of God, and made for worship, we must worship something. If we will not worship God, then we worship created things.[4] Indeed we end up worshipping the self.

Western civilisation has been described as a 'culture of narcissism'.[5] We have become 'lovers of self ... lovers of pleasure, rather than lovers of God'.[6] In particular our present generation has become obsessed with the worship of the body.

---

[1] ESV marginal translation.

[2] Quoted in Hebrews 10:5-7.

[3] From the hymn by Isaac Watts: 'Alas! And did my Saviour bleed'.

[4] Romans 1:23, 25.

[5] The title of the book by the American historian Christopher Lasch, first published in 1979.

[6] 2 Timothy 3:2, 4.

This manifests itself in various ways. A glance through the (many!) pages of advertising in even the 'reputable' glossy magazines proves the point. Many of them focus on, or employ as attractions, the elegance or beauty of the body in one way or another: what you put into it, onto it, or take off of it. Another striking expression of this is found by watching sporting occasions that involve physical prowess. The time taken for the match may be insufficient for you to count the number of tattoos you see. For all our sophistication (not to say riches) the western world may not have seen so many tattoos since the days of paganism.

Why this upsurge today? Because when secular humanism dominates a culture it abandons the biblical teaching that we have been made as the image of God.[1] Under the appearance of exalting man to be the measure of all things, it actually demeans him, and destroys his true dignity. It reduces man to biological functions. Now the body is everything, whether it be the human body, animal bodies, or the earth body.[2] The proverbial visiting man from Mars could be forgiven for reporting back to his fellow Martians that on the earth the body is the object of highest devotion, and is constantly adorned or adored. We are surrounded by voices that are in essence saying: Worship your body; preserve it; beautify it. The sub-text is: Your body is all you have; it is yours; you own it and you can do anything you want with it.

The gospel stands in stark contrast to this. It calls us to the thankful and joyful worship of the Lord in which we give our whole lives to him, including our bodies. In such worship we discover

[1] Genesis 1:26.

[2] Of course it is not possible to live consistently with any sense of real purpose or ethic if at the end of the day men and women are merely biological mechanisms predetermined by genetic structure. Both purpose and an ethic require that human beings have a dimension that transcends the merely biological. Tragically, but predictably, secular humanism has never grasped that its anthropology, rather than exalt our significance, ultimately robs us of our true and lasting dignity.

self-forgetfulness and Christ-glorifying consecration. This is why, even although it is true that who we really are as Christians is not visible to non-Christians,[1] holiness cannot remain hidden. It shows itself in how we use our bodies.

Principle 3: Mind renewal

If you were to ask Paul, 'Explain the key to the way the gospel transforms and sanctifies us', his answer might surprise us. 'It is what happens in your mind!' He says: 'Don't let the world around you squeeze you into its own mould, but let God re-mould your minds from within.'[2]

That is a vivid way of describing what actually happens. This worldliness may impact us in sudden and violent ways. But characteristically it does so by insistent, prolonged, constant pressure. This present age, this fallen world (and its citizens) gradually, imperceptibly squeeze us into their mould. In sharp contrast Christians become non-conformists, counter-culturally shaped and transformed *by the renewing of the mind*. There is a premium attached to the mind in biblical teaching.[3]

Notice the balance in what Paul says here. It illustrates a constant feature of his thinking about sanctification, as we shall see again later: there is always a negative and a positive element involved.

Negatively he urges non-conformity with respect to the present world or age in which we live. Positively he urges transformation by means of the renewal of the mind.

[1] See 1 John 3:1-3.
[2] Romans 12:2. J. B. Phillips, *The New Testament in Modern English* (London: Geoffrey Bles, 1960), 332.
[3] For a fine brief treatment see J. R. W. Stott, *Your Mind Matters* (Leicester: Inter-Varsity Press, 1972).

DEVOTED TO GOD

Non-conformist

From the biblical point of view the whole of time is divided into two ages: the present age and the age to come. The present age is dominated by the world, the flesh and the devil.[1] But in the Old Testament Scriptures God promised an age to come, the time of the kingdom of God; an age of renewal, a time of resurrection and triumph, of new life and the new creation.[2]

At the heart of Paul's gospel is a startling truth. The resurrection of Jesus Christ as the firstborn from the dead[3] means that this new creation has already broken into our world and the new age has already begun. What was expected at the end of history has been inaugurated in the middle of it—in the resurrection of Jesus Christ. Those who belong to him already begin to share in this new age. Thus, Paul says (literally) 'If anyone in Christ, new creation. The old has gone; behold the new has come.'[4]

As Christians we have been 'rescued from the present evil age'.[5] We are those 'on whom the end of the ages has come'.[6] We already experience 'the powers of the age to come'.[7] For us the day has already dawned, the light has begun to appear.[8] True, the full light of noonday is not yet shining. But we are no longer living in the

[1] 1 John 2:15-17. Cf. Paul's similar thinking in Ephesians 2:1-4.
[2] Envisaged for example in Isaiah 65:17-25.
[3] Colossians 1:18. The same idea is present in Paul's harvest metaphor of first fruits, 1 Corinthians 15:20, 23.
[4] 2 Corinthians 5:17. In an effort to translate Paul's words into understandable English, our Bible versions can somewhat obscure the full force of what Paul is saying here. He is not describing simply what happens to me as an individual when I become a Christian—I become a 'new creature' in Christ. While true, Paul has a much bigger concept in view—I enter a new creation. Raised into new life with Christ I am now living as someone belonging to the resurrection age even while I am still living in the present age.
[5] Galatians 1:4.
[6] 1 Corinthians 10:11.
[7] Hebrews 6:5.
[8] Romans 13:11-13.

46

darkness. And because we know that we are already living in the early hours of the new day, we live as children of the light, not as children of the darkness.[1]

This magnificent theological vision has very practical significance. Knowing who we are will shape how we live. Conversely, not knowing who we are as Christians will leave us muddled and confused in our lifestyle. *So we need to learn this new way of thinking about both the gospel and ourselves if we are to be transformed into the likeness of Jesus Christ by the renewing of our mind.*

But learning a new way of thinking is never easy. It always involves repentance in the mind (indeed the New Testament's word for repentance, *metanoia*, means 'change of mind'). And this is precisely what the gospel produces in us.

Another grammar lesson

Paul's grammar here is once again significant. While most of us find grammar fairly boring we understand that without it languages cannot function properly and communication tends to break down. For grammar is not something distinct from language but a description of how it works. It gives structure to our communication. In this sense it is worth paying attention to the way Paul's use of grammar expresses the inner structure of God's sanctifying work in us.

This is true here of Paul's verb: '*be transformed* by the renewing of your mind'.

Verbs have tenses (various forms of past, present, and future), moods (indicative and imperative) and also voices (active and passive). '*Be transformed*' is:

- *Tense:* the present continuous tense (*go on being* transformed). It refers not to a once for all event but to an ongoing reality.

- *Mood:* the imperative mood (it is a command, something to be done).

[1] Ephesians 5:8-14.

• *Voice:* the passive voice (it refers to something that happens to us).

We might translate the verb: *Be* (imperative) *being* (continuous present) *transformed* (passive).

Notice what is unusual and surprising here. Paul seems to be exhorting us to actively engage in something in which we ourselves are passive.

How can that possibly be? How can we be engaged in an activity in which we are going to *be* transformed? The explanation is that we are to allow this to take place in our lives by yielding to what God does through an instrument in his hands. In this case the means by which life-transformation takes place is 'the renewal of your mind'. The instrument that God uses is the word of the gospel. The truth of the gospel informs and illumines our thinking. It thus begins to permeate our mindset and influence our dispositions. This in turn, recalibrates our affections to love what we have now come to understand, and to bow our wills in a new desire for conformity with God's will.

This is how the gospel works. This is why Paul preached and wrote letters: he believed that God's word has power to renew minds and transform lives. As the greatness of the gospel begins to fill and to expand our minds, as we come to know God's Son, through God's word, by God's Spirit, a process of change takes place in our thinking, feeling, desiring, willing, and living. God's word and Spirit work together and actively and powerfully change us.

Our Lord himself prayed for this to become a reality: 'Father, make them holy through the truth. Your word is the truth that will make them holy.'[1] God's truth (given now to us in Scripture[2])

[1] John 17:17.

[2] This is made clear in the context of Jesus' prayer: The Father sent the Son into the world and gave him the word; he in turn gave the word to the apostles; the apostles were then sent into the world to give the word to the world (by preaching and to the wider world by giving the Scriptures); John 17:8, 14, 18, 20.

expresses the power of Christ and the grace of Christ that transforms and renews our way of thinking and then our manner of living.

The role of the ministry of the word

This, incidentally, is why it is so important for Christians to place their lives under the preaching of God's word. For in receiving it we are actively passive. It is expounded *to* us, not *by* us; and yet it appeals to our minds, reshapes our thinking, penetrates our consciences, and at this level engages us in intense activity.

Although set at a discount today by comparison with participation in either personal Bible study or more particularly group Bible study, neither of these, valuable as they may be, can substitute for the transforming power of the preached word. While today this is a controverted, even controversial view, in the present writer's experience it is controverted only by those who have little or no experience of it (or, sadly, have declined to participate in it and receive it).

This is partly illustrated by the fascinating difference there is between morning and evening services.[1] Even when the same people in approximately the same numbers are present at an evening (or 'second') service there is almost invariably an 'extra' which everybody notices, even if they do not pause to analyse the reason for it. While formally the morning or first service may be regarded as the

---

[1] The particular illustration here is of more than passing importance. Sadly the principle mentioned in the final sentence of the previous paragraph is itself illustrated by the virtually complete demise of a second service, so that the subtle but muddle-headed subliminal response to the statements above tends to be 'How can this be true since we have not experienced it?' The difficulty church leaders have in establishing a second service of worship and ministry seems to be proof positive of a loss of appetite for both worship and the word of God. This in turn may explain why responding to those who explain to us that 'experts' have informed them that the quality of their morning worship is outstanding by saying that 'perhaps the best test of the quality of morning worship is the quality of evening worship', is often received in a deeply self-defensive and even hostile spirit. But surely no young man in love with a young woman would be content to arrange to meet her for only one hour a week, always at the same time? The ultimate issue here is one of desire.

'main' service, it is the second service that is the high point. What explains the difference?

Doubtless there are several factors, but the major one is the cumulative impact of the word of God, expounded in the context of the worship of God by the people of God. We come on Sunday morning out of a world that has sought to squeeze us into its mould. We add to that our own spiritual lethargy. But then we are fed in God's presence by God's word, read, sung, spoken, and prayed. We are sanctified through the truth. Thus when we come together later in the day, some degree of this transforming of our lives through the renewing of our minds, has already taken place. We find ourselves as Jesus prayed we would be, cleansed and sanctified. Our thinking has been recalibrated in a Godward direction; our affections have been cleansed and drawn out in love for our Lord; our desires to serve him are purer, our affections for God's people are greater, and our wills are more submissive to his word. The more we are thus fed the more we want to be fed and to feed.

We have become such an activist generation of Christians that we can scarcely grasp that our first and greatest need is to be in this sense passive—being fed the good food of the word of God so that we may 'be being transformed'.

It should sadden us but perhaps not surprise us when analysts tell us there is often little difference between the lifestyle of profess-ing Christians and those who are not. For the fact is that we are very undernourished spiritually. Our stomachs have shrunk, but we scarcely notice. We judge ourselves by ourselves and conclude we are doing relatively well. But we are in fact demonstrating how little we really understand.[1] It seems 'normal' to us to make do with Bible 'snacks'. In our evangelical sub-culture there is a heavy emphasis on what we must do—including what we must do with our Bibles.[2] But

[1] 2 Corinthians 10:12.

[2] Thankfully there may be a slight turning of the tide, but a glance at most lists of best-selling Christian books suggests we continue to have a voracious appetite for

there is almost no emphasis that accords with the stress in the New Testament on what our Bibles will do to us! People are still called to consecration; but if little or nothing is said or done about the renewal of the mind, the summons is largely in vain.

This brings us to a fourth principle.

Principle 4: The effect

The effect of the process Paul describes is remarkable: by testing we learn to discern and approve the will of God, and see it as 'good and acceptable and perfect'.

Romans was not in fact written by the apostle Paul. He was its author—but it was written by an otherwise unknown secretary called Tertius.[1] He was surely a highly privileged man. Writing was a much slower business then than it is today.[2] So perhaps we can imagine him at this point putting down his writing implement and turning to Paul with a question: 'What do you mean that "by testing" we "may discern what is the will of God"? And how do we discover that it is "good and acceptable and perfect"?'

Although we do not have access to Paul to ask him to explain this further, certain things are clear. As we respond to the gospel we put it to the test. Faith in Christ involves an experiment—we trust him, but we cannot second-guess what the consequences will be in our lives. We learn to discover what God's will is in each situation only as we find ourselves in it and as his providence slowly unfolds his purposes. Moreover, we see only a small part of his world-wide and history-long plan. Thankfully we know enough about his ways to know that he does all things well.

'the project of the self', what we can accomplish, and how to do it, while we have little appetite for the knowledge of God and Christ which constitutes eternal life, according to John 17:4.

[1] Romans 16:22. At one time he was thought to be Silas.

[2] Both the materials to write *on* and *with* made the process more difficult and laborious.

What a privilege this is—not to be left in the dark; to know that we are not the victims of chance; and especially to know that God's will for us is good. After all, he makes all things work together for the good of those who love him.[1] And this 'good' ultimately is the way in which God's will is always engaging our lives in order to conform us to the image of his Son that he might be the firstborn among many brothers.[2] His will is good because it has the best of all possible purposes in view—his glory in our Christlikeness.

More than that, God's will is 'perfect' because his wisdom is flawless. We see this in small things, perhaps sometimes in great things. The Lord is the master of the jigsaw puzzle of our lives. The pieces may be strangely shaped; often we cannot see how they fit together; but eventually when the big picture is complete we will see that each piece was perfectly shaped. He leads us by ways we could not have guessed, into situations we never expected, to fulfil purposes we never could have imagined.

When we thus yield our lives to the Lord, and our thinking is renewed by his word, we also begin to find God's will is acceptable—it becomes a delight to us. We yield to it gladly. In it we experience the pleasures of knowing God and discovering his unfolding purposes for us. We taste and see that he is good.[3]

This, perhaps, is the most obvious contrast between life in sin and life in grace. To the unregenerate, God's will is inevitably unpleasant, simply because it is *his* will and not *their* will. They do not know that he wills much better for us than we can ever will for ourselves.

But to those who are being transformed, God's will brings pleasure.

Paul knew this and had experienced it. That is why he urged the Christians in Rome—and through his letter to them also urges us—

[1] Romans 8:28.
[2] Romans 8:29.
[3] Psalm 34:8.

to wholehearted devotion, to real repentance in which we turn away from the old life, no longer allowing ourselves to be squeezed into the world's mould, but instead allowing ourselves to be transformed by the renewing of our minds through the instrument of his word.

The result? The gospel turns the duty of doing and experiencing God's will into a delight.

3

Prepositions of Grace

W

e must now take a deep breath and plunge into one of the most important, thrilling, and challenging areas of the New Testament's teaching: the Christian's union and communion with Jesus Christ. This is the heart of sanctification, the soul of devotion, and the strength of holiness. It will be a dominant theme here and in the chapters that follow.

We have seen that sanctification, like justification, is rooted in the grace of God and in its reception and outworking. Now we must ask and try to answer the question: What does God do in order to bring us to the Christlikeness which is his ultimate goal?

The New Testament answer is found especially but not exclusively in the correspondence of the apostle Paul: God's grace transforms us through our union and communion with Jesus Christ.

Paul's most succinct statement of this is found in Galatians, possibly his earliest extant letter.

The Epistle to the Galatians is by no means the easiest of Paul's letters. In it he is battling with a group of people who were insisting that Gentile believers needed to be circumcised if they were fully to belong to the people of God.[1] In the midst of his argument there is one verse that seems to stand out like a bright star in the night sky. In the past it was one of the first verses new Christians were

---

[1] Galatians 5:2-6.

encouraged to memorize. It served as an identity card, providing a brief summary description of the Christian life. What precedes Paul's monumental statement scarcely prepares us for it. To read it for the first time is like turning a corner in Zermatt in the Swiss Alps and catching one's first sight of the Matterhorn, arising as it were out of nowhere. Nothing can quite prepare us for Galatians 2:20:

> I have been crucified with Christ. It is no longer I who live, but Christ who lives in me. And the life I now live in the flesh I live by faith in the Son of God, who loved me and gave himself for me.

These words harmonize well with some of the notes we have already sounded. They emphasize that the resources for our Christian life are in Jesus Christ and not in ourselves. They serve to remind us—and we need to be reminded of this until we are almost exhausted hearing it—that our sanctification takes place in union with Christ and not apart from him. In addition, the teaching here links in with the sphere in which we have seen our sanctification is to be worked out—in our bodies: 'The life that I now live in the flesh [*sarx,* physical body] I live by faith in the Son of God.'

The gospel never emphasizes the body at the expense of the spirit; but by the same token it never minimizes the importance of the body. Rather it changes the kind of life we live in the body. Thus Paul provides us with a brief summary of what he elsewhere calls 'my gospel'.[1] He does so in a particularly memorable way. For here his use of *prepositional phrases* leads us into the heart of his whole theology. Four of them highlight the force of his exposition:

1. The Son of God ... loved me and gave himself *for* me.

2. The life I now live, I live by faith *in* the Son of God.

3. I have been crucified *with* Christ.

4. Christ lives *in* me.

[1] Romans 2:16; 16:25.

Preposition 1: The Son of God ... gave himself FOR me

The Lord Jesus Christ has given himself *for* me. This is the foundation of my union with him.

Paul has in view here the way in which Christ gave himself for us in his death on the cross.

The Son of God came into the world for us by taking and sharing our human nature. This, his union with us in our flesh, and not our faith union with him, is the foundation of our fellowship with him. His uniting himself to us in our human nature is the basis for our uniting ourselves to him in faith.

At the beginning of his life on earth, conceived by the power of the Spirit in the darkness of the womb of the Virgin Mary, the Son of God took human nature, in all its frailty and poverty, in order to live a perfect life for us, in our place. At the end of his life he was carried by friends into the darkness of the garden tomb, having died the death we deserve because of our sins. Because he has taken our human nature and lived in perfect obedience to his Father for us, and died for our sins and been raised into new life, and ascended to his Father in the nature he assumed, there are now resources in the hands of the Holy Spirit both to justify us and sanctify us, indeed even to glorify us.

Abraham Kuyper expressed real insight in this connection when he wrote that what a sinner needs is the transformation of his sinful human nature. But he continues:

> The Holy Spirit finds this holy disposition in its required form, not in the Father, nor in Himself, but in Immanuel, who as the Son of God and the Son of Man possesses holiness in that peculiar form.[1]

---

[1] Abraham Kuyper, *The Work of the Holy Spirit*, tr. H. De Vries (New York: Funk & Wagnalls, 1900), 461. Abraham Kuyper (1837–1920) was successively minister, newspaper editor, politician, founder of the Anti-Revolutionary Party in the Netherlands, founder of the Free University of Amsterdam and Prime Minister of The Netherlands (1901–05). He is best remembered today for the famous statement in his inaugural lecture, that 'There is not a square inch in the whole domain of our human existence over which Christ, who is sovereign over all, does not say "Mine!"'

If there is to be both justification and transformation for sinful *human* nature, then the resources for both must come from one who has shared that nature, and in it lived obediently for us, and then, in further obedience to his Father, died in our place for our sins and broken the power of death in his resurrection. Only a Saviour who accomplishes this double obedience for us can resource a full and real salvation in which we are not only forgiven but also counted righteous, and then are transformed into his likeness by the Spirit.

The author of Hebrews provides us with the clearest statement of this principle when he writes:

> For it was fitting that he, for whom and by whom all things exist, in bringing many sons to glory, should make the founder of their salvation perfect through suffering.[1]

'Founder' here is the Greek word *archēgos* which means 'pioneer', 'founder', 'author', or 'trail-blazer'. It denotes a person whose actions lead others to share in the reality or consequences of his individual accomplishments. It is used only four times in the New Testament, always of Jesus.[2]

Jesus lived a life of complete obedience and perfect sanctification. He then died for our sins. As one man he brought to an end the reign of guilt, sin, Satan, and death. However he did this not as an isolated individual but as our substitute and representative. Thus what he has accomplished benefits us. He blazed the trail as our representative. Now all those who belong to him can share the fruit of his sanctification.

But the author of Hebrews adds a further important consideration. For this to be so, both the one who makes men holy (that is, Christ), and those who are made holy (that is, believers), 'must all have one origin' that is, they must all be members of the same

---

[1] Hebrews 2:10.
[2] Acts 3:15 ('Author'); 5:31 ('Leader'); Hebrews 2:10; 12:2 (both 'founder').

family.[1] The Sanctifier must share the same nature, and in that sense be one flesh, with those he sanctifies.

Jesus accomplished precisely this. By coming into the family of flesh and sanctifying his whole life, then by dying our death and being declared righteous or justified in his resurrection,[2] he became the 'pioneer' or 'author' of both justification and sanctification. Having been borne along by the Spirit and bearing him throughout his life and ministry, the ascended Saviour is able to say to him: 'Now all the resources of my incarnation, life, death, resurrection, ascension, and heavenly session are available for sinners, because they were all accomplished for them not for me. I am sending you to bring my people into union and communion with me so that they may be made like me.' This is what Jesus prophesied on the evening of his crucifixion:

> When the Spirit of truth comes ... He will glorify me, for he will take what is mine and declare it to you.[3]

Thus, through the Spirit's uniting us to Christ we have been connected to the source of our salvation. His justification—God's declaration that he was righteous—is our justification; his sanctification—since he sanctified himself for our sakes[4]—is also ours. Thus, everything Christ did he did for me in obedience to his Father. All that he has done is therefore mine as a gift. He gave himself *for* me, in his love to me; and now through the Spirit all that he did is mine.

Preposition 2: I live by faith IN the Son of God

Paul now goes on to speak about the instrument or means by which we are united to Christ: through the Spirit we are brought into living union with him *by faith*: the life that I now live, I live by faith in the Son of God who loved me and gave himself for me.

[1] Hebrews 2:11; literally 'of one'.
[2] This is implied in 1 Timothy 3:16.
[3] John 16:13-14.
[4] John 17:19.

Faith means responding to Christ's invitation, 'Come to me ... and I will give you rest.'[1] With all the burden of my sin and guilt, in my weakness and failure, I rest on Jesus Christ and receive his gracious pardon and power.

The language of the Old Testament informs that of the New Testament here.

In the Old Testament 'to have faith' meant resting your weight, and the burden of your sin and need upon the Lord as your Saviour. On one occasion the language of 'roll on' to him is used.[2] In the same way in the New Testament 'to believe', 'to have faith', means to transfer trust from self to Christ, all the while recognizing that I cannot carry the heavy load of my sin and guilt, but he can. We trust him because his strong shoulders were stretched out on the cross as our sins were 'rolled onto' his body on the tree.[3]

New language?

New concepts often require a whole new vocabulary to describe them properly. The full revelation of the gospel is new wine. Old wineskins are inadequate to hold it. Thus we find that there are occasions when Paul seems to have created a new use of language, or moulded his grammar to fit the newly revealed final shape of the gospel. So while the Old Testament Scriptures prepared the way for Christ,[4] they presented only a shadow picture. The full colour version required a new use of language to describe it. So the early Christians, perhaps led by Paul himself, occasionally employed language in novel ways in order to express what was new and unique about the gospel.

One particular expression Paul uses seems to be without parallel in ancient Greek literature. He speaks not only about believing *in*

[1] Matthew 11:28.
[2] Psalm 22:8 (*galal*).
[3] 1 Peter 2:24.
[4] Romans 1:2.

Christ (*en Christō*) but also about believing *into* Christ (*eis Christon*). Faith *in* the Son of God means believing *into* Jesus Christ.

First century people no more thought or wrote about 'believing *into*' someone else than we do. But Paul realized that this is in fact what faith effects. When we believe *on* or *in* Christ, we actually believe *into* him. Faith brings us into a person-to-person union and communion with Jesus Christ so that what is ours becomes his and what is his becomes ours. This perspective was so central to Paul's thinking that (in contrast with ourselves) we *never* find him describing believers as 'Christians'. In fact the expression is used very rarely in the New Testament.[1] Instead because we believe *into* Christ believers are most frequently described as those who are 'in Christ'.

I remember as a young teenager reading the famous passage in which Paul describes his 'thorn in the flesh'.[2] He introduces it by saying that he knows 'a man in Christ' who experienced a memorable revelation fourteen years previously. I naïvely wondered who this anonymous man might be whom Paul seemed to know so well! It slowly dawned on me that Paul was, of course, talking about himself. This for him was the essence of being a Christian—being united to Jesus Christ by faith, so that he typically described believers as those who were *in Christ*.

If by any chance you have never noticed this expression, or its parallels, now that you have been alerted to it you will notice it on every page of Paul's letters. On average it appears in his letters in one form or another between two and three times per chapter.

The point to grasp is this: believers are so united to Christ that all he is and has done for us becomes our possession too. When Christ died upon the cross, in some sense we died with him; when he rose from the grave, we also rose with him. Because we are united to him

[1] Remarkably only in Acts 11:26; 26:28; 1 Peter 4:16.
[2] 2 Corinthians 12:1-10.

everything he has done on our behalf is so embodied in him that when we believe 'into' Christ all that is his becomes ours.

Later we will see Paul unpacking this and working out its implications in considerable detail.

Larger than we first thought?

Most of us begin the Christian life knowing that we need to trust in Jesus so that our sins will be forgiven. That is true. But there is much more. In fact 'every spiritual blessing' becomes ours in Christ.[1] When we 'get' Christ by faith, we 'get' everything that is in him to pardon, liberate, and transform our lives. All the resources that God deployed in his Son—in his death, resurrection, ascension, and heavenly reign—we now inherit. If this is true then every resource stored up for us in Jesus Christ is now available to us through faith, to enable us to live for his glory.

In the second part of *The Pilgrim's Progress* John Bunyan describes a scene in the House of the Interpreter. Christiana, the wife of the Pilgrim, who has now followed him on her own journey to the Celestial City, is shown a strange sight:

> a man that could look no way but downwards, with a muck-rake in his hand. There stood also one over his head with a celestial crown in his hand, and proffered to give him that crown for his muck-rake; but the man did neither look up, nor regard, but raked to himself the straws, the small sticks, and dust of the floor.

It is a vivid picture of someone so enamoured of this world that he gives no attention to the treasures and pleasures of the gospel. So Christiana's response is as telling as it is wise. She does not say 'I am glad that's not me!' Rather, writes Bunyan:

> *Christiana.* Then said Christiana, O! deliver me from this muck-rake.

[1] Ephesians 1:3. In one extended Greek sentence (our versions verses 3-14) Paul enumerates these blessings.

Interpreter. That prayer, said the Interpreter, has lain by till 'tis almost rusty: 'Give me not riches' is scarce the prayer of one of ten thousand. Straws and sticks and dust with most are the great things now looked after.

With that Mercy and Christiana wept, and said, 'It is alas! too true.'[1]

This is indeed a portrait of a non-Christian. But Christiana's prayer is on the mark. She knows how easily we can slip back into finding our treasure on earth rather than in heaven—despite Jesus' words.[2] Sadly we often live the Christian life setting our hearts on lesser treasures and pleasures than those that are our inheritance because we are in Christ 'in whom are hidden all the treasures of wisdom and knowledge'.[3] It is hardly surprising therefore if our lives express so little of 'the praise of his glorious grace' and 'the praise of his glory'.[4] Only a new appreciation of what it means to believe in Christ—to believe into all he is for us—will introduce or recover the deep melody of grace.

But Paul presents us with another perspective on being 'in Christ':

Preposition 3: I have been crucified WITH Christ

The *heart* of union with Christ, Paul emphasizes, is this: when we trusted *into* him who was crucified for us there is a sense in which we also came to share in his crucifixion. Paul does not mean that we died physically but rather that united to Christ all the implications of his being crucified for us become our possession. Thus in Christ we 'died' out of the old family to which we belonged by nature—the family of Adam. What Paul elsewhere calls 'the old man'[5]—the

---

[1] John Bunyan, *The Pilgrim's Progress* (Penguin Books: Harmondsworth, 1965), 247-8.

[2] Matthew 6:19-21.

[3] Colossians 2:3.

[4] Ephesians 1: 6, 12, 14.

[5] Romans 6:6. The translation 'old man' is a more precise one here than 'old self' (ESV).

person I was in Adam—was crucified with Christ. As a result, all the claims the old fallen order had on me have come to an end.

But the crucified Christ to whom I am now united is also the risen Christ. I cannot be united to him in his crucifixion without being united to him in his resurrection as well.[1] When Christ rose, all the implications of his resurrection became my possession too, even if they are not yet all worked out completely.

Thus a Christian is inseparable from Christ in both his death and his resurrection. 'I have been crucified with Christ' ... yet, as Paul adds 'I live'! I died to the old life and now I have been raised into a new life altogether.

Yet more grammar

It is important to be clear about what Paul is *not* saying.

- He is not *currently crucifying* himself (present tense) with Christ, although it is true that he believes we must currently 'put to death the deeds of the body'.[2]

- Nor is he saying, as he does later in Galatians, that 'those who belong to Christ Jesus *have crucified* (past tense) the flesh with its passions and desires'.[3] That took place in the initial act of faith in which we abandoned everything to Christ when we first came to trust him. In that sense it is a decisive past event.

In fact Paul is not describing something he has done, but what has been done for him and to him, what has happened to him through being united to Christ in his death. He has been *co-crucified with Christ.*[4]

Later in his ministry Paul expounded this principle in greater detail.[5] For the moment we should notice that he is not speaking here

[1] Romans 6:4, 5, 8.
[2] Romans 8:13.
[3] Galatians 5:24.
[4] In Paul's Greek 'with' is part of the verb 'crucify' and not a separate preposition.
[5] See below, Chapter 4.

about something we believe because *we feel* it is true of ourselves, but because *God says* it is true of us. In fact we do not naturally feel or think of ourselves in this way. Paul is grinding spectacle lenses for us according to the gospel's prescription. We need to wear these spectacles in order to see ourselves more clearly and to recognise and benefit from our new identity in Christ—for if we have been co-crucified with him we have died to the old order that formerly dominated our whole lives.

So we must learn to follow the gospel order and view ourselves through gospel lenses—since only when we know, understand, and believe this truth can we begin to live in the light of it. And only then does it make a difference in our lives.

This is profound theology, but how does it make any difference to us? We have already seen the answer: *our lives are transformed only when our minds are renewed.* Knowing that we have died to the old order and have been set free from the old age in which we were held captive[1] provides us with a new sense of who were are in Christ that drives the new life we have been called to live.

Paul now takes our thinking one step further:

Preposition 4: I no longer live, but Christ lives IN me

In order to understand the undergirding logic of the gospel we have taken Paul's prepositional phrases in their *theological* order rather than in the order in which they appear in the text.

- Christ gave himself *for us.*

- We live by faith *in him.*

- We are those who have been crucified *with him.*

Now Paul leads us into one further dimension of our new identity in Christ:

- It is no longer I who live, but Christ who lives in me.

[1] Galatians 1:4.

Christ now comes to dwell *in us* through the Holy Spirit. We can say 'Christ lives in me.' This is the New Testament doctrine of the indwelling of Christ.

The importance of this is demonstrated by the emphasis Jesus placed on it in the teaching he gave his disciples in the upper room. Consider his promises:

- When the Spirit came at Pentecost they would realize that 'I am in my Father, and you in me, *and I in you.*'[1]

- United to the vine, Christ himself, they were encouraged 'Abide in me, *and I in you.*'[2]

- Thus 'Whoever abides in me, and *I in him*, he it is that bears much fruit.'[3]

- When Jesus prayed for his disciples to be one, he spoke about the foundation of this union and communion: '*I in them* and you in me that they may become perfectly one.'[4]

- In fact his deepest longing (and his final petition for the church) was that 'the love with which you [the Father] have loved me may be in them and *I in them.*'[5]

The same reality lies at the heart of Paul's prayer for the Ephesians: 'that *Christ may dwell in your hearts* through faith.'[6] This fills him with awe when he thinks about the implication, namely 'Christ in you, *the hope of glory.*'[7]

We will see later that this indwelling of believers by Christ through his Spirit has very significant implications for Christian

---

[1] John 14:20.
[2] John 15:4.
[3] John 15:5.
[4] John 17:23.
[5] John 17:26
[6] Ephesians 3:20.
[7] Colossians 1:27.

fellowship.[1] Jesus more than hinted at this in his final prayer that the union of believers in the church might be analogous to his union with the Father.[2] We need to try to grasp the enormity of what is being said.

Our forefathers used to speak about 'living below the level of our privileges'. How true that is—and often because the sheer enormity of them has never really dawned on us. And perhaps, sadly, because we have either never known what they are, or never taken time to reflect on their significance for our lives. We have been too busy *doing* to take time to reflect on *being*. As a result we suffer from a loss of our Christian identity. We live as spiritual paupers when in fact we are indwelt by the Lord of glory. But grasp the indwelling of Christ and a new dynamic is released, and a new melody is introduced into our devotion.

It is a truism that we become like the people with whom we live. That is the case with of married couples. In many respects, often quite mundane, they seem to become mirror images of each other—their thoughts, dispositions, words, even sometimes their facial expressions, reflect each another. Why? Because the intimacy of life and love together has brought them to think, act, and react, as one. Something similar is true of the closeness and depth of our union with the Lord Jesus Christ. As in marriage so when our husband is Jesus Christ we become one with him. When we come to faith we put on Christ.[3] But in another sense Christ also puts us on—he dwells in our hearts through faith.[4]

Perhaps most Christians can remember years later—as I can—when and where and from whom they first heard about the indwelling of Christ in believers. I was a relatively young Christian, fifteen years old, listening to a sermon on Paul's words 'Christ in you

[1] See below, 127-128.
[2] John 17:21.
[3] Romans 13:14; Colossians 3:12.
[4] Ephesians 3:17.

the hope of glory'.[1] I left the service knowing that my perspective on life had been changed. Christ was dwelling in me! I looked to make sure that no one was watching and skipped all the way home. It was one of the most exhilarating moments of my young life. Now I knew who I was—someone in whom the Lord Jesus had come to dwell. Yes, it takes a lifetime for this truth, grasped in a moment, to penetrate to every element in one's life. But it will never do that until we have begun to grasp its reality.

All biblical truths are important and relevant. Some have the potential to change in a fundamental way how we live the Christian life. This is one of them.

As a recently arrived alien resident in the United States in the early 1980s I heard a speech by Wilson Goode during his successful campaign to become Mayor of Philadelphia. He spoke, as I recall, words to this effect: 'My grandfather was born into slavery.'

To a thirty-something Scotsman this statement from the lips of a man only a decade older than myself was emotionally staggering. I was stunned to think that someone of roughly my own generation could have known and talked to a close relative who had actually been a slave (even if he was probably still a child when the Thirteenth Amendment to the Constitution was passed in 1865[2]). Now I could understand why a person my own age would still 'feel' the painful emotions of those days and the lingering dark shadows of past oppression. Of course this would make an impact on how you would think about yourself. I remembered that I had read years earlier that when slaves in the South were emancipated some of them were incapable of taking it in; externally they were free, but

[1] Colossians 1:27.

[2] The Thirteenth Amendment decreed that 'Neither slavery, nor involuntary servitude, except as a punishment for crime whereof the party shall have been duly convicted, shall exist within the United States, or any place subject to their jurisdiction.'

internally the marks, the habits, the dispositions and mentality pro-duced by years and generations of enslavement remained. They were free men, but they were never able to enjoy that freedom.

In some ways, sadly, the same can be true for Christians. We have been set free; we have received a new identity in Christ; we have been crucified with him who died for us; we have been raised into the new life we live by faith in him who dwells in us.

But is it too much for us to take in?

If it is, make it a priority to reflect on these gospel principles:

• The Son of God loved me and *gave himself for* me.

• I have been *crucified with* Christ.

• I live *by faith in* the Son of God.

• Christ *dwells in* me.

And then go and begin to live in the light of it.

4

A Different Kind of Death

We have already noted a surprising statistic in Paul's letters. He *never* describes believers as 'Christians'. For him the 'big idea' of the gospel is that the believer is 'in Christ'—as he makes clear on virtually every page of his letters.

For Paul this union with Christ is multi-dimensional.

It has an *eternal* dimension, since God 'chose us in him before the foundation of the world'.[1]

It has a *covenantal* and *incarnational* dimension, since in his incarnation Christ was obedient as the second man and last Adam.[2]

It also has an *existential* dimension, since the Holy Spirit brings us into a real spiritual bonding with the risen and ascended Lord.[3]

The corollary for Paul is that because we are 'in Christ' it follows that we may be said to have been 'with' him in everything he did for us as our representative and substitute. We have already seen the relevance of this: we have been crucified with Christ.

Later we will consider Paul's fullest exposition of this principle.[4] Christ is our life: we died, were buried, raised, have ascended, and will appear in glory with him.[5] This is union with Christ viewed

---

[1] Ephesians 1:4.
[2] Romans 5:12-21.
[3] See for example Romans 8:8-9; 1 Corinthians 6:17.
[4] See below, chapter 6.
[5] Colossians 3:1-4.

through a wide-angle lens. But Paul also wants us to view this same union under a microscope—so that we get a close up view of its important details. This he provides for us in his *magnum opus*—his letter to the churches in Rome:

> What shall we say then? Are we to continue in sin that grace may abound? By no means! How can we who died to sin still live in it? Do you not know that all of us who have been baptized into Christ Jesus were baptized into his death? We were buried therefore with him by baptism into death, in order that, just as Christ was raised from the dead by the glory of the Father, we too might walk in newness of life. For if we have been united with him in a death like his, we shall certainly be united with him in a resurrection like his. We know that our old self was crucified with him in order that the body of sin might be brought to nothing, so that we would no longer be enslaved to sin. For one who has died has been set free from sin. Now if we have died with Christ, we believe that we will also live with him. We know that Christ, being raised from the dead, will never die again; death no longer has dominion over him. For the death he died he died to sin, once for all, but the life he lives he lives to God. So you also must consider yourselves dead to sin and alive to God in Christ Jesus.
>
> Let not sin therefore reign in your mortal body, to make you obey its passions. Do not present your members to sin as instruments for unrighteousness, but present yourselves to God as those who have been brought from death to life, and your members to God as instruments for righteousness. For sin will have no dominion over you, since you are not under law but under grace.[1]

These are among the most important verses in the whole of Romans, indeed the whole of the New Testament. No less a figure than Thomas Chalmers stated at the beginning of his lecture on Romans 6:1-2 that

> We have ever been in the habit of regarding this chapter as the passage of greatest interest in the Bible—as that in which the greatest

[1] Romans 6:1-14.

quantity of scriptural light is thrown on what to the eye of the general world is a depth and a mystery—even on that path of transition which leads from the imputed righteousness that is by faith, to the personal righteousness that is by new and spiritual obedience. We know not a single theme in the whole compass of Christianity, on which there rests to the natural discernment a cloud of thicker obscurity, than that which relates to the origin and growth of a believer's holiness.[1]

A similar conviction seems to have been held by D. Martyn Lloyd-Jones who probably more than any other preacher in the twentieth century gave concentrated attention to expounding Romans (as he did at Westminster Chapel in London for some fourteen years). He gives us a fascinating insight into the 'back-story' of his preaching:

> One Sunday evening at the close of an evening service at Westminster Chapel, somewhere about 1943, a certain well-known preacher came into my vestry and said to me: 'When are you going to preach a series of expository sermons on the Epistle to the Romans?' I answered immediately: 'When I have really understood chapter 6.'[2]

These comments suggest that perhaps this is one of the passages Simon Peter had in mind when he commented on the writings of 'our beloved brother Paul' that 'There are some things in them that are hard to understand.'[3] Peter is not suggesting that Paul is an abstruse and difficult author. Rather the gospel contains truths so profound that they challenge and stretch the best of intellects. After all, as Chalmers indicated, the patterns of gospel truth run counter to the instincts of our fallen understanding. So we should

---

[1] Thomas Chalmers, *Lectures on the Epistle of Paul the Apostle to the Romans* (Edinburgh: Thomas Constable, 1856), 1:297. Chalmers first gave the majority of his lectures to his own congregation in St John's Church, Glasgow from 1819–23, and later completed and published them in 1842.

[2] D. M. Lloyd-Jones, *The New Man* (Edinburgh: Banner of Truth Trust, 1972), xi. The substance of Lloyd-Jones' expository sermons on Romans can be found in fourteen volumes published between 1970 and 2003.

[3] 2 Peter 3:15-16.

not assume, and we certainly dare not demand, that everything about the gospel should be elementary and that there will be no mind-stretching involved in understanding it—not if we are to take seriously the principle that sanctification comes through the renewing of our minds.[1]

This is certainly true of what Paul says here. It would not be claiming too much to say that the church is still trying fully to understand some of the details of his teaching in Romans 6. So there is room here for a lifetime of reflection. That is part of the divine plan, as we know, precisely because life-transformation takes place through the ongoing renewal of our mind.

A major key to Christian life

The fundamental significance of Paul's teaching here is highlighted by the question he asks:

> Do you not know that all of us who have been baptized into Christ Jesus were baptized into his death?[2]

He appeals to both the *fact* of baptism and to its *meaning*. It is the action by which we were publicly 'named' for the Father, Son, and Holy Spirit.[3]

Paul's teaching here can be something of a challenge for evangelical Christians—especially if we have assumed or been taught that baptism is basically a sign of *what we have done*, namely trust in Christ. Here, as elsewhere, Paul implies that baptism symbolizes not what we have done, but *what has been done for us*. His verb is in the passive not the active voice: we have '*been baptized* into Christ Jesus'. It is not something we do ourselves because it does not primarily signify anything we ourselves have done.

---

[1] As we have seen in Romans 12:1-2. Note also the words of Hebrews 5:11-14 in this context.
[2] Romans 6:3.
[3] Matthew 28:19.

To understand rightly how baptism functions in our Christian lives we must first recognise that it points to Jesus Christ and to union with him by faith.[1] It does not point *at* faith so much as summon us *to* faith. Christ himself, and, yes, all that faith finds in him, is the point—not primarily what we ourselves have done in coming to faith. Baptism says: 'Look at what is yours in Christ', not 'Look at the faith that brought you to Christ.' This—the dynamic and direction of baptism's symbolism—is of fundamental importance if it is to nourish us in the lifelong way Paul believes it should.

There is a further aspect of baptism we need to grasp. Christ has given it to us as a naming ceremony: 'Go … make disciples … baptizing them *in the name*[2] of the Father and of the Son and of the Holy Spirit …'

There is an important paradox to grasp here. Naming ceremonies do not transform us inwardly. Yet they make a lifelong difference to us.

Our parents went through a kind of 'naming ceremony' when they registered our birth. They were asked 'What is the name of your child?' That naming ceremony did not change us inwardly. Even if it had taken place when we were adults that would still be true. Yet this 'naming ceremony' has had a lifelong impact on us. We hear one or two words and we instinctively respond, 'That's me!' As I hear it, that name identifies me, and tells me who I am. My full name reminds me where I have come from, what privileges I have had; it even reminds me of the lifestyle I am expected to live as a member of my family.

If all this is true of a secular 'naming ceremony' how much more significant is the 'naming ceremony' of baptism! For here we are named for the Trinity. Baptism therefore does not so much speak *about faith* but *to faith* and says:

[1] In this respect baptism and the Lord's Supper function in parallel ways.
[2] Literally 'into' the name.

You are being named for the Father, the Son, and the Holy Spirit. The Father has sent his Spirit to unite us to Jesus Christ. In him we are given the rich inheritance of all the gracious resources we will ever need to be brought from sin to salvation, from death to life, and from earth to heaven.

In essence, then, Paul is saying: 'Look at what your baptism pictures; listen to what your baptism says; and as faith takes hold of its message remember what it tells you about who you are in Christ!'[1]

The background

Like so much of Paul's teaching what he says here is drawn out of him by muddle-headed thinking; in this case the notion that if his claim is true that 'where sin increased, grace abounded all the more', then we can surely 'continue in sin that grace may abound'.[2] His answer? Those who speak like that (and most of us have heard some version of these words), understand neither God's grace nor their baptism. In fact, at bottom, they do not really understand what it means to be a Christian; certainly they do not grasp what it means to be 'in Christ'.

Gradually Paul turns his immediate negative reaction to this wrong-headed thinking into a positive exposition. It contains at least the following related elements.

---

[1] Baptism, like the Lord's Supper, is a gospel ordinance, and so it is not surprising that there is a symbiotic relation between the two. Unfortunately baptism has become an area of considerable disagreement in the history of the church. It is all too easy to be side-tracked into polemical issues whenever baptism is discussed and as a result be diverted from its real significance. What is said above about baptism remains true whether, for example, one is a credo-baptist or a paedo-baptist. It is not only biblically important but also wonderfully enriching for us to have the objective to subjective orientation implied here, and not to subjectivise baptism as though it were a sign of faith rather than a sign of the Christ on whom faith relies.

[2] Romans 5:20–6:1.

1. Emotion

We are often (and rightly) advised not to live the Christian life on the basis of our emotions. But it would be a mistake to think that the gospel leaves our emotions in the same condition in which it found them. In fact it both informs and transforms them.

We see this vividly illustrated in Paul's instinctive reaction to the suggestion that a Christian might go on sinning since it would simply lead to God showing more grace. His immediate response seems to be all emotion; indeed it is almost an explosion! 'By no means!' he seems to shout.

This sounds a little too upper-middle class as a response. Perhaps the older tradition of the Authorised (King James) Version better captured the vigour of Paul's reaction ('God forbid'). 'That must never be!' Or, more colloquially, 'No way!'[1] His words seem to emerge without much thought. This is a gut reaction; it takes place at the level of Paul's instincts. His recoil is automatic, even visceral.

But while Paul's refusal to live in sin took place 'without much thought', it was very far from being thoughtless. In fact it was the reverse; it was the fruit of much thought about what it means to be baptised and to be in Christ. Indeed his reaction is actually a striking illustration of an important aspect of sanctification: thinking through the logic of the gospel corrects, cleanses, recalibrates, transforms, and sanctifies us *emotionally* as well as *intellectually*. It leads to us responding as whole people to the situations in which we find ourselves. Instead of being captivated emotionally, our emotions are mastered by the gospel and begin to express its truth and power. We thus develop an integrated and healthy emotional life. This is the true and valuable 'emotional intelligence' the gospel produces.

But what is it about the gospel that brought about this reaction?

---

[1] I owe this suggestion to Daniel B. Wallace, *Greek Grammar Beyond the Basics* (Grand Rapids: Zondervan, 1996), 482.

2. *Explanation*

Paul's answer is that if we understood our baptism we would see that it is inconceivable, a self-contradiction, to think a Christian can simply continue in the old way of life. Baptism 'tells' faith that the old life in Adam has gone; new life in Christ has begun.[1] When I respond to my baptism in faith it tells me: 'The believer no longer has the same relationship to sin he or she used to have; you are no longer under its dominion as you once were; you have been raised into new life with Christ—that is why it is inconceivable that you would continue in sin.' For in Christ's death and resurrection the dominion of sin was broken and a new age dawned. If this was true of Jesus Christ himself it is also true of those who are in him. Indeed it cannot *not* be true of them. It is true of them *by definition*.

Paul has his own distinctive way of making this point. Follow his reasoning. He asks: How can we who died to sin still live in it?[2]

You cannot both have died to something and still be living in it. There is a law of non-contradiction: you cannot be in one and the same sense, at one and the same time, in one and the same realm, both dead and alive. If you have died, you do not live. Those who died to sin therefore cannot go on living in sin.

Significantly here Paul does not use the regular pronoun (*hos*) but a form of it which implies the idea of belonging to a category (*hostis*—those who belong to a specific category). In this instance, Christians belong to a category sharing this defining feature: they are 'those-who-have-died-to-sin' people. They cannot still belong to the opposite category of 'those-who-continue-to-live-in-sin' people. That would be a kind of ontological contradiction, an amnesia in relation to our true identity in Christ.

---

[1] Notice that the conceptual background to all that Paul says in Romans 6:1-14 lies in Romans 5:12-21 and his description of our old identity in Adam and then our new identity in Christ.

[2] Romans 6:2.

This is gospel logic. It is worthwhile labouring the point because—as Thomas Chalmers suggested—it is such a counter-intuitive way of thinking about ourselves. Unfortunately that leads some Christians to regard what Paul is saying here as too difficult to grasp or to be of any practical importance. But once again we need to remember that in any discipline—and living the Christian life is a complex discipline of its own!—we need to apply our minds to thinking clearly. In the case of this particular teaching the effort to grasp what Paul is saying and to work out its implications is vital.[1]

Perhaps an illustration will help. Many years ago now the president of the seminary in which I taught asked me—a native Scot—'Have you become an American citizen yet?' I replied—with self-control!—in the negative. But then he asked: 'Why not?' Taken somewhat aback by the very question itself I immediately (and perhaps less than tactfully!) blurted out: 'But I'm a Scot!'

Was it not obvious therefore why I had not become a citizen? I wasn't an American; I was a Scotsman. Why would a Scotsman want to become an American! Was this ethnic prejudice on my part?—Don't almost all of us feel this way about our native land and our nationality?

Of course the illustration breaks down. I have friends who have become American citizens with good reason (and in good conscience!). But the point is surely taken. We are born with our

---

[1] A point made with particular force by John Murray: 'We are too ready to give heed to what we deem to be the hard, empirical facts of Christian profession, and we have erased the clear line of demarcation which Scripture defines. As a result we have lost our vision of the high calling of God in Christ Jesus. Our ethic has lost its dynamic and we have become conformed to this world. We know not the power of death to sin in the death of Christ, and we are not able to bear the rigour of the liberty of redemptive emancipation. "We died to sin": the glory of Christ's accomplishment and the guarantee of the Christian ethic are bound up with that doctrine. If we live in sin we have not died to it, and if we have not died to it we are not Christ's. If we died to sin, we no longer live in it, for "we who are such as have died to sin, how shall we live in it?" (Rom. 6:2).' John Murray, *Principles of Conduct* (Grand Rapids: Eerdmans, 1957), 205.

distinctive nationality; we grow up in its culture; we love our people; we love our land and its topography; this is where our parents and grandparents lived; here lie the influences that have shaped us; this is what in many respects defines who we are. Even for those who decide to become citizens of another country it must feel in some measure like a denial of their identity to become a citizen of a nation to which they have not 'belonged'.

Of course there are circumstances and situations where this illustration breaks down. But the spiritual analogy never breaks down. As believers we possess a permanent and irreversible new citizenship.[1] We are 'in Christ'—that is who we are. He once died to sin and now lives forever to God.[2] We are inseparably united to him in this. It is what constitutes our 'national identity' our 'spiritual ethnicity'. To continue living the old life in sin would be a denial of who we really are.

The challenge? Until we grasp this teaching we do not yet fully understand what it means to be a Christian.

If we are to understand the implications of this for sanctification, we need to turn to Paul's third step:

3. Exposition

We are 'those who have died to sin'. The significance of the expression 'died to sin' has been much discussed. I take it to mean something like 'died to the reign, the dominion, the authority, and the rule of sin'.[3] Paul helps us grasp its implications by spelling out in detail what 'we know' about ourselves as those 'who have been baptized into Christ Jesus' and have 'died to sin':

(1) *The fact* is that 'our old self was crucified with him [Christ]'.

---

[1] Philippians 3:20.

[2] Romans 6:10.

[3] For an extended exposition and discussion of this understanding of 'we who died to sin' and the later statement (6:10) that the death Christ died 'he died to sin' see Appendix 2 below.

(2) *The end in view* is that 'the body of sin might be brought to nothing'.

(3) *The result* is that 'we would no longer be enslaved to sin'.

(4) *The reason* for our new freedom is: 'one who has died has been set free from sin'.[1]

These are critical statements; yet they have challenged interpreters largely because Paul does not use this wording elsewhere in his letters. So what do these statements mean, and what do they imply?

From one point of view we could simply omit any discussion of these nuances of interpretation (after all we do that often enough in reading the Bible—some things we 'leave to the experts'). But there is an important reason for giving patient consideration to this passage: these words are of major importance in determining the way we think about ourselves as Christians. They contribute significantly to what in recent years has been called our 'self-image'. True, the pursuit of a 'self-image' can be a bondage all of its own. But part of the beauty of the 'self-image' the gospel gives us is that it delivers us from narcissism, and from seeing 'self' as the central project of our lives. It produces a blessed release by inducing a new self-forgetfulness in us precisely because we now know who we really are.

Track then with Paul's words:[2]

We know that our old self was crucified with him. Literally Paul says 'the old man (*ho palaios anthrōpos*) was crucified with him [Christ]'. While this is often taken to refer to Paul's life as Saul of Tarsus, before his Damascus Road experience, it has a much larger framework of reference. In the immediately preceding section in Romans Paul had set our lives in a much bigger context. By nature we were *in Adam*, but now we are *in Christ*. In Adam we were under

[1] Romans 6:6-7.
[2] Romans 6:7.

the dominion of sin and death; in Christ we are in the dominion of grace and life. Sin once reigned, but now grace reigns.[1]

The 'old man' in view here is therefore not simply 'my former self' (say fifteen or thirty years a non-Christian) but the person I was *in Adam* and not simply *in myself.* When I was united to Jesus Christ I was transferred from Adam-Land to Christ-Land, from the Adam Family to the Christ Family. By God's grace my past was forgiven. But there is more to it than that: I died out of an entire world order—the Adamic order—and was thus delivered from a fallen and condemned race under sin's reign, through union with the Christ who died to sin and was raised to new life.

This has happened—

In order that the body of sin might be brought to nothing. Here Paul uses a verb ('brought to nothing', *katargeō*) that expresses the idea of rendering something inoperable, or barren, of no effect, no longer able to exercise the authority it once had. The same verb is used by the author of Hebrews when he says that Christ came 'to *destroy* the one who has the power of death'.[2] It suggests not annihilation but disabling.

But what is 'the body of sin' that is 'brought to nothing'? Commentators have often taken this to be a metaphorical way of describing sin as a mass, and in that sense as a 'body'. But later in Romans Paul gives us a key to its meaning when he uses a similar expression: 'Who will deliver me from this *body of death*?'[3]

Paul does not mean he wants to escape bodily existence. He did not share the view of the Greek philosophers summed up in the adage *sōma sēma*, the body is a tomb.[4] And it is probably stretching a point to think he has in mind the grotesque punishment employed

[1] Romans 5:12-21.
[2] Hebrews 2:14.
[3] Romans 7:24
[4] A point he makes with vigour in 2 Corinthians 5:1-5.

in antiquity in which a murderer would be tied face to face with the corpse of his victim.[1] Rather Paul is probably thinking here of his physical body as one which exists under the reign of death. He does not desire a non-bodily existence. But he does long to be free from a bodily existence that is subject to death. And he knows Christ will one day set him free.[2]

In a parallel way, when Paul speaks about 'the body of sin' he is probably thinking of his physical body—himself viewed from the physical point of view. Sin once exercised total dominion over his body. It was in this sense 'the body of sin'. Sin exercised its rule through his mortal body. But now, in Christ, that dominion has been broken. Grace now reigns through righteousness leading to eternal life.[3] As a bodily individual he has been set free from his old 'ethsinity'[4] and brought into the kingdom in which Christ now reigns. His body is no longer the fertile soil for the weeds of sin to grow as it once was.

Thus—

We are no longer enslaved to sin. Yes, sin continues to indwell us. Yes, we must battle against its influences. But it no longer *reigns over us.* It no longer has a legitimate or legal claim on us, for in Christ we have died to the realm in which sin reigned. We are no longer sin's citizens.

As I write a young, world-class, South Korean golfer who plays on the USPGA tour has been called up to do military service for his country. No appeals on the basis of his stellar talent have availed. Now for an extended period he must set aside his multi-million dollar career. Who knows what the lasting effects will be? But he is a South Korean; he has no option.

[1] Most vividly described by the Roman author Vergil, *Aeneid*, VIII.483-488.

[2] Romans 7:25a.

[3] Romans 5:21.

[4] Not a misprint for 'ethnicity' but a coinage attempting to capture the idea that by nature we are citizens of the kingdom in which sin reigns.

But imagine before his call-up papers had arrived this young man had become a citizen of the United States of America. He could have written in response to the call-up letter: 'I am no longer under your dominion; you have no claims on me; I am free now. I am an American citizen!' Even although his genes were still Korean, and the past influences on his life South Korean, his *status* would be radically changed. He would be free from the old authority because he was living under the new. The 'South Korean' he once was now was no more; the American he had become—no matter what he felt inwardly—that would have become his true identity.[1]

This is, surely, what Paul has in view here.

He is not saying that sin has been destroyed—as though Christians lived in a perfect world.

He is not saying that we no longer experience the influence and impact of our past life as though we had never been in Adam.

He is not saying sin's presence has been eradicated in our lives—as though Christians were already perfect.

But he is saying that we are no longer citizens of the kingdom in which sin reigns. We are no longer its slaves or its subjects. We have become citizens of the kingdom of Christ in which grace reigns.

He summarizes this in the simple statement:

The one who has died is freed from sin. However, his statement is not quite that simple! For Paul uses language here that we associate with justification. Literally it could be translated that someone who has died has been 'justified from sin' (*dedikaiōtai apo tēs hamartias*).

Because of this language some interpreters suggest the apostle's reasoning is as follows: 'Since you have been justified you must not fall back into a sinful lifestyle.' In other words 'died [to sin]' refers to being united to Christ in his death *for our sins.* Since Christ *died for our sins* we should *no longer live for them.* We have 'died to sin'

---

[1] It need hardly be said here that commitment to our country of birth is an admirable quality, not least if it comes at personal cost.

in the sense of being justified from sin; therefore we must no longer contemplate living in sin.

This is certainly true. And it is indeed the teaching of Scripture. But it is doubtful if it is the teaching *of this particular passage of Scripture*. What then is Paul saying?

Suffice it here to say that our standard translations (most of which translate 'freed' rather than 'justified'[1]) seem to assume that, in keeping with the context, the meaning is 'freed from the reign or dominion' of sin.

- This translation is substantiated by a number of elements in the context. Paul's concern is not now with the *guilt* of sin (as in Romans 3:21ff.), but with its *reign*.

- Paul appears to emphasize the notion of sin as dominion by a series of personifications: it reigns as a king; dominates like a slave-master; deploys the members of our bodies as if it were a military general using them as weapons; and as an employer it pays the wages of death.[2]

- Although it is not obvious in our translations (and would be difficult to represent in literary English), Paul regularly uses the definite article before the word 'sin' throughout this whole section of Romans. In fact it virtually becomes a title—'The Sin' (*hē hamartia*). The term proliferates as if to impress on the reader (or hearer) that sin (singular) is being personified here and viewed in terms of its dominion and not, as elsewhere as 'sins' (in the plural) in terms of its guilt.[3]

---

[1] KJV, RSV, NIV, ESV. Other translations introduce the nuance of deliverance in their translation e.g. *The Moffatt Translation of the Bible* ('absolved from the claims of sin'), and *The Jerusalem Bible* ('finished with sin'). This same nuance appears in an old Scots use of the term 'justify' in relation to capital punishment. Notice of an execution would indicate that the prisoner had been 'justified', i.e. all claims on him were now null and void.

[2] See Romans 5:21; 6:6; 6:13; 6:23 for each of these personifications.

[3] Although it remains unexpressed in our translations, Paul employs the definite

- As if to underline this point Paul later states quite specifically that believers have been 'set free' from sin, in the sense of being delivered from bondage.[1]

- Plus, despite views to the contrary, it is in this sense that Paul claims Christ died—not only *for* sins, but also *to* sin.[2]

Christ died to sin's reign and has now been raised up to live in newness of life to God. We are united to him. Therefore we have died in a death like his; we too have been raised into new life. Yes, there is a difference[3]—we are still in the pre-resurrection body, and we live in a pre-resurrection world. But we do so as those who have already died to sin's dominion and been raised into the kingdom of our Lord Jesus Christ. The end of the ages has dawned on us; the new creation has already been inaugurated and we are part of it. When we realize this we know that life can never be the same again. The old has passed away; the new has come.[4] Now grace, not sin reigns!

This brings us immediately to consider the major implication of what Paul is saying.

---

article in an emphatic way throughout this section of Romans. Thus 'The Sin' appears in 5:12 (twice); 5:20; 5:21; 6:1; 6:2; 6:6; 6:7; 6:10; 6:11; 6:12; 6:13; 6:17; 6:18; 6:20; 6:22; 6:23; 7:7; 7:8; 7:9; 7:11; 7:13 (twice); 8:2; 8:3. Contrast 1 Corinthians 15:3 ('Christ died for our *sins*'); Galatians 1:4 ('[Christ who] gave himself for our *sins*'; and in an interesting use of both singular and plural, 1 Peter 2:24 ('He himself bore our *sins* in his body on the tree, that we might die to *sin* and live to righteousness').

[1] Romans 6:18, 22, where he uses the standard verb for setting free (*eleutheroō*). The verb is used in this sense of freedom from slavery in Jesus' statement: 'everyone who commits sin is a slave to sin … if the Son sets you free, you will be free indeed' (John 8:32, 36). The adjective (*eleutheros*) is used specifically of those who have been set free from slavery. See Galatians 4:22-23, 30.

[2] Romans 6:10. For further discussion of this see below, Appendix 2.

[3] Signalled by the fact that we have died in a death 'like his'.

[4] 2 Corinthians 5:17.

4. Implication—back to baptism

Paul began by asking the Romans, in essence, whether they understood their baptism. Were they living the baptized life? Had they really 'heard' what their baptism was telling them? Perhaps we have the same problem today.

We can probably assume that Paul's first readers never debated the divisive issues in baptism[1]—whether subjects (converts, or converts and their children) or mode (immersion, affusion, or sprinkling). These issues, however important they may be, have a way of diverting us from the biblical teaching on what baptism itself *means*. Our interest then tends to lie in defending our denominational views, or—as is commonplace—seeing baptism as a sign of something in us (our trust in Christ) rather than understanding that it is a sign of what Christ has done and is for us. We thus too often focus not on what it says *to us about Christ* but on what it says *to others about ourselves*.

This is almost an epidemic among evangelical Christians. Ask (1) 'What does baptism mean?' and (2) 'What does faith grasp in baptism?' and we are *unlikely* to get the answers, (1) 'It means fellowship with the Trinity through union with Christ in his death and resurrection', and (2) 'It teaches me that through faith I am united to Christ, have died to sin and been raised into a new life.' But to the extent to which those answers are lacking we have lost hold of baptism's power and usefulness in our lives. We do not get much beyond thinking about ourselves, and our faith in or 'decision for' Christ. We therefore forfeit the life-long blessing baptism is intended to be. And so our baptism fails to accomplish its purpose of defining our daily life in Christ.

---

[1] At least it cannot be proved that they did. Some scholars have detected language in the New Testament that they believe hints at answers to one or two of the questions that were later debated, thus indicating that already in the early church theological questions that required answers were being raised.

Contrast what baptism says, and the message faith receives from it:

- I am no longer the person I was in Adam; I am a new person in Jesus Christ.

- In Christ I am someone who has died to the dominion of sin and been raised to new life.

- In Christ I am someone who has been delivered from the dominion of sin and has been transferred into the kingdom of God.

This is foundational to the logic Paul now develops. Know your new identity and it will determine how you live—just as hearing the name your parents gave you causes you to respond in a deep seated and instinctive—and perhaps distinctive—way.

But, Paul concludes, recognize our new name (one baptized into Christ, and thus into his death to sin and resurrection to new life) and we are in a position to respond to these powerful imperatives:

- Reckon on it. It is true. So think about yourself as someone who has died to sin and been raised to new life in Christ.

- Reject the efforts of 'King Sin' to reign again.

- Refuse to give yourself to 'King Sin's' control; but give yourself to righteousness.

- Realise that if the dominion of sin is broken, it has lost its right to exercise dominion over you again.[1]

This, then, is the rhythm of the baptized life of faith: knowing that we are united to Christ; believing that this is so and acting on that conviction; and then discovering the power of the gospel to transform and sanctify.

---

[1] This is Paul's logic in Romans 6:11-14.

What's in a name?

I once had a delightful doctoral student from the Far East. His name was 'Timothy', but his family name was obviously oriental. Once we got to know each other well enough I engaged him in the following dialogue:

'Timothy, what's your *real* name?'

'Timothy', he replied.

'Yes', I said, but (referring to his native language), 'what's your *real* name?'

Once again he replied: 'Timothy'.

Realizing Timothy was leading me on, I tried once more, and this time asked him:

'What name did your parents give you?'

Timothy responded with an oriental name.

'So', I continued, '*that's your real name?* You just chose "Timothy" because it would be familiar and easy for us Westerners?'

Perhaps you can guess what he said?

'No', he replied, '*Timothy* is my *real* name.'

And then he added:

'That's the name I was given when I was baptized.'

I found his words deeply moving. But more than that, it made me realize that this scholarly young man understood his baptism. The name he was given then was his *real* name. It was the name that reminded him of who he really was—someone who, in Jesus Christ, had been named for the Trinity. As it happens, 'Timothy' means 'honoured by God'.

Paul is saying here: 'Christians, do you know your real name?'

Do you know who you really are in Christ? Do you understand what it means to be renamed in Christ? Do you think of yourself each day as someone who has died to sin and been raised into newness of life and therefore cannot go on living in sin?

Immediate, but also long term

Union with Christ in his death and resurrection is ours the moment we trust in him. But since this involves nothing less than being brought into a new creation, understanding what has happened to us takes longer. Our foolish hearts have been darkened and our minds are ingrained with a false perspective on everything. Our regeneration certainly involved radical surgery; it removed our spiritual cataract. But there is a long process involved in rehabilitation. We will need to repeat the same exercises again, and again, and … again.

A physician whose expertise was in the field of addiction-recovery once told me that in his experience, although an addiction might be decisively broken in someone's life, two considerations needed to be borne in mind:

(1) It may still take eighteen months or longer before that person begins to think about himself or herself instinctively in a new way— no longer under the addiction, but now a former addict seeking to remain strong.

Thus, for example in the case of an eating disorder, it may take the person who has been 'fat' but has now developed a different eating pattern an extended period of time before they think of themselves not as a fat person trying to become slim, but as a 'normal' person who is sensibly maintaining their weight.

(2) The decisive break with the addiction is not the same thing as the destruction of the substance to which we have been addicted— be it food, alcohol, drugs, or anything else. In addition, we have created a weakness, a tendency, and developed an appetite for the subject of our addiction. We are not people who were never addicted to it. We therefore need to exercise lifelong vigilance against it.

A similar dynamic is true for us as Christians. We were born addicted to sin and under its dominion. Now we are in Christ, 'set free from sin'. But it may take us some time to realize that we are new men and women in Christ. And lifelong vigilance is now our calling, for the old way of thinking can linger long; the power of temptation has not been destroyed. We need to keep coming back to the teaching of the New Testament, and remind ourselves of the truth about our lives in Christ. We need to keep recalibrating our lives in terms of Paul's exhortation not to let sin reign.

John Owen once wrote that in a sense there are only two basic issues with which a minister of the gospel has to deal.

The first presents an evangelistic challenge: persuading those who are under the dominion of sin that this is the truth about them.

The other? It is the pastoral challenge: persuading those who are no longer under sin's dominion that this is who they really are.[1]

Who do you think you are?

Do you understand your baptism?

Do you know who you are—in Christ?

---

[1] John Owen (1616–83), *A Treatise of the Dominion of Sin and Grace* in *The Works of John Owen*, ed. William Goold (1850–55; repr. Edinburgh: Banner of Truth Trust, 1965–68), 7, 517.

5

Conflict Zone

———

We have noticed several times already the importance of the shape of the New Testament's teaching on sanctification and our devotion to God. No matter which apostle's writings we examine, the same pattern is present with an identical undergirding structure. Exhortations to be holy are always derived from an exposition of what God has done and provided for us in Christ and through the gift of the Spirit. Indicatives are always the foundation for imperatives even if they appear in the reverse order.

God never throws us back to rely upon ourselves and our own resources. He encourages us rather to grow up as Christians by digging down ever more deeply into the riches of his grace in Jesus Christ. Christ himself is the rich and fertile soil in which Christian holiness puts down strong roots, grows tall and bears the fruit of the Spirit. Thus the New Testament always links two things together in an important piece of spiritual logic. The new situation creates the new lifestyle:

God has been or done this—*therefore* you should be or do that.

Or:

Be this, or become that—*because* this is who God is and what he has done.

The pattern reappears in Galatians 5:16-17:

But I say, walk by the Spirit, and you will not gratify the desires of the flesh. For the desires of the flesh are against the Spirit, and the desires of the Spirit are against the flesh, for these are opposed to each other, to keep you from doing the things you want to do.

Here there is an exhortation to live by the Spirit. It arises from the new situation into which we have been brought by becoming Christians. The, perhaps unexpected, new reality in our lives is that the presence of the Spirit brings us into a conflict zone—we are now involved in a Spirit-against-flesh war. There are forces loose 'to keep you from doing the things you want to do'.

We may have experienced inner conflicts before we became Christ's. But any conflict we experienced then with the flesh was *in the flesh!* In a sense we were simply battling with ourselves, experiencing what the Roman author Ovid described:

> I see the better and I approve it,
>   but it is the worse that I pursue[1]—

a point vividly and sadly illustrated in the writings of the famous English diarist Samuel Pepys. We know we should do better and be better. That produces an inner conflict. Small libraries of works of psychology and psychiatry have been built on this universal reality: we want what we know we should not; we do what we know we ought not to do. Every schoolboy confronted with the sign 'Keep off the grass' has shared the experience.

But Paul is speaking here of a new and more radical conflict—not between flesh and flesh, but between flesh and Spirit. He explains that only if we live by the Spirit can we avoid gratifying the desires of the flesh.

It is important to underline that *we cannot do this simply by trying to avoid sin*. We can do it only by refusing the desires of the flesh *and simultaneously* living in the power of the Spirit.

---

[1] Ovid (43 BC – AD 17), *Metamorphoses*, VII.20 (*Video meliora, proboque, deteriora sequor*).

Here we should notice two features in Paul's teaching:

1. When he speaks about the 'flesh' and its desires he includes what goes on in our minds and hearts as well as what we do with our bodies.[1]

2. When he employs his basic gospel structure of indicatives leading to imperatives he tends to join to this a further structural element. We might call it 'The simultaneity of negative and positive.'

Positivity and negativity

'Positivity' is an 'in word'. Purists might find its over-use an irritating novelty, although the word itself has a long and honourable pedigree.[2] Today, however, sportsmen learn to 'banish negativity' and often speak about having a high degree of 'positivity' in the way they played. Thus negativity is little more than feeling badly, while positivity is simply feeling confident.

Living the Christian life is not a sport. But if we are going to do it well there needs to be *both* negativity and positivity at a very profound level. After all, our entire Christian experience is built upon the ultimate negativity—the crucifixion, and the ultimate positivity—the resurrection. So when you hear a Christian say he or she does not like to be negative, you should listen carefully to what they mean. They could be quite seriously confused about the gospel and its implications for living the Christian life. For Paul (following Jesus) teaches us that to live well requires being both negative and

---

[1] See Romans 8:6-7; Galatians 5:19-20.

[2] The term is absent from the 1,600 pages of *The Concise Oxford Dictionary* 12th edition, ed., A. Stevenson & Maurice Waite (Oxford: Oxford University Press, 2011). But its use can be traced back to at least 1659 in the title of a book by H. Hickman, *A Justification of the Fathers and Schoolmen; shewing, that they are not selfe-condemned for denying the positivity of sin*. In view here is the (Augustinian) rejection of the idea that sin is an independent substantial entity (a positive 'something').

positive—denying the flesh with its desires, and living under the lordship of the Holy Spirit. This—while expressed in a variety of different ways—is always the biblical pattern.

Paul puts it in stark terms. If you are going to resist the desires of the flesh (negative), you will need to live in the power of the Holy Spirit and walk according to his disciplines (positive).

Do you follow Paul's reasoning here?

Three principles help us to understand it. We need to be prepared to put on our thinking-caps as we grapple with the teaching here.[1]

1. 'Flesh' and 'Spirit' are not only two aspects of a Christian's being; they are characteristics of the two ages or epochs in which the Christian lives.

Sometimes the Bible speaks about men and women being flesh and spirit meaning roughly the same as 'body and soul'. We are made for this material world, and have bodies, or flesh. But we also transcend it: we were made for fellowship with God, and are souls, or spirits. We are psychosomatic unities—physical-and-spiritual beings. This being the case we naturally tend to view these two terms, 'flesh' and 'spirit', as references to aspects of our individual person. Often that is exactly right.

But Paul sets this in a wider context, and it may require some lateral thinking for us to follow him. Here 'flesh' and 'spirit' are bigger concepts, characteristics—almost atmospheres—of two ages—this present age (dominated by the flesh) and the age to come (ruled by the Spirit).

In Scripture 'flesh' can carry several different shades of meaning:

(*a*) The skin, or more generally our physical framework, as in the phrase 'flesh and blood'.

---

[1] Notice Paul's exhortation to Timothy to do precisely this: 2 Timothy 2:7, 15.

(*b*) Human beings in their weakness and frailty. Humanity contrasted with deity.

(*c*) Human nature not only weakened but twisted and enslaved to the power of sin, alienated from God and in the grip of the evil one.

In this last sense, 'flesh' is human nature under the dominion of sin, corrupted by it, and powerless to reverse its effects. Thus Paul can not only speak about 'the flesh' being *in us*, but about our being '*in the flesh*'.[1] We live in, breathe the atmosphere, and share the nature, of a fallen world. Flesh is another way of describing the domination and impact on our lives of 'the present evil age'.[2]

How does this come about? Paul's answer is that we are not simply isolated individuals who begin our lives in a neutral relationship with God, innocent until we have sinned and only then guilty. Rather we are all by nature 'in Adam',[3] deeply implicated in his fall, sharing in his subsequent alienation from God. Powers have been released into the human blood-stream with the result that we are—

> dead in … trespasses and sins … following the course of this world, following the prince of the power of the air, the spirit that is now at work in the sons of disobedience—among whom we all once lived in the passions of our flesh, carrying out the desires of the body and the mind, and were by nature children of wrath, like the rest of mankind.[4]

But Christians are no longer in Adam. Therefore we are no longer 'in the flesh'.[5] By definition we are 'in Christ' and participate in the

---

[1] Romans 8:8.

[2] Galatians 1:4.

[3] Paul expounds this principle in Romans 5:12-21; 1 Corinthians 15:20-28.

[4] Ephesians 2:1-3.

[5] Romans 8:9. Notice that this is not the same as saying that 'the flesh is no longer in us.' The difference highlights the fact that Paul can have a larger concept in view when he uses the term 'flesh' (*sarx*).

new creation. We are possessed by the Spirit, live under his lordship, and are breathing his atmosphere.

Yet, at the same time we remain in the same old world which is infected by Adam's fall, as well as by the power of sin. We live in an atmosphere of flesh, in a social order under the influence of the devil. Thus we are alien residents, living here as citizens of a new order, as those who are under King Jesus, who are indwelt by the Spirit of the kingdom of God. Here we are strangers, exiles for the moment. We have no continuing city in the present world order.[1]

So long as this is true we will find ourselves under threat from the old order. And like recovering addicts we will need to make daily decisions and commitments to live out the new life. This involves conflict and requires resolute resistance. For the world of the flesh continues to breathe out its own polluted atmosphere into lives that once gladly breathed it in.

A friend who in earlier life had smoked cigarettes, and found pleasure in doing so, once explained to me that every time he sensed the aroma of smoke from someone's cigarette he felt the old instincts and attractions surround and invade him, and pull at his desires. It was a battle to resist. His addiction had been broken. Otherwise there would not have been a battle. But it was a struggle. This is but a hint and pale reflection of the nature and magnitude of the conflict between flesh and Spirit. The world is full of smoke.

2. Being 'in the flesh' and being 'in the Spirit' also denote two different periods in the life of someone who has become a believer.

The very fact that the Spirit is now influencing our lives, and that a conflict with the flesh has resulted, presupposes that Christ has come as the second Adam and has reversed the sinful disobedience of the first Adam. Instead of disobeying, he obeyed; instead of bringing in sin, he brought in righteousness; instead of bringing us into

[1] Hebrews 13:14.

death, he has brought us into resurrection life—a new order of life, a new native atmosphere dominated by the presence and power of the Spirit. We now live in a kingdom in which Jesus Christ is Lord, where the Holy Spirit governs the environment, and where grace and righteousness reign.[1]

Paul had already laid the groundwork for this earlier in Galatians. God sent his Son to redeem us; he then sent the Spirit of his Son to bring us into his family (calling him 'Abba, Father'). In doing so he has rescued us from the present evil age.[2] We live in its dominions, but we are no longer under its dominion.

Being in the Spirit and no longer in the flesh therefore represents a larger and more significant reality than that we merely experience competing desires, good and bad. The reality is that (*the world of*) *the flesh* once dragged me down into sin and death in Adam; but now I live in (*the world of*) *the Spirit* and have been lifted up into righteousness and life. I used to be a citizen of the first. I have become a citizen of the second. Paul summarizes this later when he says that Christians are no longer *in the flesh*, but are now *in the Spirit*.[3]

Notice that Paul is not saying: the flesh is no longer in you.

Rather, he is saying that, by the power of the Spirit, I am no longer what I was. Now, delivered from the evil age into the age of grace, I am no longer in the flesh but in the Spirit, and therefore no longer under obligation to the flesh. I have no taxes to pay to it. I owe no loyalty to its institutions. It has no claims on me. I have abandoned my natural relationship for citizenship in my adopted country, the truly 'united kingdom' and the 'empire on which the sun never sets', the kingdom of God the Father, the Son, and the Holy Spirit. Now I am a child of God; I am in Christ; the Spirit indwells me. I live in the old realm as someone who already belongs to the new.

[1] Romans 5:12–8:39.
[2] Galatians 1:4; 4:4.
[3] Romans 8:9.

The implication is clear. Because we have been brought out of the dominion of the flesh into the dominion of the Spirit, we are responsible to live according to the principles of this new kingdom. So, says Paul: Walk by the Spirit, in such holy power that you will not yield or give way to the lingering influences of the flesh.

What does it mean that I was 'in the flesh' and under its dominion? It means I lived out of a centre in myself, absorbed in myself and with my own perspective, devoted to this world and its values and standards. It means I viewed the temporal as more significant than the eternal, this world as bigger than the world to come, and made man rather than God the measure of all things. Life 'in the flesh' was centred on a this-worldly system of thought and life rather than in God himself—the only true and eternal centre of all things. This is the story of life apart from Christ, and therefore was the story of my life prior to coming to faith in Christ.

Another characteristic of life in the flesh is that, in both obvious and subtle ways, the self hides from and defends itself against God. My flesh wants to glory in the flesh. But this is one thing that God will never permit.[1] So what does the flesh do? Tragically it protects itself because it fears that because God destroys the glory of the flesh, he will also destroy us. It cannot grasp that this same divine glory is committed to doing us good. It cannot see that self-protection against God's glory leads only to our own ultimate loss.

More subtle forms of self-protection can appear clothed in religious garb. The history of the Christian church is punctuated with examples. For the self is constantly insisting on weighing in the scales the good things it has done to balance its sin. Although such good works profess to be spiritual, they are in fact further evidence of being under the dominion of the flesh, whose chief form of pride is believing that we can make ourselves acceptable to God.

[1] Isaiah 42:8; 48:11; 1 Corinthians 1:29.

All this—the mindset of the flesh—is condemned and banished by faith in Christ. It belongs to the old order and to the old life. Now in Christ and through the Spirit all things become new.

Why then would we want to return to, or look back on, the world we have left—like Israelites complaining that when they were in Egypt they had 'fish … cucumbers … melons … leeks … onions … garlic'?[1]

Yet Paul recognizes that remnants of this same subtle thinking can take hold of the Christian believer as well. He found himself writing to the Corinthians as though they were 'fleshly' and not 'spiritual'.[2] They were displaying some of the ugly marks of the old world from which they had come. The cross should have brought all that once and for all to an end—as Paul also had to remind the Galatians: 'Far be it from me to boast except in the cross of our Lord Jesus Christ, by which the world has been crucified to me, and I to the world.'[3]

On the one hand, then, flesh and Spirit are epochs, worlds, kingdoms, dimensions, not simply aspects of my individual life. On the other hand, being in the flesh and being in the Spirit denote two identifiable periods in my individual life. Before I came to faith in Jesus Christ I was in the flesh and under its dominion. Now that I have come to faith in Jesus Christ, I am no longer under that dominion. I have torn up my citizenship papers; now by the grace of God I have been brought into the Father's new creation, the kingdom of the Son, and the dominion of the Spirit.

Just here a tendency creeps in to dilute the radical teaching of the New Testament. We may feel that it does not easily harmonise with the struggles we experience. But, as we are about to see, Paul helps us to think much more clearly.

[1] Numbers 11:5.
[2] 1 Corinthians 3:1.
[3] Galatians 6:14. Cf. 5:24.

3. Paul's exhortation not to walk or live living according to the flesh but according to the Spirit underlines the fact that these powers remain competitors for our lifestyle as Christians.

The New Testament teaching has brought us from the *large scale picture* (flesh and Spirit as aspects of two cosmic ages) to the *personal picture* (flesh and Spirit as aspects of our personal history). Now we move on to the *immediate picture*. Paul brings us right up to date: we are faced with a daily choice between walking according to the flesh or according to the Spirit. These two lifestyles are constantly bidding for our allegiance. One does so illegitimately. But that does not mean its bid is not real, or that it lacks the power of attraction. The Christian life involves us in an ongoing, lifelong conflict. The gospel therefore calls us to live under the reign of the Spirit in a world order dominated by the flesh. We do so as former 'addicts' to the flesh, perhaps for many years. In the process we may experience many painful withdrawal symptoms. There will be many battles. Hence the urgency of Paul's exhortation. Daily, hourly, we need to keep walking in the Spirit, refusing to return to the flesh.

We are in a war zone, and therefore we cannot live any way we please. That would be the mindset of the flesh. But the lordship of Christ and the promptings of the Spirit lead us to obey the Lord even when it hurts. In bodies that have been under the dominion of the flesh, we must keep deciding that now that we are in Christ we will live consistently with our new identity and not according to the old order. Just as initial deliverance from addiction does not mean we will never again be troubled by it, so it is here. We need to live out the consequences of our decision. We may have given our whole lives to Christ; but it will take the rest of our lives to work that out in practice. And we can only do that if we keep on walking in the Spirit.

Sin and the life of the flesh together constitute a spiritual addiction that leads to spiritual death:

Those who live according to the flesh set their minds on the things of the flesh, but those who live according to the Spirit set their minds on the things of the Spirit. To set the mind on the flesh is death, but to set the mind on the Spirit is life and peace. For the mind that is set on the flesh is hostile to God, for it does not submit to God's law; indeed it cannot. Those who are in the flesh cannot please God.

You, however, are not in the flesh but in the Spirit, if in fact the Spirit of God dwells in you …

So then, brothers, we are debtors, not to the flesh, to live according to the flesh. For if you live according to the flesh you will die, but if by the Spirit you put to death the deeds of the body, you will live.[1]

Addiction to the flesh has its manifestations in all the specific addictions of life—to alcohol, drugs, sport, money, sex, work, and a myriad of other forms of bondage. But believers have made the decision to reject it all. 'Those who belong to Christ have crucified the flesh with its passions and desires.'[2] That was a once-for-all action when we came to Christ. But now its consequences have to be lived out on a daily basis. The future is a series of small decisions to live the new life and not to fall back into the old. Living in the Spirit therefore means a daily commitment to please Christ and not to please self.[3]

But *how* can we do this?

The how-to question

We might be tempted to think that here (and perhaps elsewhere) the apostle Paul is at his weakest. Was he strong on indicatives, and good on imperatives, but weak on directives? Was he simply not skilled at helping people at a practical level to transition from the old pattern of life in the flesh to new life in the Spirit?

---

[1] Romans 8:5-9, 12-13.
[2] Galatians 5:24.
[3] 2 Corinthians 5:14-15.

That might be understandable. Was it perhaps just as true of apostles as it is of pastors, teachers, and Christians in general that while we all have the same Spirit we do not all have the same gifts?[1] Was Paul perhaps a better teacher than he was a counsellor, better at exposition than at application?

We would need strong evidence before we drew that conclusion. In fact this is one area where our earlier reflections on patiently thinking through the teaching of Scripture are particularly relevant. Here Paul's words to Timothy are applicable: 'Think over what I say, for the Lord will give you understanding in everything.'[2] For in this context, as elsewhere, he has woven a series of principles into the warp and woof, into the very fabric of his teaching. If we grasp them, they will provide practical guidelines to enable us to walk in the Spirit and not in the flesh.

To fix them in our memories we will think of them here as sanctification's 'five Rs': Recognize, Remember, Realize, Respond, and Reap.

(i) Recognize the enmity there is between the flesh and the Spirit

The more sensitive we are to the fact that we are living in a warfare context, the more successful we are going to be in living in the Spirit. The Christian who succeeds here is the one who recognizes the reality, the urgency, and also the magnitude of the conflict. We are in the middle of a battle between the flesh and the Spirit. Like cosmic super-powers they are waging a war against each other. Our lives form the battle ground in which it takes place. Knowing this creates the alertness we tend to lack and provides us with the motivation we need. Only those who are on their guard will be protected against temptation. We need to 'watch and pray' because while the spirit is willing the flesh is weak.[3]

---

[1] Romans 12:4-5; 1 Corinthians 12:4.
[2] 2 Timothy 2:7
[3] Mark 14:38.

(ii) Remember the new status you have been given in Christ

Yes, there is a war on for our lives; the flesh battles against the Spirit. But we are not living in a no-man's land in between. We belong to the new creation; we are in the Spirit, and we are indwelt by him! If the Spirit of Christ dwells in us, says Paul, we have all the resources of the victorious Son of God to enable us to conquer in the battle. The Father's love is ours in his Son, the Son's gift is ours in his Spirit:

> Think what *Spirit* dwells within thee;
>   What a *Father's* smile is thine;
>   What a *Saviour* died to win thee,
>   Child of heaven, should'st thou repine?[1]

(iii) Realize the calling you have been given—to live by the Spirit and not to gratify the flesh

When Paul urged the Christians in Rome to 'Put on the Lord Jesus Christ' he was also saying: 'Put on the fruit of the Spirit that you see in Christ.' That means, inevitably that we are to 'make no provision for the flesh to gratify its desires'.[2]

This is the very text that helped Augustine into the kingdom of God. As he sat in a friend's garden he overheard a child's voice calling in a sing-song fashion (apparently as part of a game): '*tolle lege, tolle lege*' (take it and read it). He picked up the copy of Paul's letters lying on the table and read the first words he saw. They were from Romans 13:14:

> Not in orgies and drunkenness, not in sexual immorality and sensuality, not in quarrelling and jealousy. But put on the Lord Jesus Christ, and make no provision for the flesh, to gratify its desires.

---

[1] From the hymn by Henry F. Lyte (1793–1847), 'Jesus, I my cross have taken, all to leave and follow thee.' Lyte, who was born in Scotland and educated in Ireland, spent most of his ministry in England. He wrote many hymns, but is best known for 'Abide with me, fast falls the eventide.'

[2] Romans 13:14.

Augustine did precisely that. He put on Christ and refused thereafter to make provision for the flesh. He had spent much of his previous life making the kind of provision for the flesh that any self-indulgent young man could. Doubtless there were times when his flesh struggled against the flesh. But since he was 'in the flesh' he could not overcome it until he had put on the Lord Jesus Christ. And this he did—with effects of untold significance.[1]

We must learn more and more to do this day by day. 'No provision for the flesh' is an essential motto for the growing Christian. And we are enabled to make it ours when we take hold of Christ and all that he is for us and to us,—perhaps saying each morning with Patrick:

> I bind this day to me for ever,
> by power of faith:
> Christ's incarnation;
> His baptism in the Jordan river;
> His death on cross for my salvation;
> His bursting from the spicèd tomb;
> His riding up the heavenly way;
> His coming at the day of doom;
> I bind unto myself today.[2]

Have you ever done that? Have you, by faith, put on Christ and his resources deliberately and consciously? Do you refuse to make provision for the flesh? This is the way to live in the Spirit.

(iv) Respond sensitively to the Spirit

If you are led by the Spirit, says Paul, you are not under the law[3]—in the sense that you are not under its condemnation.

What is his logic? It is this: You cannot have the Spirit as your Leader unless you have Christ as your Saviour, because you cannot

---

[1] Augustine tells this story in *Confessions*, 8.12.
[2] From what is usually described as 'St Patrick's Breastplate.'
[3] Romans 8:14.

have the Spirit without having Christ, and vice-versa.[1] But if you have Christ there is no condemnation for you.[2] And being led by the Spirit will deliver you from a lifestyle in which you find yourself constantly coming under the condemnation of the law.

But if this is Paul's logic, what does he mean by 'led by the Spirit'?—the expression found in Romans 8:14: 'All who are led by the Spirit are sons of God' and 'have received the Spirit of adoption as sons, by whom we cry "Abba! Father!"' As his sons we know we belong to his family. We learn to put out of our lives everything that is not in keeping with the family lifestyle. This is what it means to be 'led by the Spirit'. We begin to be sensitive to him. He is the Spirit of our Father and of our Saviour. We avoid anything that would bring shame on the family name. Our Father's smile has come to mean everything to us; his frown would be our greatest loss. This is what it means to be 'led by the Spirit'.[3] This is the *fear* of the Lord' which Scripture tells us stimulates obedience and holiness.[4]

(v) Reap what you sow

In the context of his teaching on the conflict between flesh and Spirit, Paul goes on to say:

> Do not be deceived: God is not mocked, for whatever one sows, that will he also reap. For the one who sows to his own flesh will from the flesh reap corruption, but the one who sows to the Spirit will from the Spirit reap eternal life.[5]

The more we offer ourselves to the Spirit as seed to be fructified by him, and the more we ask 'what will please him?', the more we will produce the fruit of the Spirit. And the more we produce the

---

[1] As Paul makes clear in Romans 8:8-9.
[2] See Romans 8:1-4.
[3] See below, pp. 150-151.
[4] See Exodus 1:17; Philippians 2:12-13.
[5] Galatians 6:7-8.

fruit of the Spirit, the less nourishment will be found in the soil of our hearts for the weeds of the flesh.

Paul's agricultural metaphor reminds us of the importance of thinking long term. This means we will always be asking the question 'What will be the final harvest, the ultimate fruit of this thought, act, or pattern of behaviour?' Trace the pattern of sin in the lives of the characters described in the Scriptures. You cannot avoid noticing that they did not see far enough, or think clearly enough, about their decisions and actions. From Eve in the Garden of Eden, through David on the rooftop of his Jerusalem palace, to Demas the erstwhile companion of the apostle Paul, they thought 'What *now?*' rather than 'What *then?*' They tended to see with their eyes in terms of their own perceptions rather than—as God's children must learn to do—with their ears in terms of the teaching of God's word.

We will return to these principles again. But we must begin to put them in place now. We battle with the flesh. But it is never enough to concentrate our attention only on the flesh. We must give our attention to the Spirit. The general in an army never under-estimates, but nor does he focus all of his attention on, the enemy. He must also give detailed attention to his resources and his strategy for victory.

The battle in which we are engaged is ongoing, long, and weari-some at times. We may feel we are making little headway. But Paul urges us not to grow weary. Spiritual agriculture and horticulture are long-term activities. We are sowing to the Spirit. The final harvest may seem a long way off, far out of sight. But we will reap in due season. We must not give up.[1]

Some Christians feel they make little headway in this. One com-mon reason is that, in seeking to make no provision for the flesh, they have become so engrossed in the flesh that they lose sight of the Spirit. This inevitably leads to losing sight of Christ. But it is only

---

[1] Galatians 6:9. Cf. 1 Corinthians 15:58; 2 Corinthians 4:16-18.

in him that we will find the resources we need to overcome the flesh and deny it the provision it demands.

So keep your focus on Christ. Make sure you are familiar with the provisions for victory God has given you in him. He has made it possible to say 'we are more than conquerors through him who loved us'.[1] And do not fail to notice that Paul characteristically uses the *second person plural* when he writes his letters. Of course we each apply them individually to our own lives. But sanctification was never intended to be an individualistic project. We are in this battle together. Many Christians are wounded soldiers; we need to get round one another, encourage one another, and say to each other: 'Onwards and upwards! Let us be people who walk in the Spirit! Let us not make any provision for the flesh!'

This is the only way to live the Christian life. It is, by definition, the pathway to holiness. This is part of what it means to be devoted to God.

[1] Romans 8:37.

6

The New Rhythm

T he New Testament passages that are basic for our understanding of sanctification are related to each other like a
set of Russian dolls, all with the same characteristics but
coming in different sizes and fitting into each other. They are either
miniaturized or enlarged versions of the same basic structure. Each
passage has its own context, emphasis, and level of exposition. But
the underlying patterns are the same: indicative and imperative,
objective and subjective, negative and positive. They all have their
foundation in the undergirding reality of union with Christ.

No passage more clearly illustrates this, or provides a more
expansive illustration of it, than Colossians 3:1-17:

> If then you have been raised with Christ, seek the things that are
> above, where Christ is, seated at the right hand of God. Set your
> minds on things that are above, not on things that are on earth.
> For you have died, and your life is hidden with Christ in God.
> When Christ who is your life appears, then you also will appear
> with him in glory. Put to death therefore what is earthly in you:
> sexual immorality, impurity, passion, evil desire, and covetousness,
> which is idolatry. On account of these the wrath of God is coming.
> In these you too once walked, when you were living in them. But
> now you must put them all away: anger, wrath, malice, slander, and
> obscene talk from your mouth. Do not lie to one another, seeing
> that you have put off the old self with its practices and have put on
> the new self, which is being renewed in knowledge after the image

of its creator. Here there is not Greek and Jew, circumcised and uncircumcised, barbarian, Scythian, slave, free; but Christ is all, and in all. Put on then, as God's chosen ones, holy and beloved, compassion, kindness, humility, meekness, and patience, bearing with one another and, if one has a complaint against another, forgiving each other; as the Lord has forgiven you, so you also must forgive. And above all these put on love, which binds everything together in perfect harmony. And let the peace of Christ rule in your hearts, to which indeed you were called in one body. And be thankful. Let the word of Christ dwell in you richly, teaching and admonishing one another in all wisdom, singing psalms and hymns and spiritual songs, with thankfulness in your hearts to God. And whatever you do, in word or deed, do everything in the name of the Lord Jesus, giving thanks to God the Father through him.

Notice the features: *indicative* ('if then you have been raised with Christ') gives rise to *imperative* ('... Therefore'); *objective* (all that Christ is) is the foundation for *subjective* (all that we experience); *negative* ('put to death') is accompanied by *positive* ('put on'). And everything is related to our *union with Christ* (we have been 'raised with', are 'hidden with', and will 'appear with' him). There is a wonderful rhythm to the entire process.

Some scholars have thought that these words could have begun life as part of a homily or sermon Paul preached at baptismal services, expounding the significance of the new name given to the Christian believer, and explaining his or her new identity in Christ.[1]

We are now familiar with Paul's thought forms:

As Christians we have been given a new identity in Christ since we

- have died with Christ
- have been buried with Christ
- have been raised with Christ

---

[1] He makes specific reference to baptism in Colossians 2:12.

- are 'hidden with Christ in God' and

- are intimately and permanently united to Christ so that when he appears at the end of all things, we will also appear with him in glory.

We have been united to Christ and given his name. All that he has accomplished for us in his death, burial, resurrection, and ascension to the right hand of the Father, and indeed everything he will accomplish when he comes again in glory, constitutes our inheritance.

We do not know if these words formed the substance of a baptismal sermon. But it would certainly have been an appropriate context for Paul to emphasize these truths.[1]

It is not easy to take in all that Paul is saying here at first reading— or for that matter after several readings. For once again we do not naturally think about ourselves in these terms. Yet this perspective is clearly vital to the Christian's 'self-image'. For unless we are processing this new paradigm we are not yet thinking clearly about who we now are 'in Christ' and what that implies for the way we live. The result for the Colossians to whom Paul was writing was that they might easily be attracted to false substitutes and artificial 'spiritual laws' that would come with a promise that they would experience spiritual 'fullness'.[2]

---

[1] If indeed this section of Colossians echoes a baptismal homily it has much to teach us about the range of biblical truth that feeds into our understanding of baptism, and takes us beyond either the apologetic or polemical elements that sometimes are far too dominant in our discussions of it. Far healthier for us to know what baptism means and how it functions in our Christian lives than that our sub-set of evangelical Christianity is 'right' and 'they' (whether credo-baptists or paedo-baptists!) are wrong. It is possible to be 'right' and yet lack any sense of the wonder of the privileges proclaimed in the 'visible word' of baptism or, for that matter, not know how to 'improve our baptism' (a practice well described in *The Larger Catechism* Q. & A. 167).

[2] This is the most likely explanation for Paul's repeated use of 'fullness' language in Colossians; see 1:9, 19, 24, 25; 2:2, 9, 10; 4:12. Spiritual 'fullness' was being offered to the Colossians by means that could never deliver it—as he makes clear in 2:23.

Who are you?

One simple way of underlining this issue is to ask the question: How do you describe yourself when someone asks you about your faith? Do you say, 'I am a believer', or some variation of 'I have been born again/am converted/am a disciple of Jesus', or 'I am a Christian'?

Probably the last of these is the most common. But, as we have seen, in the New Testament the word 'Christian' appears only three times and never in Paul's letters. Indeed the term may well have been a demeaning one used by non-Christians to describe the followers of Jesus: 'the Christ-ones'.[1] It is *not* the New Testament's description of choice. Yet it has become ours. And since we tend to think by means of words and categories, in a perfectly innocent way our thinking about ourselves may deviate from the New Testament norm.

Contrast Paul's frequent use of the specific expression 'in Christ' (over eighty times), and 'in the Lord' (over forty times), not to mention the variations of it such as 'in him'. The statistic is staggering. It is the basic way Christians in the Pauline churches were taught to think about themselves. They were 'in Christ', united to Christ, and therefore sharing 'with Christ' in all he had accomplished for them. After all, as we have seen, they had been 'baptized into Christ Jesus'.[2]

Paul is spelling out the dimensions and implications of this union at length here (and in the broader context from Colossians 2:20 onwards). *This makes it perhaps the most comprehensive passage in the entire New Testament to help us align our self-understanding to the apostolic norm.* Here what Paul had described briefly early in his ministry in Galatians 2:20 is expanded into seventeen verses which are themselves built on a foundation he laid earlier in the letter. So fully one quarter of Colossians is devoted to the theme. Thus:

[1] Acts 11:26; 26:28; 1 Peter 4:16.
[2] Romans 6:3.

Faith brings us into union with Christ. Therefore:

We *died with* Christ,

and were *buried with* him.

We have been *raised with* Christ into new life.

When Christ appears in glory, we will *appear with* him.

This is the message that baptism proclaims. This is what baptism 'says' to us; it is an expression of powerful gospel logic:

- All the privileges of union with Christ are made over to us in Christ.

- Our new identity is determined by what Christ has done for us.

- Through faith we become new men and women in Christ, people with a totally new identity.

Since this is so,

- We must get rid of everything that is inconsistent with that new identity—all that belonged to the old life in Adam.

And in addition,

- We must grow in the graces that are the hallmarks of our new life in Christ.

Thus we are to live out our new identity in Christ—as those who have died to the old, whose life in Adam has been buried in Christ's tomb, who have been raised with him into the new creation, and live as its citizens in a still-fallen world as those who are destined to share in his final glory.

Given the magnitude of this, perhaps it is not altogether surprising that the Christian church began to develop a dramatic liturgy for its celebrations of baptism on Easter Day. Converts came to their baptism wearing an outer garment which they would take off in order to be baptized. Then, having been baptized into the name of the Father, the Son, and the Holy Spirit, they would be given a new garment to wear—thus symbolically putting off the old man and putting on the new man in Christ. It was a powerful representation of Paul's teaching here.

When we come to understand our new identity as those who are united to Jesus Christ then our response to the exhortations that follow will be: Of course! There can be no other way to live the Christian life than by

(1) Putting to death the old, and

(2) Putting on the new.

The logic here is straightforward:

- Since you no longer have the old identity you once had, it would be inconsistent to live the old way you once did.

- Since you have received a new identity in Christ, you should live in a new way that is consistent with who you really are.

We have now become very familiar with this basic pattern for spiritual growth. But it bears repetition and fuller examination.

1. Putting off the old

Paul first deals with putting off the characteristics of the old life. He sees them virtually as three layers of clothing: under garments, basic garments, and outer clothing.

The first layer concerns dimensions of the old lifestyle which belong to the secret and private life of the mind. This is where we need to begin. Whatever belongs to our 'earthly' nature must be put off: 'sexual immorality, impurity, passion, evil desire, and covetousness, which is idolatry'.[1]

(i) Private life

There seems to be a development or movement in what Paul is saying here—from the outward act of sexual immorality to the

---

[1] Colossians 3:5.

inward desires that lie behind it, and then eventually to the root problem—evil desire and covetousness as idolatry.

When we have rejected or denied our basic created desire for God (we were, after all, made for him), we do not destroy our need; we only distort it. In its place we deify something that God has made. We worship a lesser god—the creature rather than the Creator.[1] Thus, as Paul notes, we claim to be wise ('I know what's best for me!'). But in fact we show ourselves to be fools.[2]

The prophets underscored this in words of powerful sarcasm. They not only spoke out against idolatry; they exposed its utter folly. A man takes a single piece of wood; he cuts it into two pieces; he uses one piece to kindle a fire and from the other piece he carves a god. He both warms himself by and worships two halves of the same piece of wood. What folly! Yet he is blind to it.[3] The human heart is indeed, as Calvin famously noted, a perpetual idol-making factory.[4]

But idols do not need to be statues.

God created us male and female, for himself and each other. But, as Paul makes clear here, when we are under the dominion of sin we rebel against his ordering of reality. Instead of loving and giving ourselves in the bond of marriage and thanking God for it, we desire, demand, lust, and distort what he has made. We turn the gifts he has given us to promote his praises and our enjoyment of him into idols that we come to serve. Then, since we discover that we 'must' have them, and actually 'need' them, we find ourselves in bondage to them. One would almost need to be blind, or at least ignore the media, not to realize that sex, in one form or another (frequently illicit), has become the idol of our day, the goddess who must be honoured. Not to do so has become a form of blasphemy against cultural

---

[1] Romans 1:25.

[2] Romans 1:22.

[3] Isaiah 44:9-20.

[4] *The Institutes of the Christian Religion* (1559), I.xi.8 (*hominis ingenium perpetua idolorum fabrica*).

norms. Nebuchadnezzar-like we have lost our minds.[1] And the problem with losing our minds is that we never know it, because they are the instruments by which we accept our folly and treat it as wisdom.[2]

The gospel reverses this. Once we were blind. But now we see. The eyes of our hearts are opened.[3] In Christ we have been renewed in the spirit of our minds.[4] We recognise immorality for what it really is—part of the old world order of the flesh. We have developed a taste for divine things, so that now the life of the flesh leaves a bad taste in our mouths. We know we are not yet what we have been called to become. But we are no longer the person we once were, in Adam. We should therefore no longer live in the old Adamic way as we once did.

Relevant today?

The letter to the Colossians while addressed to a small local church is perennially relevant.

Paul is addressing believers who may have been disappointed by their relatively small advance in the Christian life. Perhaps—as some still do—they had identified their dramatic deliverance from the *dominion* of sin with freedom from the *presence* of sin. But the two should never be confused. True, sin no longer reigns over us;[5] but it has not ceased to dwell in us. It will plague us until the end of our lives. If new believers fail to grasp this they become easy prey for false teachers peddling a 'higher' form of Christian living, free from the struggles and stresses of battling the ongoing influence of indwelling sin. 'What you Colossians need', some were perhaps saying, 'is to follow these spiritual laws: Do not touch this, do not taste that, have these spiritual experiences … and thus you will enter into

[1] Daniel 4:28-33.
[2] Romans 1:21-23.
[3] Ephesians 1:18.
[4] Ephesians 4:23.
[5] Romans 6:14.

the fullness for which you long.'[1] It was of course a lie; but it had its attractions for earnest new converts disappointed with their slow progress.

If that was true then it remains true today. Many young believers are shocked to discover that indwelling sin seems to be like an onion in the soul; the unravelling of one layer simply reveals the next—on and on continue the painful revelations of our sinfulness. It is then all too easy for false teachers to come along and say, as they still do, 'Are you disappointed with what you have experienced? There is a formula available that will deliver you.'

We must not be deceived by a 'spirituality' that masquerades as Christianity and takes the form of certain kinds of physical disciplines, special diets, 'tuning in' to spiritual beings, and experiencing 'spiritual fullness'. Not all that is spiritual is either healthy or holy. We need to remember Paul's warning: these disciplines may seem to be spiritual precisely because they are so rigorous. Indeed the more rigorous they are the more spiritual they may seem to be. They will offer much, but they can never deliver from indwelling sin; 'they are of no value in stopping the indulgence of the flesh'.[2]

The key test of any formula for sanctification is: Does this enable me to overcome the influence of sin, not simply in my outward actions but in my inner motivations? And, in particular: Does it increase my trust in and love for the Lord Jesus Christ? Is it a Christ-centred sanctification I am being offered? For that alone will enable me to put to death sexual immorality as an external act, and at the same time deal with the impurity at its root, and with its every impulse. Only thus in Christ can we squeeze the life out of lust and evil desires, and overcome the spirit of greed, which is idolatry.

So Paul is probing into the deep root of these manifestations of sin in the body, in the mind, in the soul, and in the heart. 'I want

[1] See Colossians 2:20-23.
[2] Colossians 2:23.

and will have ...' is idolatry. The root cause is the worship of self. That is why Jesus says that we must deny self.[1] True, believers have already done this in principle: 'Those who belong to Christ Jesus have crucified the flesh with its passions and desires.'[2] But now the cross must be carried on our shoulders daily.[3] This is not a matter of external action only but of inner devotion and motivation.

We should not lose sight of the fact that Paul is specifically addressing *Christians* here. He was realistic enough about the continuing presence of indwelling sin in believers to speak honestly about the nature of the battle.

Not only so, but Paul lists the very same sins he had told the Ephesians 'must not even be named among you'.[4] What explains such a paradox? He had long experience of his own and others' struggles in seeking to live wholeheartedly for Jesus Christ. In our private life, and in the hidden recesses of the mind, and in the way we use our bodies, the old lifestyle needs to be put off. It needs to be 'put to death'. But if we are to do so we must learn to be specific. It is not enough to say 'Help me overcome sin.' We must learn to say, 'Help me to overcome sexual immorality, or impurity, or passion, or evil desire, or covetousness, which is idolatry.'

(ii) Everyday life

Paul now expands his teaching beyond the hidden life of the mind and our *private life* behind closed doors. He turns to the *everyday life* of the believer. 'Now rid yourselves of all such things as these ...'.

What heads the list? 'Anger'—by which he means expressed hostility directed towards someone or something.

---

[1] Mark 8:34.

[2] Galatians 5:24.

[3] Luke 9:23.

[4] Ephesians 5:3 (they are 'sexual immorality and all impurity or covetousness'). By saying that these should not enter into our general conversation he is not for a moment pretending that Christians do not inwardly struggle with them.

Paul is obviously not saying we should never be angry. There are times when we should be. Our Lord Jesus was angry on occasion,[1] and there is such a thing in the New Testament as righteous anger— anger without sin. Such anger does not fester and last beyond the time of its appropriate expression.[2] But here Paul is speaking about settled hostility—a basic inner disposition manifested in our attitudes, speech, and actions.

Paul adds, we are to put away 'wrath'. This seems a straightforward enough exhortation. If all Paul means is that Christians should not fly off the handle, extract vengeance, or explode into a rage we would all nod our heads in agreement.

Some are blessed with the kind of personality that seems almost incapable of such explosive reactions. We are phlegmatic by nature.

But what if—as one scholar has suggested—we translate Paul's term here (*orgē*) as 'exasperation'?[3] That gets under the skin! If all Paul meant was 'rage' we might think of others to whom these words apply, but hardly ourselves. But 'exasperation'? Respectable impatience? Irritation when things go wrong? Surely these cannot be classed as *real* sin? But this is to remove God from our perspective. For the root cause of impatience and exasperation lies in our response to the providence by which God superintends our lives. At the end of the day the deep object of our exasperation is the Lord himself. For it is his sovereign purposes and detailed plans, and the way in which he has ordered our steps to bring us into the situation, that has been the catalyst of our exasperation.

So in fact 'exasperation' spells spiritual danger. Yet most of us do not think of it as serious sin. In fact we may have said (even with a sense of pride): 'I am not the kind of person to suffer fools gladly.

[1] Mark 3:5.
[2] Ephesians 4:26.
[3] 'Boiling agitation of the feelings; i.e. "exasperation".' R. C. H. Lenski, *The Interpretation of St Paul's Epistles to the Colossians, to the Thessalonians, to Timothy, to Titus and to Philemon* (Minneapolis: Augsburg Publishing House, 1961), 160.

I am easily exasperated by them.' But if so we have become deaf to what we are really saying. For such exasperation is an expression of the warped and distorted old way of life in Adam. It is un-Christlike and needs to be put off. At its heart is a self-exaltation over others, and a dissatisfaction with the way God is ordering and orchestrating the events of our lives.

In addition Paul adds that we should put off 'malice, slander, and obscene talk'. This refers to attitudes and speech which destroy the character (and therefore the reputation and the life) of another. Jesus said that there is more than one way to commit murder.[1] A Christian too can have 'a tongue as sharp as a knife'. Will we use it to cut someone's throat, or to cut their food? Do we use words that work to demolish or to reconstruct, to pull down or to build up?

Paul stays with the tongue. We are to get rid of filthy language. Impure vocabulary can never be consistent with the purity of the new creation. The tongue is the 'small member'; but it is the hardest thing in the world to tame. That is so because spiritually, if not anatomically, the tongue is directly attached to the heart.[2] Only when we have made some progress in mastering it have we begun to grow in maturity.

Providing motivation

We must not leave this catalogue in which Paul names what 'ought not to be named' without noting that it also contains a motivational supplement.

Sin causes us to suffer from a spiritual anaemia that in turn affects our vision—we no longer see things as they really are, but through diseased lenses. We no longer see sin clearly for what it really is. Paul reminds us of its nature by the sudden introduction of two vision clarifying statements:

[1] Matthew 5:21-22.
[2] James 3:5; Matthew 12:34.

(*a*) Sin brings divine wrath: 'On account of these things [sexual immorality, impurity, passion, evil desire, and covetousness, which is idolatry] the wrath of God is coming.'[1]

(*b*) This clothing belongs to your former life[2] as 'the old self [*anthrōpos*]' not to the present life of the 'new self [*anthrōpos*]' which is in process of being transformed into the renewed image of God.[3]

It is a commonplace to say that 'the punishment must fit the crime'. But that can be a half biblical truth. It can encourage us to assess the nature of the punishment by what *we consider* to be the severity of the crime. Paul reverses this. We learn the magnitude of the crime by means of the severity of the punishment it deserves. The dispositions and actions he delineates merit the wrath of God— *that* is the measure of their true nature. In addition they besmirch the believer (think of yourself attending a grand occasion only to discover that your elegant clothes are torn and covered in filth).

These are not the only motives for putting off the old. Nor are they in themselves sufficient to enable us to do it successfully. But they are important. We need to learn from the gospel to see our sin in its true light.

(iii) Church life

But then there is a third area in which we need to overcome sin: in the fellowship of the church, in our life with '*one another*'.[4]

What would be the first on the list of shortcomings that you think need to be *put off* in the Christian fellowship to which you belong?

Top of Paul's list is, 'Do not lie to one another.' His verb (*pseudo-mai*) is recognizable even to non-Greek speakers because we are familiar with the prefix *pseudo*. Paul's exhortation probably extends

---

[1] Colossians 3:6.
[2] Colossians 3:7.
[3] Colossians 3:10.
[4] Colossians 3:9.

beyond 'Do not lie to one another' to 'Don't play "Let's pretend"' in church; let us have honest and real relationships with each other. We are new men and women in Christ after all. Those who know who they are in Christ no longer need to pretend and to hide themselves behind a mask. He expresses the positive side of this in the parallel passage in Ephesians when he says 'speaking the truth [literally, *truthing*] in love we are to grow up in every way into him who is the head, into Christ'.[1]

A word of caution may be in order here, because Paul's exhortation has sometimes been misapplied. Living in the truth with one another is not the same as telling people everything about ourselves.

From time to time in the church's history teaching has been given which insists that Christians should be 'open' with each other. Well and good, so far. But when this is interpreted as hiding nothing, revealing everything, including private thoughts and feelings, it loses biblical balance. It can do much harm, not least when such 'openness' is viewed as a hallmark of the 'really committed' Christian. Colossae-like this has the aura of serious spirituality; but it goes beyond Scripture. And that can be just as damaging as falling short of it.

In fact we know that our Lord did not conform to this 'super-spirituality'. John specifically tells us that 'Jesus on his part did not entrust himself to them, because he knew all people.'[2] He did not reveal his inmost thoughts to all and sundry. Indeed he knew that was not a safe or wise way to live. Furthermore he knew that there were some things even his closest disciples would not be able to handle if he told them.[3] So we need to beware of teaching that has the appearance of maturity and impresses us because it makes rigorous demands but is not in fact scriptural. Private thoughts and feelings should ordinarily be kept just that—private.

[1] Ephesians 4:15.
[2] John 2:24.
[3] John 16:12.

Yet the relationships between and among those who are in Christ should be marked by reality rather than pretence, honesty rather than dissimulation—otherwise we will not grow together into the transformed community the church is called to be. Pretending to be something other than what we are is destructive of true fellowship. The reason is obvious. It means we are constantly keeping at arm's length those who are 'in Christ' along with us. By contrast the sanctification of the church involves 'the whole structure, being joined *together* [growing] into a holy temple in the Lord. In him you also are being built *together* into a dwelling place of God in the Spirit.'[1]

There is no need to hide. As sinners we cannot shield ourselves from God's gaze by weaving fig leaves together, but only by trusting in his righteousness. By faith we learn that he has accepted us, sinners though we are. If that is true then we no longer need to hide from him or pretend to him. But if we have been accepted by the One who knows our darkest secrets, we should also be increasingly delivered from the fear of others' opinions about us. In God's justification and acceptance of us we learn to accept each other for his sake. But constantly pretending to be something we are not gives the lie to our acceptance with God. The result is a loss of fellowship; all becomes either superficial or artificial—and that is a mark of the old life, not of the new. It is the way of the world, not the way the church should be. By contrast God has called his people to be different and to experience a special quality of fellowship which is found nowhere else. After all, if we are in Christ our lives are now part of a new family altogether.

So Paul says, Don't lie to one another; and don't be unreal with one another. Notice how he spells out the reason:

> You have put off the old self with its practices and have put on the new self, which is being renewed in knowledge after the image of its creator ... Here there is not Greek and Jew, circumcised and

[1] Ephesians 2:21-22.

uncircumcised, barbarian, Scythian, slave, free; but Christ is all, and is in all.[1]

A more literal translation would be, 'You have put off the old *man/person* with its practices and have put on the new *man/person*, which is being renewed in knowledge after the image of its creator.'

Paul is bringing us back again to the undergirding structure of a gospel way of thinking. He is not speaking here about the (modern) concept of the self (*anthrōpos*) as 'the individualised self' but about what we were *in Adam* (the old self) and what we have become *in Christ* (the new self). We once belonged to the old order, to a world and community dominated by the world, the flesh, and the devil—fallen in Adam, with the image of God in ruins if not totally destroyed. We now belong to the new world inaugurated in Jesus Christ; we are part of a new humanity in him. We have put off Adam and have put on Christ!

Once again then Paul bases his exhortation on our new identity and citizenship. He is not merely saying 'Remember how bad you used to be' but 'Remember the family to which you used to belong and the influences that shaped you. You are now in a new family in Christ, experiencing holy influences on your life. Remember who you really are!'

In the context of Colossae that was all the more important because they had either never known, or were in danger of forgetting their true identity in Christ. Or worse, they were suffering from identity theft. They needed to be encouraged to see themselves in the mirror of the gospel, as new men and women in Christ. Then the divisions that characterise all societies would cease to be relevant. They would be left at the church door, as it were:

Here there is not Greek and Jew, circumcised and uncircumcised, barbarian, Scythian, slave, free ...

[1] Colossians 3:9-11.

for here

Christ is all, and is in all.[1]

What makes the fellowship of the church stand out as different or 'holy' is a twofold reality: (i) Jesus Christ means everything to all the members; and, in addition, (ii) he comes by his Spirit to dwell in each of the members. Other kinds of fellowships are united by different principles. There *we* are everything, or *what we do* is everything. But in the church family Jesus Christ is everything all of the time, and he indwells each and all of the members.

This creates a double unity. Grasp this principle and our church fellowship will be transformed; holiness in our mutual devotion will mark it out. There is no intimacy in the world deeper or closer than this: there is only one Christ—and he dwells in each believer. We cannot get closer to each other than this! Here, then, is the often undetected secret of a fellowship that is growing in grace: *the Christ who is all to each one is also the Lord of glory who indwells every one.*

What is the first thing you see when you think about the Christian fellowship to which you belong? What is the first thing you look for? Is it this? 'What an enormous variety there is here. But in all the variety there is something—no, there is *Someone*—we have in common: the same Christ who indwells him also indwells her, and indwells me too! And he is everything to each of us!'

If we really thought this way about our fellow believers, and saw them as people in whom the Lord Jesus dwells, would we not treat each other differently? Surely this perspective would evoke love for them and a desire to serve them? That is why Paul sees this as one of the great features of a Christian fellowship that grows in holiness and consequently makes an impact on the world.

In the 1960s a memorable account of a London murder trial was published in one of the British national newspapers. The murder

[1] Colossians 3:11.

had taken place in a Chinese restaurant. One of the waiters was a key prosecution witness because he had been only a few feet away when the crime had been committed. The prosecuting counsel asked him if he was able to recognize in the court the person who had committed the murder. The Chinese waiter's response stunned the court. He apologised that he was unable to identify him. Pressed by the exasperated prosecuting counsel, he acknowledged that he had indeed witnessed the murder at close quarters. But under further questioning he eventually responded, 'I am very sorry, but I *cannot* identify the man. You see *all you Englishmen look alike to me!'*

To Westerners that may seem highly amusing. But if you were an *English* waiter working in a Beijing restaurant might you not in similar circumstances say '*All you Chinese men look alike to me*'?

We are all familiar with this phenomenon. Until we get used to looking at people who share the same ethnic features we tend to 'see' only those they all have in common. The same is true of twins. We do not notice the minor differences at first because of the major similarities.

Paul is saying something similar about the 'third race', the fellowship of the church. When we are in Christ it should be natural for our eyes to focus first on what we have in common, and especially on the fact that Christ indwells each of us. If this is so—if the Lord Jesus indwells other believers in love—should we not love them too? If Christ is really everything to us then of course we will.

But, we may say, 'Not all Christians are equally easy to love!' Not so. It is more accurate to say 'Not all Christians are equally easy *to like*'. But the sanctification of our relationships is not a matter of *liking*; it is a matter of *loving*. We may like other Christians because of what they are in themselves (and perhaps because they are like us and like us in return!). However, we come to love our fellow believers not because of what they are in themselves but because of what Christ is in them and to them and because of what they have become and will become in Christ. This is where we begin. If the Lord of glory is prepared to live *in them* with love, should we not be prepared to live *with them* in love too?

Just here we need to pause once more and draw a deep breath. For again, Paul's teaching on sanctification illustrates one of his key principles: *We must never stress the negative* ('put to death') *on its own.* That would lead to spiritual disaster. It must be accompanied by the positive ('put on').

When we are unwell we need medicine that will clear up the sickness. Perhaps even surgery will be required. But we also need nourishment to build up our strength. This principle—expulsion and restoration—also applies to our spiritual health. Unless graces take the place sins once occupied in our lives we will have no ongoing resistance to the old lifestyle or its habits. They will simply return to master us all over again. As Jesus noted: if we sweep the house clean of one demon but do not furnish it properly, then the old demon will return with seven more, and the last state will be worse than the first.[1] We therefore need to experience what Thomas Chalmers called 'the expulsive power of a new affection'[2] if we are to make progress. Expulsion and infilling must accompany each other.

Paul regularly illustrates this principle in his teaching. Thus even when he was dealing with the old life that we are to put off, he was already beginning to speak about aspects and elements of the new lifestyle that we are to put on.[3]

He now turns more directly to this.[4]

But before we continue with Paul, for a moment let us turn back to first principles (which is itself a vital lesson for us to learn). He has

---

[1] Matthew 12:43-5.

[2] The title of a sermon preached to his congregation of St John's Church, Glasgow, *Sermons and Discourses of Thomas Chalmers, D.D., LL.D.* (New York: Robert Carter & Brothers, 1856), 2, 271-278.

[3] As in Colossians 3:10-11.

[4] Colossians 3:12-17.

enunciated them in Colossians 3:1-4:

- You are in Christ,

- You therefore share in the significance of his death, resurrection, and ascension.

- You are permanently united to Christ; therefore you will share with him in his glory.

- This being the case do you not realize that through faith in him you have put off the old man with his old way of life? You are no longer in Adam. You have put on the new man. You are now in Christ and living in a new atmosphere. You are now being renewed into the image of God.

- So put off everything that would be inappropriate to wear as a Christian!

This brings him to the beginning of his series of positive exhortations. These can be summed up simply: *Since you are now a new person in Christ—dress accordingly.*

2. Dress the part!

When it comes to living out the gospel, clothes make the man—or the woman! If you are a new person in Christ, having died to the old life, been buried in Christ's tomb, been raised with him, ascended in him, now have your true life hidden in him, and are destined to be with him in his glory—then *live as though these things are true of you*—because *they are true!* Do not go about in soiled garments or spiritual rags. Your new identity requires a new wardrobe.

Paul presents us with an entire catalogue of clothing appropriate for life in Christ.

We are to put on Christ-like graces. God's chosen people, holy and dearly loved, should clothe themselves with Christlike characteristics: compassion, kindness, humility, gentleness and patience. Everything Paul mentions here is, in one way or another, a description of the character of the Lord Jesus himself. But perhaps it comes as a surprise that he prefaces his comments by saying these characteristics are appropriate for the Colossians because they are 'God's *chosen ones*'.

What word or words come immediately to mind at the mention of 'divine election'? Would *any* of the five words Paul associates with it? Compassion? Kindness? Humility? Meekness? Patience?

Paul, like Peter, sees election as a motivation for sanctification.[1] How does election bear such fruit? What is the gospel's logic here?

It is a first principle of the gospel that unless God had set his love upon us long before we turned to him we would never have come to Christ. His choice of us preceded our choice of him. He loved us before we loved him. He had compassion on us before we showed any interest in trusting in him. He has been kind to us. He has been gentle with us. He has shown us divine meekness in Christ. He has been patient with us. No wonder then that God's chosen people should react to others in exactly the same way. No wonder we should want to dress, spiritually, like him and grow in godliness, reflecting his moral beauty.

Paul's comment, mentioned almost in passing, presents a challenge to us. On the one hand, we readers may be somewhat allergic to the doctrine of election, or even critical of it under the misconception that a person who knows he or she is elect would simply live any way they pleased. If so we are not thinking biblically. Over and over again the Scriptures make clear that the knowledge of our election in Christ provides us with a powerful motivation to live godly lives. For God 'chose us in him before the foundation of the world, *that we should be holy* …'[2] On the other hand, election and predestination have usually been associated with Augustinians in the early church and Calvinists in the later church. If we share their biblical

---

[1] 1 Peter 1:2.
[2] Ephesians 1:4.

theology then our lives should, indeed must, bear these hallmarks: compassion, kindness, humility, meekness, patience. Striking thought, isn't it?

Do these clothes fit well on us, and suit us? If not, perhaps it is because we have never allowed ourselves to be humbled by the knowledge of God's election—and therefore never fully sensed the overwhelming privilege it is to be Christ's.

This clothing is attractive; but it is not 'showy'. It does not draw attention to itself, and yet it draws the eye.[1] Take kindness as an example. It seems a very modest fruit of God's electing love and of the work of Christ. You do not need to have a vast following on Facebook or Twitter, or host a television programme, or have a ministry named after you for this to be a sure sign that you are filled with the Spirit. It is an internationally transportable grace. Paul sees it as of the very essence of the new life. Not only so, but it wonderfully reflects the character of the Lord Jesus and powerfully displays his grace. Alas for us if we have confused the price tags God has placed on the fruit of the Spirit with those (lower!) price tags he has placed on the gifts of the Spirit (especially those that seem to bring position in the church or public recognition). Do we doubt this? Then we doubt Scripture. For Paul makes clear that this—the way of love—is 'a still more excellent way'.[2]

Augustine provides us with a remarkable illustration of the reality and power of these less spectacular evidences of the Spirit's work.

As a young man his theme-song might well have been the Rolling Stones' 'I can't get no satisfaction, and I've tried, and I've tried, and I've tried.' He tells us in his *Confessions* how he eventually applied for a teaching post in the city of Milan where Ambrose served as

---

[1] Notice the striking parallels in Paul's teaching: 'Put on the Lord Jesus Christ' (Romans 13:14), 'Put on then, as God's chosen ones …' (Colossians 3:12). His list of 'the fruit of the Spirit' (Galatians 5:22-23) and his exposition of love (1 Corinthians 13:4-7) say essentially the same thing.

[2] 1 Corinthians 12:31b. This is Paul's climactic statement on spiritual gifts.

the bishop. We can listen to Augustine telling the story in his own words (he is addressing God, rather than his readers):

> And so I came to Milan to Ambrose the bishop, known through-out the world as among the best of men, devout in your worship. At that time his eloquence valiantly ministered to your people 'the abundance of sustenance' and 'the gladness of oil' (Ps. 44:8; 80:17; 147:14), and the sober intoxication of your wine.[1] I was led to him by you, unaware that through him, in full awareness, I might be led to you. That 'man of God' (2 Kgs. 1:9) received me like a father and expressed pleasure at my coming with a kindness most fitting in a bishop. I began to like him, at first indeed not as a teacher of the truth, for I had absolutely no confidence in your Church, *but as a human being who was kind to me* ... gradually, though I did not realize it, I was drawing closer.[2]

What impressed Augustine about Ambrose? Despite the fact that he was one of the greatest preachers of his century, it was not his rhetorical skills in the pulpit, but the eloquence of his life. It was—although at the time Augustine could not have expressed it this way—his Christlikeness. He 'was kind to me'.

You could be that to someone, couldn't you? To say this does not diminish the importance of preaching or of personal witness; but it does stress the significance of wearing life-clothing that is the fruit of the gospel message and that enhances it. And, as it happens, few things are more helpful and encouraging to those who do preach than knowing that if strangers are present they will also encounter illustrations of the gospel when they later meet members of the congregation.

We are also to 'wear' Christlike responses to one another: 'Bearing with one another and, if one has a complaint against another,

---

[1] He is referring to the knowledge of God.

[2] Augustine, *Confessions*, 8.13 (23), translated with an Introduction and Notes by Henry Chadwick (Oxford: Oxford University Press, 1991), 87-88. Emphasis added.

forgiving each other; as the Lord has forgiven you, so you also must forgive.'[1]

The fact that Christ has died for us and brought us forgiveness is (i) the *foundation*, (ii) the *motivation*, and (iii) the *model* for our forgiveness of others. This is where the rubber meets the road, where union with Christ issues in likeness to him. In what other society is it true that the complaints department becomes the pardon department? This is what happens when we 'put on the Lord Jesus Christ and make no provision for the flesh'[2]—the very words that finally brought Augustine to the point of unreserved commitment to Christ. The flesh has a complaint and retaliates; the flesh is complained against and enters self-protection mode. But when new men and women in Christ are complained against they seek reconciliation through forgiveness. And when they have a complaint, they forgive. This is what the sanctified life looks like in practice. It has a dignity all of its own.

Here then is the clothing that Jesus Christ gives to us by the power of his Spirit indwelling us.

But Paul is not quite finished with his clothing catalogue:

We are to wear the love of Christ as our belt. Over all the fruit of the Spirit we are to 'put on love, which binds everything together in perfect harmony'.[3] We may have many gifts and graces but if they are not held together by love for Christ and for one another then our poor dress sense will be evident to all.[4] What is the point of possessing and wearing fine clothes if they do not fit together?

Have you ever said about someone (or perhaps thought but wisely *not* said), 'Why does she never dress properly?' or 'Why does

[1] Colossians 3:13.
[2] Romans 13:14.
[3] Colossians 3:14.
[4] Paul is here repeating the principles of 1 Corinthians 13:1-3 but using a vivid metaphor to do so. In antiquity, without a belt a person's clothing would come loose and his movements and activity would therefore be hindered.

he not wear clothes that suit and fit him?' or perhaps, 'Do they have no dress sense?' There is a spiritual analogy. Paul is saying: Clothe yourself in grace-attire that suits who you are in Christ. In order to do that everything needs to be held together—all your gifts, all your graces, all your talents, all your energies—with the belt of *love*. Otherwise you will be like a woman who has bought an expensive dress, is wearing a beautiful necklace, has marvellous shoes on her feet, but has forgotten the belt that would have prevented her from tripping up as she made her grand entry to the function. Everybody can see that the one essential item is missing—and it spoils the whole effect. Everything looks out of place. People will say 'How silly!'

In the same way Paul is saying, 'Dear Colossian Christians, don't you see how silly you will look—for all the gifts you have—if you do not show the love of Christ?'

We are to have Christ's peace ruling over us: 'Let the peace of Christ rule in your hearts, to which indeed you were called in one body.'[1] We are *called* to peace. It is not an added extra, an elective subject; it is a summons, a required course.

Paul is not referring to the kind of thing Christians sometimes say: 'I am sure it is right to do this—I have such a feeling of peace about it.' He is thinking here about Christ's peace serving as a referee, as an umpire in the church. In other words our life together in Christ, the decisions we make, the way in which we are shaped as a fellowship, are to be determined according to this rule: the peace of Christ. That is, by the answer to the question, 'What will best promote the *shalom*, the peace, wholeness, and well-being of the gospel here in the life of our fellowship?' This means being willing to deny ourselves, to silence insistence on our own way, or our personal desires, and to pray: 'Lead us on whatever path will bring most glory to your name and harmony in our fellowship.'

[1] Colossians 3:15.

These words should not—any more than other biblical state-ments—be read in isolation. This is not a plea for 'peace at any price'. Paul is not encouraging us to turn a blind eye to sin or self-seeking 'just for the sake of peace'. Nor is this an encouragement to ignore doctrinal confusion or false teaching. But in Christ we must seek the peace as well as the purity of the fellowship. For how can those who do not submit to Christ's peace ruling in their hearts claim that, despite this, they are at peace with Christ, or that they love their brothers and sisters? It makes a huge difference to the life of a church when everyone knows that in making any decision the first question that will be asked will always be, 'What will most promote Christ's glory? How best can we allow his *shalom* to rule in our hearts?'

We are to have Christ's word indwelling us. 'Let the word of Christ dwell in you richly' is a beautiful expression. Paul tells us that this should be especially evident when we are 'teaching and admonishing one another in all wisdom, singing psalms and hymns and spiritual songs, with thankfulness in your hearts to God'.[1]

Do you ever think about this when you gather with others for worship? Yes, you are praising God. But sanctified praise will have a manward as well as a Godward dimension. The Psalms well illustrate this. Perhaps one third of them are addressed to God himself ('Lord, you have been our dwelling place in all generations'[2]); in another third the psalmist is addressing himself ('Bless the Lord, O my soul, and all that is within me, bless his holy name!'[3]); and in a final third he is addressing others ('Oh give thanks to the Lord, for he is good'[4]). Thus, as we sing we are instructing, exhorting, encouraging, and teaching one another. This is one reason the words are always more significant than the music—important though the music is. It is also the reason *sanctified* believers will be *singing* believers. The word

[1] Colossians 3:16.
[2] Psalm 90:1.
[3] Psalm 103:1.
[4] Psalm 107:1.

that indwells them comes with such power to them that it issues from them in heart-felt sung proclamation. Our singing of psalms, hymns and spiritual songs is therefore our corporate ministry of God's word, a kind of mutual prophesying to one another to hear and live by the gospel. The more the word of Christ fills us by means of the words we sing, and as we sing them with understanding,[1] the more we will be able to bless God, encourage one another, and be strengthened in ourselves.

Finally, *we are to live in fellowship with one another making Christ's glory pre-eminent*: 'whatever you do, in word or deed, do everything in the name of the Lord Jesus, giving thanks to God the Father through him'.[2]

Paul has now brought us full circle in one half chapter of his letter.

In Colossians 3:1-4 he taught us about our new identity and encouraged us to set our hearts on heavenly things.

In Colossians 3:5-11 he traced the character of the old lifestyle back to the idolatry that dwells in our hearts by nature.

In Colossians 3:12-17 he has brought us from the pit of our own hearts to the height of God's glory.

The difference between the old lifestyle and the new lifestyle can be summed up in this contrast:

• The old is marked by sin, idolatry and our worship of self.

• The new is marked by the enthronement of Jesus and our worship of him.

The corporate result of this is that in our Christian fellowship our Lord Jesus Christ is all and is recognized to be in all.

Thus, growing in sanctification means:

---

[1] Notice in this connection the way Paul seems to relate both prayer and singing to the idea of prophecy and emphasizes the role of the mind and understanding in each. Cf. 1 Corinthians 15:15.

[2] Colossians 3:17.

- Understanding that I am a new man or new woman in Christ.

- Recognizing the traits in my life that are inconsistent with that new identity.

- Dealing death blows to my sins.

And simultaneously

- Clothing myself in the graces of Jesus.

When this is true of us our very presence enhances the lives of others in our church family. In addition, outsiders are attracted to the fellowship to which we belong—even if they do not yet understand why. It is because the 'holy church' is attracting them as the divine magnet it was meant to be.

How different this is from the individualism, self-interest, and narcissism that so many social commentators see as dominant features of modern society. In sharp contrast, success in the Christian life never means that we live for ourselves or see ourselves as superior to others. No, the real success the gospel effects releases us from our self-obsessions and self-interests, so that at last we are free in Christ to love and serve others. When this is true our fellowship becomes a powerful expression of the gospel. It becomes wonderfully attractive and compelling to some—even although others may hate or despise the gospel that produces such grace.

But then, if it was that way for Jesus, it will also be that way for those who grow in likeness to him.[1]

---

[1] John 15:18-21.

7

In for the Kill

———

The story so far is as follows. The basic pattern of sanctification is rooted in our relationship with Christ—our union with him in his death and resurrection. In him we have died to sin and been raised into newness of life. Building on this foundation involves putting off what belonged to the old lifestyle in Adam, and putting on and growing in the graces appropriate to the new humanity to which we now belong in Jesus Christ.

All this, as we have seen, was vividly symbolized in the early Christian centuries when, on Easter Sunday morning, new converts would gather wearing one set of outer clothing which would be removed as they came for baptism. Then after being baptized into the name of the Father, Son and Holy Spirit, they would be given new clothes to wear. They had put off the old life and put on the new.

What thrilled the apostles—John, Peter, and Paul all comment on it—was that this new life not only meant freedom from their former enslavement to sin, but also included an assurance that when Christ appeared they would appear with him, see him in his glory, and become like him.[1]

All this is true. Yet at the same time we continue to be troubled by the presence of indwelling sin. Thus there is a kind of inner

[1] Colossians 3:4; 1 Peter 1:7; 5:4; 1 John 3:1-2.

contradiction in the believer: Christ now dwells in us and yet sin also continues to indwell us. So long as this is true we face an ongoing conflict.[1] We need to learn how to deal with it.

We have already considered the guidance Paul provides in his comprehensive summary of union with Christ penned for the Colossian church. But it is worth noticing now how he put one aspect of that teaching under the microscope when he later dictated his letter to the churches in Rome:

> So then, brothers, we are debtors, not to the flesh, to live according to the flesh. For if you live according to the flesh you will die, but if by the Spirit you put to death the deeds of the body, you will live.[2]

Since this is so obviously basic to our sanctification, we might easily assume that almost every Christian is familiar with it, and can explain to others how to 'put to death the deeds of the body' and overcome sin. But it is doubtful if this is true. So for a moment we will press the pause button and ask the question: How then do you, in the power of the Holy Spirit, 'Put to death therefore what is earthly in you'?[3] How do you 'by the Spirit ... put to death the deeds of the body'? If we succeed in doing this, Paul says, we will live. But the opposite is also true: fail to do so, live instead 'according to the flesh', and we will die.[4]

A frustrating apostle?

Here again it is possible to become a little frustrated with Paul. Once more we find him issuing directives—*put on, put off, put to death*. But we may feel like saying, 'It is all very well for you to keep talking about these things, Paul, *but how are we to do them?*'

---

[1] In addition to the statement in Galatians 5:17 (which we examined in chapter 5), Romans 7:14-25 has often been seen as Paul's sharpest exposition of this inner conflict in the believer. See, Sinclair B. Ferguson, *The Holy Spirit* (Leicester: IVP, 1996), 155-62 with references for discussion of the varying interpretations.

[2] Romans 8:12-13.

[3] Colossians 3:5.

[4] Romans 8:13.

But what if, as we saw in his letter to the Colossians, we linger on these words, and chew on them like a dog with a bone? Perhaps again we will find that the answer to our 'How do you do this?' question is already embedded in the passage in which we were given the 'This is who you are and what you are to do' teaching. We have simply not noticed it, or perhaps never expected to find it.

It is always a good practice prayerfully to ask questions of Scripture as though you were having a dialogue with God as he speaks to you through it—which is exactly what happens. 'Lord, what are you saying here not only about *who* I am in Christ, and *what* I am to do, but also about *how* I am to accomplish it?'

The value of such catechizing of Scripture becomes almost immediately clear in the context of Paul's words in Romans 8:13. It would be too much to claim that he tells us everything we need to know about how to overcome sin (it takes the whole Bible to do that); but he certainly provides us with pointers in that direction.

Three central principles are expressed in this context—each of which breaks down into its own subsections.

Principle number one: Developing a mindset

The first principle is: *The Spirit of God is given to us to enable us to put sin to death.*

The Spirit does not bypass our minds and work directly on our emotions or affections.[1] It would be both bad theology and poor psychology to think so. Rather he addresses our minds through the word of God, simply because we are created as rational, thinking beings. How and what we think determines how we feel, will, and live. There is more to it than that, of course, but never less. As we

---

[1] A point made with particular force by Jonathan Edwards in the context of one of the criticisms levelled at preaching during the Great Awakening in North America. See *The Works of Jonathan Edwards* (1834; repr. Edinburgh: Banner of Truth Trust, 2005), 1, 404-405; or Jonathan Edwards, *Thoughts on the New England Revival* (1742; repr. Edinburgh: Banner of Truth Trust, 2005), 174-183.

have already seen, we are transformed through the renewing of our minds, and this involves the creation of a new mindset.

But what is this new mindset? Paul provides several clues.

(i) Necessity

It involves the recognition that I *need to* put sin to death in my life. It is my God-given responsibility if I am to 'keep in step with the Spirit' and not 'grieve' him.[1]

Sometimes people who come to Christ in a dramatic way experience an enormous sense of deliverance not only from the burden of the guilt of sin, but also from their bondage to it and their sense of hopelessness under its power. But we can mistake this for entire deliverance from the very presence of sin.

The danger at this point is to look for as dramatic and immediate an experience of sanctification as we had of justification. If only we could 'get' holiness by a simple act of faith, the same way we 'got' Christ!

Some have believed and taught this very possibility. There is a well-known view taught by Christians who believe in such 'sanctification by faith'. It is often associated with interpreting Paul's words in Romans 7 as a description of the 'defeated Christian'. It speaks of needing to 'get out of Romans 7 and into Romans 8' (seen as an expression of the life of victory). Another expression of it alluded to what Paul had taught in Romans 6:

> Buried with Christ and raised with him too,
> What is there left for me to do?
> Simply to cease from struggling and strife,
> Simply to walk in newness of life,
> Glory be to God!

This leaves very little place for the older (and more biblical) teaching that spoke in such vigorous terms as 'putting a knife to the

---

[1] Galatians 5:16 (NIV); Ephesians 4:30.

throat' of our sin!¹ Thus the *Westminster Confession* speaks about the believer's experience of 'a continual and irreconcilable war' between the flesh and the Spirit.² This war is *possible* only because we have already been delivered from the reign of sin. For only then are we free to fight against our former sovereign. The war is also *inevitable* because we have not yet been fully and finally delivered from the presence of sin. It remains like a squatter in our lives—and squatters are notoriously difficult to evict. In the case of sin the only remedy for the situation is that we put it to death.

Think about it this way. Paul says that two things are true of Christian believers:

(*a*) Jesus Christ dwells in them

(*b*) Sin continues to dwell in them.

So long as these are both true, so long will we need to go on putting sin to death.

Growing in holiness, enjoying closer fellowship with God, brings with it an ongoing and very painful revelation of layers of sin that have been subtly hidden in our hearts but rarely if ever exposed.

The term Paul uses here ('deeds' of the body) occurs outside the New Testament in reference to acts of subtle intrigue. It is well chosen. Sin lies hidden within the deep folds of our hearts, in the dark recesses of our ambitions, desires, and aspirations, and even in our gifts—no, if Isaiah's confession is anything to go by, *especially* in our areas of giftedness.³ It is so subtle it is capable of hiding from us until the Spirit uses God's word and superintends his providences to

---

¹ Alexander Whyte would re-wrap and send back any commentary on Romans that took the view that Romans 7 described 'the defeated Christian' and famously told his congregation 'You'll not get out of Romans seven so long as I am your minister!' It might have been more Pauline to have said 'You'll not get out of Romans 6, 7 or 8 so long as I am your minister!'

² *Westminster Confession of Faith*, XIII.2.

³ Although the most eloquent of the prophets he confessed 'I am a man of unclean lips' (Isaiah 6:5).

penetrate our consciences.[1] Only then do we see the twistedness that needs to be untangled, and patterns of mind and spirit that need to be confessed and abandoned. Only then do we fully realize that we *need* to go on putting sin to death. Otherwise as Paul hints here, we will be in danger of sin putting us to death. For 'if you live according to the flesh you will die'.

(ii) Responsibility

The second aspect of the mindset produced by the Spirit is a recognition that *we are personally responsible* to put sin to death. It will not simply vanish on its own accord. No, says Paul: '*You* are the one who is responsible to put sin to death.'

We may be tempted to respond: 'But Paul talks here about the Holy Spirit's work; surely this is his task, not mine? Surely he alone can really put sin to death?'

But look again at what Paul says: *not*, 'Let *the Spirit* put sin to death …' but 'If … *you* put to death …'. Yes, the Spirit enables us. Without him we are powerless. But he never turns us into automatons. He never relieves us of the responsibility of living for the glory of Jesus Christ. Since he is holy in himself, he wants us to be holy in ourselves (but not by ourselves). And holy people do holy things—such as resisting and mortifying sin.

So here we have a particular application of the more general principle, 'Work out your own salvation with fear and trembling, for it is God who works in you, both to will and to work for his good pleasure.'[2] We do not say, 'If God is working in me, then I can just sit back and relax.' No, we say 'Because God is working in me I must work out what he is working in.' This includes putting sin to death.

Unless we are doing it we are not being sanctified.

[1] Hebrews 4:12.
[2] Philippians 2:12-13.

(iii) Ability

There is a further dimension to Paul's words. He implies that with the help of the Spirit we are *able* to put sin to death. We may not see its presence disappear from our lives, but we can keep resisting its influence.

On the one hand the discovery of the subtle presence and power of indwelling sin may rock us back on our heels. But on the other hand we are not left paralyzed and despairing. We must not become discouraged by how far we still have to travel. For one thing, we know that the decisive victory over sin has already been won—we are no longer its slave.[1] Now we are involved in the mopping-up operations. There may still be sore conflict; we may still suffer wounds and discouragements. But through the enabling of the Spirit it is possible to be successful in overcoming sin in an ongoing way. There is every reason for encouragement, hope, and joy.

But there is a further vital element in the mindset Paul is encouraging.

(iv) Will

During one of his visits to Jerusalem, Jesus met an invalid at the pool of Bethesda. He asked him what, at first sight, is a surprising question 'Do you want to be healed?'[2] If it were not Jesus asking it we would probably think 'Silly question!'

What did Jesus mean? 'Do you *want* …?' or 'Do you want *to be made whole*?' or 'Do *you* want to be made whole?' Certainly the verb 'to will' occupies the emphatic position in John's account. Is it possible that after almost four decades as an invalid, this man had given up both the hope and the desire for healing? We speak about people

---

[1] Romans 6:1-14. Robert Murray M'Cheyne wrote that Romans 6:14, 'Sin shall not have dominion over you', 'is the sweetest word in the Bible'. Andrew Bonar, *Memoir and Remains of R. M. M'Cheyne* (1844; 1892 enlarged ed. repr. Edinburgh: Banner of Truth Trust, 2009), 42.

[2] John 5:6.

losing the will to live. Had this man lost even the will to be healed? Was he paralyzed in his will as well as in his body?

We might ask a parallel question: What do we *want* Christ to do for us? Do we really *want* to grow in holiness? Or has our failure left us content with mediocre levels of sanctification? Or worse, are we still in the spiritual wasteland in which Augustine prayed 'Give me chastity; but not yet'?[1] Can we perhaps substitute for 'chastity' the antidote for some prevailing sin in our own lives?

So here is a critical issue in our progress: *Do we really want to overcome sin?* For there seems to be a principle in sanctification: in some measure we get what we desire. Or, to put it more bluntly, we get what we are prepared to pay for. For the language that both Paul and Jesus use about dealing with sin is tinged with personal cost, indeed with violence and pain:

> If your right eye causes you to sin, *tear it out and throw it away*. For it is *better that you lose* one of your members than that your whole body be thrown into hell. And if your right hand causes you to sin, *cut it off and throw it away*. For it is better *that you lose* one of your members than that your whole body go into hell.[2]

> If then you have been raised with Christ, seek the things that are above … *Put to death* therefore what is earthly in you …[3]

There are no spiritual gains without pains. So we must be willing to act with spiritual violence against our sin. It is enmity against God and it distorts his purposes for our lives. It offends him and it destroys us. Only when we grasp this will we begin to develop the mindset which the Holy Spirit seeks to produce in us. Spirit-led believers are willing to break the neck of sin, or to stab it in the heart, or to pull out the weeds it sows, in the knowledge that what we are doing may feel like a death.

[1] *Confessions*, 8.7.
[2] Matthew 5:29-30.
[3] Colossians 3:1, 5.

In his book *The Great Divorce* C. S. Lewis provides a dramatic illustration of this. In his guided tour of the heavenly world the central character, the Narrator, sees a ghost ('unsubstantial') 'who carried something on his shoulder … a little red lizard'. The creature dominates and controls the ghost's life. A 'flaming Spirit' appears, an angel who offers to 'make him quiet' and thus set the ghost free:

'Would you like me to make him quiet?' said the flaming Spirit …

'Of course I would,' said the Ghost.

'Then I will kill him,' said the Angel, taking a step forward.

'Oh—ah—look out! You're burning me. Keep away,' said the Ghost, retreating.

'Don't you *want* him killed?'

'You didn't say anything about *killing* him at first. I hardly meant to bother you with something as drastic as that.'

'It's the only way,' said the Angel, whose burning hands were now very close to the lizard. 'Shall I kill it?'

The dialogue continues for another page until the Ghost says:

'Get back! You're burning me. How can I tell you to kill it? You'd kill *me* if you did.'

'It is not so.'

'Why, you're hurting me now.'

'I never said it wouldn't hurt you. I said it wouldn't kill you.'

Readers of *The Great Divorce* will remember well how the passage ends. The Angel does his deadly work. But the result is that the Ghost turns into a man and the lizard turns into 'the greatest stallion I have ever seen' onto which the new man leaps and rides away.

The narrative concludes with a dialogue between the Narrator and his Teacher:

'Do ye understand all this, my Son?' said the Teacher.

'I don't know about *all*, Sir,' said I. 'Am I right in thinking the Lizard really turned into the Horse?'

'Aye. But it was killed first. Ye'll not forget that part of the story?'[1]

Perhaps you recognise yourself? For 'Ghost' substitute yourself; for 'lizard' substitute indwelling sin. For 'Angel' substitute Holy Spirit. Of course like all allegories this one has its limitations, but the point is surely well taken. Only the death of sin leads to a life of freedom. Yes, it hurts. Yes, it may feel like getting dirt out of a wound, using a needle to get a splinter out of your finger, trying to remove an eyelash from your eye. It feels as though it is yourself dying. But 'if by the Spirit you put to death the deeds of the body, you will live'!

Paul now adds a second principle—

Principle number two: Motives

The apostolic letters often weave together the new mindset the Spirit creates with new motives the gospel provides. So here.

But what motives?

(i) Think of the harvest

The first motive is enshrined in the statement: 'If you live according to the flesh you will die, but if by the Spirit you put to death the [mis]deeds of the body, you will live.'

In the Christian life we always reap what we sow. The relationship is inexorable:

- Live to the flesh—and die.

- Put the flesh to death—and you will live.

That actions have consequences is a proverbial principle in life. Look at the faces of men and women who have been addicted to

---

[1] The narrative is found in C. S. Lewis, *The Great Divorce* (1946, repr. Glasgow: William Collins, Fount paperbacks, 1977), 89-96. As with all of his writings it would be far from wise to build a theology on Lewis's imagination. Nevertheless he presents us with a powerful allegory of the effects of sin, of the work of the Spirit, and of the biblical principle that the way to life involves death.

drugs or alcohol, or the medical condition of people whose bodies have been abused.

But then, consider saints who have gone through much and are now grown old. The outer person perishes, but the inner person is renewed.[1] At times we catch sight of the work of the Spirit transforming them already. There is the gentle glow of grace and the subtle beauty of Christlikeness in their character. They have already begun to reap what they have sown. The best is yet to come, but their lives already taste of it. By contrast, for the ungodly the best lies in the past, and as the future rushes upon them they have no glory to reap, for they sowed only to the flesh.

The Christian life has both seed-time and harvest. We therefore need to take a long-term view. If I sow to the flesh I will always reap from the flesh corruption; sow to the Spirit and I will enjoy a spiritual harvest in eternal life. That is an unchanging law in the kingdom of God.

So at least here Ralph Waldo Emerson was right:

> Sow a thought and you reap an action;
> Sow an action and you reap a habit;
> Sow a habit and you reap a character;
> Sow a character and you reap a destiny.

It is hardly surprising to learn that Emerson's answer to the question 'What is the hardest thing in the world?' was: '*To think.*' Yes, *think* of the harvest; it will transform your view of what you are doing here and now. It will encourage you to tend the garden of your soul, weeding, planting, nourishing it patiently. You will then accept short-term pain, or self-denial, or loss, for the sake of long-term gain. And you will not die but live.

Nor does the harvest come only at the end. It sprouts up already in the development of Christian character. And the more these good

[1] 2 Corinthians 4:16.

crops grow the less nourishment remains for the weeds of the flesh. In this as in so many other things, success breeds success. As the children's hymn says, 'Each victory will help you some other to win.'[1]

(ii) Be sensitive to the Spirit

Notice too, the way in which Paul's words about the mortification of sin are linked with the statement that follows:

> If by the Spirit you put to death the deeds of the body, you will live. *For* all who are led by the Spirit of God are sons of God.[2]

These words 'led by the Spirit' tend to be used (and therefore interpreted) out of context, as though Paul were speaking here about special and individual experiences of God's guidance ('The Spirit led me to take the job.' 'I feel led to marry …').

There is no doubt that the Lord leads his people, guiding and directing them in such matters as vocation and marriage. But Paul is not describing that here, and therefore we should be cautious about applying his language in that way. Here he is speaking about the leading or guiding the Spirit gives all the time to all who belong to Christ: *The Spirit leads us to put to death the* (mis)*deeds of the body so that we will live.* Those who follow this guidance are God's sons. What this 'leading' has in view is not the job we should take, the place we should live, or the person we should marry, but our responsibility to mortify sin!

In thus being sensitive to the Spirit's leading we show that we really are the children of God. For the Spirit through whose power we overcome sin is the same Spirit of adoption who enables us to call God 'Abba, Father.'[3] As God's sons, who love our heavenly Father and are sensitive to his indwelling Spirit, we refuse to bring anything

[1] From the hymn by Horatio Richmond Palmer (1834–1902), 'Yield not to temptation'.
[2] Romans 8:13-14. In Roman law only sons inherited.
[3] Romans 8:15.

home, or into our lives, that would spoil the family atmosphere, distort the family likeness, or grieve him. For those who experience the Father's love and enjoy the family privileges know there are also family obligations to fulfil and a family lifestyle to express.

So there is a quadruple motivation here: love for the Father, knowing that Christ is our Elder Brother, learning to be sensitive to the Spirit's holiness, and also our responsibility for the family honour. Taken together these realities produce the impetus we need to turn our backs on sin in any and all of its forms.

To fail to do so would be to forget who we really are in Christ— *children of the living God.*

(iii) Remember Calvary and Pentecost

Christ died for our sins in order to give us his Spirit to enable us to overcome them.

This is the foundation on which Paul builds his teaching:

> God has done what the law, weakened by the flesh, could not do. By sending his own Son in the likeness of sinful flesh and for sin, he condemned sin in the flesh, in order that the righteous requirement of the law God might be fulfilled in us, who walk not according to the flesh but according to the Spirit.[1]

The Father, in his love for us, has given us his Son; he has also given us his Holy Spirit—his two most precious gifts, indeed everything he possessed before his first act of creation—his own love, his beloved Son, and his Holy Spirit![2]

The teaching here makes two points about sin: *First,* our Lord Jesus came from the glory of heaven to the shame of the cross in order to die for our sin. He suffered, exposed to the world's gaze, in pain and isolation, for the sin that continues to lurk within our

[1] Romans 8:3-4.
[2] Cf. Galatians 4:1-6.

hearts. *Second,* the Holy Spirit has come to indwell us in order to deliver us from the influence of that sin for which Christ died, and to make us more and more like our Saviour.

Thus in giving his two most precious possessions for us and to us, the Father has also given us the strongest possible motives and the greatest possible assistance for deliverance from sin's guilt and also from its ongoing influence.

Why then would we live for that for which Christ died? Why then would we continue in the sin from which the Spirit has come to deliver us? Why then would we say to our Father, 'Despite your best gifts I will retain my love of sin'?

What motivation this provides! When I am tempted and feel the power of sin and its tug on my affections, the gospel gives me something to say: 'Christ bled and died for this sin—I will therefore have nothing to do with it. I am now united to Christ by the indwelling of the Spirit—how can I drag him into my sin?'

Recall Paul's dramatic words to the Corinthians. We are united to Christ as whole people, body and soul: 'Do you not know that your bodies are members of Christ?' We belong entirely to him. We are joined to the Lord. But some members of the Corinthian church were apparently engaging in blatant sexual immorality— with prostitutes. And so Paul appeals:

> Don't you understand? Don't you see what you are in effect doing? Anyone who joins himself to a prostitute becomes one with her. But you are already one with Christ, united to him. Don't you see that you are, in effect, dragging him into your sin? Don't you see that you are uniting someone united to Christ to a prostitute?[1]

We can substitute our own sin here, to help us to see it in true perspective. If we are united to Christ we are not able to place that union temporarily in abeyance, and say to the Lord Jesus 'Let's leave our union to one side for a few minutes while I sin.' No. Rather it

[1] 1 Corinthians 6:15-17.

is as though we do not even care if we drag Christ himself into the sin—the very sin for which he died!

Surely if I realize that sin is an offence of this magnitude, I have motivation sufficient to resist it in the power of the Spirit and to put it to death? It is significant, surely, that in the space of only five verses Paul asks the Corinthians three times, '*Do you not know this?*'[1]

Well, *do we?*

Principle number three: *The Method of Grace*

When these principles are worked into our thinking, adding nitty-gritty instructions about what we are to do seems almost superfluous. The motivations themselves carry with them the impetus to live wholly for Christ. But even here, Paul weaves in practical directives for dealing with sin. We can summarize them as follows:

(i) Deal with the root

Essential to dealing with *any* particular form of sin is a willingness to deal with *all* sin. Paul does not tell us to put some sin, or only embarrassing sin, but all sin to death.

The older Christian writers—much more skilled in these things than we usually are—placed great emphasis on the difference between *mortifying* sin (i.e. putting it to death), and merely *diverting* it—so that it lives on in a different but less obvious guise.

We are all past-masters of doing this. Social pressure, or expectations within Christian fellowship, cause us to divert obvious sin to some other less obvious sphere. Sin is not so much put to death as channelled in a different direction.

In 'the old days' when toothpaste came in metallic rather than in plastic tubes, eventually after much pressing and bending the casing of the tube tended to crack. When it was squeezed the toothpaste would come out of the crack rather than the mouth of the tube.

[1] 1 Corinthians 5:15, 16, 19.

You could cover the crack, put finger-pressure on it to block the toothpaste—and most of us did! But then what? It simply emerged from another crack.

Sin is like that. Cover over the crack through which it emerges, stem the flow because it embarrasses us, and all we do is divert its activity to another area of our lives. We have not made any real progress in overcoming sin *as sin*.

When Paul speaks about putting sin to death, he means much more than covering it over or diverting it. He means dealing with the reality which lies behind, and comes to expression in, any and every pattern of sinful behaviour.

Here is a further context in which Augustine of Hippo's great text is so helpful: 'Put on the Lord Jesus Christ, and make *no provision* for the flesh, to gratify its desires.'[1]

This is not just an encouragement to mortify sin in the area in which you happen to be particularly troubled by it, but to make no provision whatsoever for the flesh in any shape or form. Neither a medical sticking plaster nor drugs can cure us when what we need is surgery. We simply mask the problem. Similarly, neither disguise nor diversion of sin provides the lasting solution we need. Only seeking to put it to death does.

Think of what happens when people go on a diet. They thought the problem was food. But in the process they discover that the problem is not the food but the reasons for the 'snacking' or for that matter the 'binging'. It is a manifestation of other issues with which they must deal. They need to get to the root of the matter if they are to deal with its fruit.

The same is true in dealing with sin. Unless we get to the root of the matter, we will never be able to divest ourselves of its fruit. It will simply grow on another branch.

[1] Romans 13:14, emphasis added.

And so we need to return to and apply the basic biblical principle with which we began: Commit yourself *unreservedly* to holiness in *every* aspect of your life.

Taking that exhortation seriously is an important first step. It may touch a raw nerve and expose patterns in our lives that we secretly love but have never fully and honestly admitted to either the Lord or ourselves. Only if we bring them from their hiding places, and (as we have seen) give them their proper names, can they be dealt with effectively.

In this connection think back to the paradox enshrined in Paul's letters to Colossae and Ephesus. To the Colossians he wrote:

> Put to death what is earthly in you: *sexual immorality, impurity,* passion, evil desire, and *covetousness* …[1]

But in his Letter to the Ephesians he said:

> *Sexual immorality* and all *impurity* or *covetousness* must not even be named among you, as is proper among saints.[2]

We noted earlier the paradox in the highlighted words. In Ephesians he 'names' the very sin-patterns that he told the Colossians 'must not even be named among you'.

Recall why Paul names the not-to-be-named. He knows that only when we name our sins, confess them for what they really are, and seek forgiveness and deliverance, will we make headway against them. Some people are proud of 'calling a spade a spade' until it comes to the patterns of sin in their own lives. But only when these are exposed in their true colours are we able to overcome them. Confessing that we are sinners in general will not enable us to make lasting headway against our sins in particular.

---

[1] Colossians 3:5.
[2] Ephesians 5:3.

(ii) Guard the mind

Second, we must learn to guard our mind against dwelling on the flesh.

We tend to distinguish between mind and body and also between mind and 'flesh'. But in the New Testament our natural mind is part of what is meant by 'the flesh'. Setting my mind on the things of the flesh—allowing my thoughts and imagination to dwell on them—is bound to lead to being captivated by the flesh. So I must guard my mind.

But how?

By consciously refusing to let my mind focus on, or drift towards, the things of the flesh.

We are easily tempted in this way, and may tend to defend, even justify, ourselves by saying 'I didn't *actually do* it; I was only *thinking* about it.' But 'thinking about it' is *already a form of doing it*. As Jesus makes clear, it is doing it mentally.[1]

What do you think about when you have got nothing special to think about? Towards what do you allow your mind to wander? Paul is saying 'Rein it in.'

I had a friend, brought up in New York City, who had a unique (and at times alarming) driving habit. If he saw another car beginning to pull out into his path he would put his foot on the accelerator and say out loud, 'Don't even think about it!'

This may not be a particularly commendable way to drive, but it well illustrates how the Christian should live. Whenever we see sin emerging from the recesses of our hearts, or temptation coming into view, we need to put the foot down on the accelerator pedal that will drive our minds quickly to Christ, and say: 'Don't even think about it!' For, sadly, one of the most common statements pastors and counsellors hear from those who have grievously sinned is 'I don't know what I was thinking about' or 'I just didn't think.'

[1] Matthew 5:27-28.

But this 'putting off' in the mind also needs to be accompanied by 'putting on', by learning to 'set the mind on the Spirit'.[1]

(iii) Fill the mind

Remember Paul's big picture: Christ has died and been raised again; we are united to Christ in his death and resurrection; we have died to sin and been raised to newness of life in him. Built on this foundation the reshaping of our lives involves putting off and mortifying sin on the one hand and putting on the graces of Christ on the other. We refuse to allow our minds to dwell on the flesh. But we must also seek to flood our minds with the things of the Spirit. This then allows us to experience 'the expulsive power of a new affection'.

Thus Paul writes:

> Whatever is true, whatever is honourable, whatever is just, whatever is pure, whatever is lovely, whatever is commendable, if there is any excellence, if there is anything worthy of praise, think about these things.[2]

When I was a young Christian this list of 'things to think about' seemed tame and overly-mundane, more like good advice than gospel grace. To a certain extent many New Testament scholars have agreed, seeing Paul's words as little more than a recognition that Christians should share qualities respected by the world at large.

But Paul never speaks in a non-gospel way. There is nothing mundane about his exhortation. It is better to understand Paul to say that any 'overlap' here between the gospel and a secular ethic lies in the fact that the gospel actually delivers what men and women at their best recognise to be the qualities of true humanity. And so we allow the fruit the Spirit produces in us to become the object of our thinking and aspiring. For what we think about and love will have a determinative influence on our character. What fills our minds will

[1] Romans 8:6.
[2] Philippians 4:8.

shape our lives. We become what we think! And like Paul's lists of the qualities of love,[1] and of the fruit of the Spirit,[2] these are ultimately reflections of the character of our Lord Jesus, who after all was the true and perfect man.

It is telling that immediately following Paul's listing of the works of the flesh and the fruit of the Spirit he adds that 'those who belong to Christ Jesus have crucified the flesh with its passions and desires'.[3] From the start of the Christian life there is to be putting on and putting off; putting off and putting on; death and life; life and death. And this begins with the renewal of our minds.[4]

How hard it is for many of us in the modern world to set our minds for any length of time on the truth of the gospel! But if we are to overcome sin we must develop the ability to fix our minds on the things of the Spirit and the glory of Jesus Christ. And that can take place only when we are being filled with the truth of Scripture.[5]

Is it cruel to suggest that many of us spend more mental time and energy on fixing face and hair and mouth and clothes before the mirror than we do fixing our minds on the mirror of God's word? We can hardly deny that we find it so much easier to be engrossed in our hobbies and interests than in Scripture. Is there a remedy?

Yes there is. Your grandmother, or at least her mother may well have known it. But we have forgotten it in a world that is awash with the immediate and the bite-size. The remedy is soaking ourselves frequently in God's word; allowing our minds to be filled to saturation point with its truth until it can be said of us as C. H. Spurgeon

[1] 1 Corinthians 13:4-8.
[2] Galatians 5:22-23.
[3] Galatians 5:24.
[4] Romans 12:1-2.
[5] Note in this connection how Paul seems to parallel the ideas of being filled with the Spirit (Ephesians 5:18) and letting the word of Christ dwell in us richly (Colossians 3:16). These are two aspects of one and the same reality.

said about John Bunyan, 'Prick him anywhere—his blood is Bibline.'[1] The old adage is still true: 'Sin will keep you from God's word; or God's word will keep you from sin.'

The remedy is at hand. There is no immediate pathway to getting to know God's word intimately. There is no quick fix. We can only do this the old-fashioned way, by reading it often and learning it well.

(iv) Live in fellowship

Each of us is responsible to put our own sin to death and to grow in Christ. But this was never intended to be a merely individualistic activity. For characteristically the exhortations in the New Testament ('you do this … or that') appear in the second person *plural*, not *singular*. Yes, we are responsible to apply them to ourselves as individuals. But we would be wrong to think we can or should always 'go it alone'. For 'On its own each member loses fire.'[2]

There are occasions, as James writes, when it is both appropriate and helpful to confess our faults to and pray for one another.[3] He is not urging the church to organise a corporate confession meeting; nor is he instructing individuals to go to 'Confession'. Rather, as the masters of the spiritual life have believed, there may be times in our pilgrimage when Satan engages in blackmailing us. We have secretly given in to sin. He whispers that we have failed; we are unworthy. He will keep our secret—so long as we keep it a secret too, and hide or disguise it. No one else must be told.

---

[1] 'The Last Words of Christ on the Cross', a sermon delivered on 25 June 1882 by C. H. Spurgeon, *The Metropolitan Tabernacle Pulpit* (London: Passmore & Alabaster, 1899), 45:495 (Sermon 2,644).

[2] From the hymn by Bryan J. Leech, 'We are God's people'.

[3] There are important general principles governing confession of our faults and sins: private sin should be confessed privately to the Lord; sin hurting a brother or sister should be confessed to the Lord and to him (or her); only where our sin has been against the whole congregation and reconciliation is needed with them all would it be appropriate for us to confess our sin before the whole church.

What is Satan's ploy? We are already ashamed, but now in addition we fear what others will think and say. The result? We become isolated within ourselves; we feel there is a secret nobody else must know, we fail to deal biblically with our sin; we develop habits of despair about it. We thus hide our sin; we do not admit it even to God. This, insinuates the evil one, is the only safe way. All very subtly we have begun to lose sight of the fact that there is forgiveness. Satan will make sure that we continue to feel our guilt and shame. What would others in the church think of us (as though they were not sinners too!)? We become paralysed.

Under these circumstances we may find ourselves incapable of breaking the dark stranglehold sin and Satan now have on our lives.

But if we are able to share our failure, our sense of guilt and bondage with a fellow Christian whom we can trust absolutely, and to whom we can open our heart—then we break the power of the blackmail, the truth is out in the presence of God, we are able to pray together honestly, and forgiveness once again flows into our hearts. Yes, there may be shame, and sorrow, and tears—but there is also pardon, forgiveness, a new beginning, and the blessing of stronger bonds of fellowship.

Part of the reason Satan manages to keep us in such a bondage state spiritually is because he convinces us that he alone knows our secret. It is a lie. The heavenly Father has long known it. A wise and loving friend may be able to reassure us from the gospel that with the Lord there is forgiveness, that he may be feared.[1]

In this way we learn not only how to mortify sin, but how to overcome the evil one. And thus we learn to live the Lord's Prayer:

> Forgive us our debts,
>   as we also have forgiven our debtors.
> And lead us not into temptation,
>   but deliver us from the evil one.[2]

[1] See Psalm 130:4.
[2] Matthew 6:12-13, ESV marginal translation.

8

The Law Goes Deep

The apostle Paul preached that it is the Spirit who produces in our lives such rich fruit as 'Love, joy, peace, patience, kindness, goodness, faithfulness, gentleness, self-control.'[1] But then he added, 'against such things there is no law'.[2]

When he preached in this way, as he must often have done, this last statement stuck in the throats of some who had heard (perhaps at second-hand) what he taught. In Jerusalem he was informed by the elders of the church that people there had 'been told about you that you teach all the Jews who are among the Gentiles to forsake Moses'. A week or so later he was waylaid by a mob and accused of 'teaching everyone everywhere … against … the law'.[3] It is clear from his correspondence that he was frequently attacked for demeaning, if not actually abandoning, the law of God. After all, did he not preach that the righteousness of God had been 'manifested apart from the law' and that 'by works of the law no human being will be justified in his sight'?[4] Was this not a recipe for license?

If this is so then we too need to ask Paul's own question: 'Why then the law?'[5] His answer, and his whole perspective on the

[1] Galatians 5:22-23.
[2] Galatians 5:23.
[3] Acts 21:21, 28.
[4] Romans 3:20
[5] Galatians 3:19.

relationship between the law and the gospel has challenged scholars and students of Scripture throughout the ages. The question has been repeated frequently: If our salvation is by grace, and our sanctification takes place through union with Christ in the power of the Spirit, what role—if any—is left for God's law? Does the gospel abolish it?

A common enough answer today is that we now live in the power of the Spirit *by love* which is the fulfilment of the law. After all, 'the one who loves another has fulfilled the law ... love is the fulfilling of the law'.[1] Does it not follow therefore that the law no longer functions in any strategic sense in the Christian's life?

This is a profound question. Our answer to it involves our understanding of the narrative thread of the entire Bible as well as its specific discussions of the nature and role of the law. And it is bound to have a significant impact on how we think about the Christian life.

Law and love

A moment's reflection should make clear that the role of the law in the sanctification of the Christian cannot be quite as simplistic as a radical *love or law* antithesis might suggest. For one thing, the law is *fulfilled* by love, it is not *replaced* by love. This fulfilment means that law is love-shaped and that love is law-shaped. Think of the way Jesus fulfils Old Testament prophecy. It points forward to him, and he 'fills out' the shape it takes. There is continuity, not antithesis, between promises in the Old Testament prophecies and their fulfilment in the Saviour. As a general principle we should think of the relationship between law and love along similar lines.

In fact love was always at the heart of God's law. It was given *by love* to be received *in love* and obeyed *through love*. The divine commandments could be summed up in the great commandment to

[1] Romans 13:8, 10

love God with heart, soul, and strength.[1] Thus Jesus himself teaches that if we love him we will keep his commandments.[2] Paul adds that rather than nullify the law the gospel strengthens it.[3] Moreover specific laws from the Decalogue are almost casually sprinkled throughout the New Testament.[4] Not only does love *not* abolish law, but law *commands* love!

The explanation for this is clear enough: love provides motivation for obedience, while law provides direction for love. This is why the new covenant promise envisaged the law being written on our hearts.[5] In the new covenant, then, obedience to God's law is driven by the love of God shed abroad in our hearts by the Spirit. This in turn produces love for God that expresses itself in obedience. The 'law' that is in view in the promise given through Jeremiah must mean the principles enshrined in the Ten Commandments in particular. It can hardly refer to the ceremonial or civic dimensions of *torah*.

So we need to take a closer look at the law of God and its role in our sanctification.[6]

God's law is central in the Old Testament Scriptures. If you had asked an old covenant believer about the way of sanctification, he

---

[1] Deuteronomy 6:5.

[2] John 14:15

[3] Romans 3:31.

[4] The United Bible Societies edition of *The Greek New Testament* lists fourteen quotations plus twelve verbal allusions found in the New Testament to Exodus 20:1-17 (the Decalogue). Of all chapters in the Old Testament possibly only Isaiah 53 is more frequently cited. *The Greek New Testament* (3rd edition, Stuttgart: United Bible Societies, 1983), 897, 902.

[5] Jeremiah 31:33, cited in Hebrews 8:10; 10:16.

[6] The contrast between older evangelical teaching on the law and its relative relegation today may be illustrated by the fact that the catechisms written by Luther and Calvin at the time of the sixteenth-century Reformation devoted considerable attention to the exposition of the law. They were followed by the *Westminster Larger* and *Shorter Catechisms* which devote around one third of their questions to the exposition and application of the Ten Commandments. By contrast, were catechisms to be written today by evangelicals it is doubtful whether the law would receive much if any detailed attention.

would have directed your attention to the law. He might well have quoted the first Psalm to you—the psalm of psalms in the sense that it describes the way of divine blessing. The blessed man is the one who loves the law and meditates on it day and night.[1] God's law could hardly be more central than this.

But Paul's teaching that we are 'justified by faith apart from the works of the law'[2] led to him being accused of nullifying the law. He therefore asks the question himself: 'Do we then overthrow the law by this faith?' His answer? 'By no means! *On the contrary we uphold the law.*'[3]

This issue did not arise first with Paul. The same accusation was made against Stephen before him: 'This man never ceases to speak words … against the law.'[4] But behind both these men lies the teaching of Jesus—and the implied accusation against him (sometimes disguised as a criticism of his disciples), that he gave too little, if any, place to the law.

Jesus and the law

It is true that Jesus did not fit in with the approach of the Pharisees who saw themselves as the self-appointed guardians of the law. Plus, when he began his famous Sermon on the Mount and described the life of blessedness, his words seemed to have little contact with the first Psalm and its description of the life of blessedness. He seemed to ignore the law altogether. His chief emphasis was on the coming of the kingdom, and on knowing, trusting, and loving God as a heavenly Father.

Was Jesus overthrowing the law?

Does he teach that it no longer has any role to play in our lives?

Are we no longer obliged to obey it?

---

[1] Psalm 1:2—a verse on which the whole of Psalm 119 is an extended commentary.
[2] Romans 3:28. Cf. Acts 21:28.
[3] Romans 3:31.
[4] Acts 6:13.

Or is his teaching more nuanced than that?

This is a tremendously important topic. How does the law of God fit into Jesus' teaching about the gospel? John Newton, the great hymn and letter writer, wrote that 'Ignorance of the nature and design of the law is at the bottom of most religious mistakes.'[1] And Martin Luther famously stated in his 1531 Wittenberg lectures on Galatians:

> Whoso then can rightly judge between law and the Gospel, let him thank God, and know that he is a right divine.[2]

So what Jesus taught about the law is immensely important for us.

Consider Christ's opening summary statement in the Sermon on the Mount. The logical flow of his teaching is as follows. He has just introduced the citizens of his new kingdom. They are the truly blessed. But notice how he describes them. They are poor in spirit, mourning, meek, hungering and thirsting for righteousness, merciful, pure in heart, peacemakers, persecuted and reviled.[3]

There is no reference here to the law of God; no exhortation to meditate on it day and night in order to be among the blessed. Does Jesus simply think that the law is irrelevant? Worse, is he ever so subtly denigrating it by ignoring it? After all he never denied the accusation that he spent time in the company of tax collectors and sinners—antinomians all.[4] Was he a theological antinomian?

Apparently not. For he goes on to say:

> Do not think that I have come to abolish the Law or the Prophets; I have not come to abolish them but to fulfil them. For truly, I say to you, until heaven and earth pass away, not an iota, not a dot, will pass from the Law until all is accomplished. Therefore whoever

---

[1] John Newton, *The Works of John Newton* (Edinburgh: Banner of Truth Trust, 2015), 1, 240.

[2] Martin Luther, *Commentary on the Epistle to the Galatians*, edited by P. S. Watson (London: James Clark, 1953), 122.

[3] Matthew 5:3-12.

[4] Matthew 9:11; 11:19.

relaxes one of the least of these commandments and teaches others to do the same will be called least in the kingdom of heaven, but whoever does them and teaches them will be called great in the kingdom of heaven. For I tell you, unless your righteousness exceeds that of the scribes and Pharisees, you will never enter the kingdom of heaven.[1]

Here Jesus brings to the surface three principles that help us to understand the relationship between the law of God and the kingdom of God, and therefore its role in the sanctification of believers.

Permanent significance

First, Jesus underlines the *permanent significance of God's law*. He could scarcely make this clearer. And like all good teachers he states it both negatively and positively.

When wise parents teach their little children, they express the lesson both negatively and positively to make it clear. It is *not* this, but it *is* that. Jesus also adopts that method:

Negative: Do not think I have come to abolish the law.
Positive: I have come to fulfil it.

Negative: Not the smallest letter or the least stroke of a pen will disappear from the law.
Positive: Every part of the law will be fulfilled and accomplished.

Negative: Anyone who breaks one of the least of these commandments and teaches others to do the same, will be called least in the kingdom of heaven.
Positive: Whoever does and teaches these laws will be called great in the kingdom of heaven.

Conclusion: I tell you that unless your righteousness surpasses that of the Pharisees and the teachers of the law, you will certainly not enter the kingdom of heaven.

[1] Matthew 5:17-20

In each of these couplets the permanent significance of God's law is underscored.

Now why did Jesus emphasize this? The answer lies in large measure in the nature of the law itself and the reasons for which it was originally given.

The law of God—in the sense of the Ten Commandments[1]—was an expression of the will of God for the people he had delivered from bondage in Egypt. But in a deeper sense it gave expression to his original design for the lifestyle of men and women made as his image.[2] But now, at Sinai, he was addressing human beings suffering from an inner distortion and living in a very different context. His will, therefore, was now clearly expressed in terms of the lives of sinners in the new land in which he would settle them.

So, from one point of view the commandments expressed God's *original* will for his image. In that sense it was by definition a kind of transcript of his character. While shaped for *later* human life in a *specific* place and time, it simultaneously gave expression to principles intended to be applicable to *any* place or time—simply because it reflected his own character which he wanted his people to reflect.

The Ten Commandments therefore expressed, largely in negative terms (because addressed now to sinners), what God originally willed in a positive way for Adam and Eve in the Garden of Eden. In a sense their failure was a breach of the inner significance of all the commandments God would later give at Mount Sinai. There God was republishing his original blueprint for life. But now it was 'contextualised' or applied to the *sitz im leben*, the life-setting of sinners. Its negative cast had the goal of preventing them from further self-destruction. At the same time, enshrined within the largely

---

[1] Exodus 20:1-17.
[2] Genesis 1:26-28.

negative commandments,[1] were the positive goals God intended us to pursue.

And so when God says, 'You are not to bear false witness', he implies that his people were to be truthful, marked by honesty and integrity in their dealings with one another. His command 'Do not commit adultery', speaks into a world in which marriage relationships have been fragmented. Woven into the prohibition is the implication that God created us to live in harmony, mutual encouragement, faithfulness, and joy—and that we should cherish and nurture this goal.

This pattern is enshrined in each of the Ten Commandments. Every one of them reflects God's original purpose for man in his unfallen condition, and applies it now to his fallen condition. The law therefore has a permanent validity since its substance predated the Mosaic covenant. The correlative of this is that if the will of God *after the exodus* reflects the will of God *before the fall*, then it remains in place *following our redemption*. It is contextualised differently at Sinai than in Eden. It naturally therefore takes on a new context and shape after Pentecost—Jesus is now the model of obedience. Yet it is, in essence, one and the same law of God. For he does not change, nor does even fallen man cease to bear his image.[2]

So the Ten Commandments looked back to creation and the fall. The people were no longer sin-free as Adam and Eve were. Nor were they living in the Garden of Eden. They were on their way to a new land, a kind of temporary Eden, flowing with milk and honey.[3] But it was also a land inhabited and surrounded by pagan nations where

---

[1] The only commandment lacking a declared negative is the commandment to honour parents. But all can be summarised positively, Luke 10:27-28.

[2] That the image of God remains despite the fall seems to be indicated in Genesis 9:6, James 3:9, and hinted at by Jesus in Matthew 21:15-22 (what carries Caesar's image—the coin—should be 'rendered to Caesar' and what carries God's image—men and women—should be 'rendered to God').

[3] Exodus 3:8.

false gods were worshipped. In such a world God's will for their blessing was no different from what it had been in Eden. What was different was the presence of sin and the context of their lives within redemptive history. Now God's revealed will for them is shaped to this new situation.

In the new land God's recently born people were to live until his ultimate purposes were fulfilled. He intended to create an international people spread throughout the earth.[1] This had been the original plan.[2] But now it would be brought about not through the first man Adam, but through the second man, the last Adam, Jesus Christ.[3] In the meantime, set between these two Adams, and in a pagan context, God 'contextualized' his will. His commandments were now expressed in a way that was calibrated to sinners, tempted to make and worship idols, living where immorality was commonplace, where men and women could be slaves, where the creation sabbath rest was ignored, and where people worked fields and owned oxen within a rural economy.

In this way the law was both preventative, preserving God's people for himself, and it was also in measure restorative of the old and original lifestyle of fellowship with God. It republished in contemporary form and on tables of stone what had originally been written on the human heart.

Paul seems to allude to this original writing of the law when he says that even in societies where the Law of Moses has not been known, to a certain extent people may still sometimes do 'by nature'—we might say 'instinctively'—the things the law of God commands. They thus show that the requirements of the law are

---

[1] He had announced this purpose already in his covenant with Abraham in Genesis 12:1-3. It was inherent already in the life of Adam, Genesis 1:26-30.

[2] We should not overlook the fact that the Abrahamic covenant also looked back to the original purposes of God, as is evident in Genesis 1:26-29.

[3] See 1 Corinthians 15:20-28.

written on their hearts.[1] The human heart retains a distorted copy, a smudged image of God's original will. All of us retain some sense that we were created in God's likeness, made to live for his glory, and hard-wired for obedience to him as it were—although now major distortions and malfunctions have affected our instincts. Were that hard-wiring totally destroyed we would cease to be distinctly human. But, in fact, relics of it remain in us, fragments of our lost destiny. Like a ruined castle it is still possible to discern the glory for which we were created.

The Law, or *torah* of God in the Old Testament was of course much broader than the Ten Commandments. It included *civil* laws to govern the people in the land; it also contained *ceremonial* laws, especially focused on the importance of holiness and the rituals of the sacrificial system, which would later be fulfilled in Christ.

From one perspective, those living in Old Testament times saw these three dimensions—moral, civil, and ceremonial—as a seamless robe. Yet, at the same time, they would have been able to grasp the inbuilt distinctions in the way the law functioned.

For example, an Old Testament believer could see that the Ten Commandments included *applications* to specific cultural circumstances (a rural economy, a world in which people had servants or slaves). If he understood the Abrahamic covenant he would have been able to work out that laws that governed the people in the land of promise would undergo a transformation when the Abrahamic covenant was fulfilled in the internationalizing of God's people. Even more than that, he would have been able to grasp that the repeated sacrifices of the law could not be the source of full and final

---

[1] See Romans 2:14-15. It has been argued that Paul must be referring to Gentile Christians here, in light of the allusion to the promise of the new covenant that the law would be written in the heart. But Paul's language is more nuanced. He refers to the 'works of the law' rather than the law itself. The sense seems to be that the Gentiles still experience the law's demands, and intermittently seek to conform to them—not that these individuals are empowered inwardly by the Spirit's work.

forgiveness. Otherwise they would not require repetition.[1] Plus he would recognize that a physical exodus from Egypt could not provide the inner moral power to keep God's law.

Thus in one sense God's law had been his first word, written into man's creation. But now that it lay broken it would not be his last word. There must be something more to come. This is what Jesus meant when he said, 'Do not think that I have come to abolish the Law or the Prophets; I have not come to abolish them but to fulfil them.'

Present fulfilment

Jesus came *not to abolish the law but to effect its fulfilment*:

- Do not think that I have come to abolish the Law …

- I have not come to abolish … but to fulfil …

- Truly I say to you, until heaven and earth pass away not an iota, not a dot, will pass from the Law until all is fulfilled.[2]

'Fulfil' means to bring out the fullness already inherent in principle in something else, to show its full significance. Already Matthew had shown how Jesus fulfilled Old Testament prophecies.[3]

This idea is familiar enough. But what does Jesus mean by saying that he came to fulfil the law?

---

[1] This argument is used in Hebrews 10:1-4. But while it appears in the *New* Testament it enshrines logic that was already available to an *Old* Testament believer: sacrifices that require repetition *ipso facto* cannot fully and finally take away sin. Hebrews uses a similar argument in connection with the promise of a priest after the order of Melchizedek: if the Levitical priesthood could bring final forgiveness there would be no need for a new order to arise (Hebrews 7:11).

[2] Matthew 5:17-18.

[3] Matthew 1:22-23; 2:6; 2:15; 2:17; 2:23.

(i) Jesus fulfilled the law by his obedience to it

He was, as Paul says, 'born of a woman, born under the law'.[1] His life revealed thereafter what perfect obedience to the law looks like. In that sense it also revealed how good it is for us. No one had ever done that before; and therefore no one had ever seen what it really looked like. In Christ we catch a glimpse of the blessedness that accompanies living in wholehearted and unreserved devotion to the heavenly Father. In him we see God's law in human form. We see that obedience to it is the pathway to glorify *and* enjoy him. At no point did Jesus find the law irritating; nor did it diminish his joy. He is the ultimate illustration of a person who says 'O how I love your law.' In that sense he is the perfect psalmist.

We live in an antinomian world in which the law of God is regarded as the enemy even if human laws are still necessary.[2] The wider western culture of the past fifty years and more has been reacting against what it calls 'Victorianism' and has established a new culture which has returned to the drivers of the French Revolution. 'Liberty and equality' (or in our times 'freedom and justice') have ascended the throne as king and queen.[3] The moral cathedrals

[1] Galatians 4:4.

[2] It almost goes without saying that when we remove the Ten Commandments from personal and civil life and from the basic nurturing values of family, our society requires to make *more*, not *less* laws in order to cope with the disorder that flows from indifference to the basic undergirding principles of a well-ordered life. It is rarely brought to public attention by politicians (who are our 'law makers') that abandoning the Ten Commandments never comes cheaply for a society. *Inter alia* it leads to the necessity of government income being redirected from positive care to dealing with the fruits of the disdain of commandments one through ten in an increase of disorder in social life, various forms and degrees of dishonesty, breakdown in marriage and family life, and an increase in crime, whether brutal or intellectually sophisticated.

[3] The third member of the French Revolutionary trilogy, 'brotherhood' vanished from the slogan within decades of it being invented—for a biblically predictable reason: where you deny the place and role of God the Father you cannot maintain the family concept beyond its genetic and nuclear context. Only a biblical worldview can adequately ground the notion of brotherhood.

established in the culture of the West are again being torn down because nothing is a greater enemy of human autonomy than divine law.

This spirit of the age has undoubtedly bled into the life of the church. Now to place any *emphasis* on the law of God is often regarded by professing Christians as 'legalism'. A new 'narrative' has arisen to interpret the 'old evangelicalism' which is now characterised—actually caricatured—as a religion of the 'dos and don'ts'. Now we frequently hear that God loves us the way we are. Any element of divine demand is seen as a return to the bad old ways and days—in a word to legalism.

But this viewpoint requires revision. For one thing this 'narrative' of the past is jaundiced. For another, the New Testament is punctuated with exhortations telling us what not to do! Plus, the truth is that since the fall of Adam God has loved only one person the way he is. We have lost sight of the fact that it is the way we are by nature that put Christ on the cross. The biblical perspective is quite different: God loves us *despite the way we are*.

So there are strong biblical and theological arguments against our contemporary indifference to God's law. Perhaps the simplest is also the most persuasive: Jesus loved and obeyed God's law. He was no legalist. In fact he was accused of being the very reverse. But, because he loved his Father, his Father's expressed will was important to him. Nor did Jesus find obeying the law an irritating restriction, a dampener on his spiritual joy. Indeed, every Christian acknowledges that if you want to see what life is really meant to be, you look at Jesus—but there is only one Jesus: Jesus the law-keeper.[1]

So Jesus fulfilled the law, just as he fulfilled the prophecies. Jesus is the person described in Psalm 1: his meditation was on the *torah*,

---

[1] Nor do Christians look at Jesus the law-keeper imagining he was thinking: 'I hate doing this; it irritates me; but *for their sake* I will put up with it'; as though his obedience was a mere means to an end and not a happy devotion to his Father.

the law of the Lord, day and night, and he flourished like a tree planted by the river. At the epicentre of that *torah* stood the Ten Commandments.

In effect Jesus says not only—

Do you want to know what these prophecies mean? Look at me!

But also—

Do you want to know what the law of God really looks like? You will not see it by looking at Adam or Abraham, or Moses, or David. They all failed. They were defeated by sin. But in me you will see the fulfilment, the joy, the beauty of the law of God displayed.

(ii) Jesus fulfilled the law by expounding its inner significance

While our Lord's life shows us the beauty of the law, his teaching further explains its spirituality and its penetration. So much so that he told his disciples that unless their righteousness exceeded that of the scribes and Pharisees there would be no place for them in God's kingdom![1]

Those words must have stunned his first hearers: this was an impossibility! But in the context of the Gospel witness in which Jesus berates the scribes and Pharisees for their externalism and their majoring on minors, we discover that true righteousness involves the devotion of a loving heart to the person of God.

The Pharisees it seems, prided themselves on their ability to keep the law and therefore remain in covenant with God.[2] But Jesus

---

[1] Matthew 5:20.

[2] In recent years in Christian scholarship the Pharisees have been somewhat rehabilitated, and the traditional view of them as legalists questioned. While it has always been a huge error to regard Old Testament religion as legalistic and merely external, it would also be a mistake to confuse what the Old Testament taught with how people lived. Probably not all Pharisees should be tarred with the same brush. Certainly not all Pharisees actively engaged in the physical persecution of the early church. But the Pharisees Jesus encountered, who were in the main deeply hostile to him, were condemned by him for their externalism and self-sufficiency. See Luke 18:9-14; Matthew 23:1-36. They may have spoken about grace, but they had not tasted it in its true form.

suggests they will not thus enter the kingdom.[1] By contrast he shows the spiritual significance of the law. It deals with inward thoughts and not simply outward actions. Adultery can be committed by a look; murder can be committed by a destructive word. The 'full' meaning of the law penetrates to the heart, and to the motives.[2] There is no point in tithing mint and dill and cumin if the weightier matters of the law, namely 'justice and mercy and faithfulness' are ignored, or of washing the outside of the plate if the inside remains dirty.[3]

Jesus thus fulfilled the law by his deeds and also by his doctrine.

(iii) Jesus fulfilled the law by making clear its three dimensions

When God gave the law to and through Moses, it was received by the people as a unified body of teaching. The Decalogue was accompanied by subsidiary laws about sacrifices for its breach (a liturgy governing the approach to God), and applications of its principles to society (a civil code). Thus the whole of life was governed by God's law.

From one perspective then, the law was a seamless robe. Even if some commandments were more fundamental than others, the people could not pick and choose which commandments they would obey and which they could safely ignore.

Yet at the same time a thoughtful old covenant believer would be able to see an inner substructure and dynamic built into the law. It was given in a three-dimensional form.

---

[1] Matthew 5:20.

[2] Matthew 5:21-48. It may be worth reminding ourselves that Jesus is not here contrasting his own teaching with the law as such. He introduces each of his contrasts with 'You have heard that *it was said*' (5:27, 31, 33, 38, 43), not by his standard formula for introducing a quotation from Scripture ('*it is written*'). He is contrasting the inadequate and behaviouristic interpretation of the scribes and Pharisees with the true meaning of God's law. In this sense Jesus *expounds* the law; he does not *add to it*; he certainly does not *repudiate it*. Indeed his whole exposition is set within the context of his statement that he has come to fulfil it.

[3] Matthew 23:23-26.

This has sometimes been called 'the threefold division of the law'. But it is probably better to say that the law was 'three dimensional'. The Decalogue was foundational. It in turn was then applied to the life of the community in the land in civil legislation and a penal code. In addition provision was made for the breach of the law in the directives given for the restoration to *sinners* of a way of access to and fellowship with God. This was the function of the ceremonial dimension of the law. In this way both the civil and ceremonial dimensions were built on the foundation of the Decalogue. In the sense that obedience was *required* by God to all these laws, all law was moral. And from another point of view all law was 'civil' because no believer exists in isolation; and furthermore since the ceremonial law gave directions about sacrifice for sin, it too had a moral dimension and inevitably bled into every area of civil life.

This way of thinking and speaking about the law was a staple of older theology. But it has come under major scrutiny and criticism in recent years. Today it is regarded as *passé* by many scholars and not infrequently somewhat demeaned. Yet reflection on the biblical text suggests that this triple dimension was already embedded in the Old Testament itself. There the Decalogue is viewed as foundational to and distinct from its local and temporal applications. This distinction is built into the very way in which God gave the laws in the first place:

- The Ten Commandments alone were spoken to the whole congregation.[1]

- The Ten Commandments alone were written on stone tablets.[2]

- The Ten Commandments alone were written by the finger of God.[3]

---

[1] Deuteronomy 4:12-13.
[2] Deuteronomy 5:22.
[3] Exodus 31:18.

• The Ten Commandments alone were housed in the ark.[1]

By contrast,

  • The civil laws were given through Moses, not directly written by God.[2]

  • The civil laws and commands were to be kept while the people were 'in the land'.[3]

  • The ceremonial laws do not appear in the words of Deuteronomy which were spoken to the people as a whole—except insofar as they involved the people's action.[4]

So in the very giving of the law distinctions were embedded in it which certainly approximate to the idea of its three-dimensionalism. And as we have seen an old covenant believer would readily have understood this.

(*a*) As he watched the temple sacrifices being repeated day after day he would realise that these sacrifices could not take away his sin. Animal sacrifices could not serve as adequate substitutes for human beings made as God's image. If they were, the priest would not need to stand at the altar making them again and again and again. So these ceremonies must be pictures of a true saving sacrifice. Consequently, when that sacrifice was made there would be no further need for these ones. In a word, the sacrificial system of the ceremonial dimension of the law was understood to be temporary.

(*b*) In addition a true son of Abraham would understand that what the kingdom God ultimately had in view was not one nation in a single land with its own distinctive civil government. For God's covenant promise to Abraham involved the blessing of all peoples in all lands. God's vision was not Israel-limited but world-extensive,

[1] Deuteronomy 10:1-6.
[2] Deuteronomy 4:14.
[3] Deuteronomy 5:30-33; 6:1.
[4] They are encoded in Exodus 25-40 and in Leviticus.

reaching people under all forms of civil government. This would take place in the coming of great David's greater son, the one he called Lord, whose kingdom would have no end.[1] In that day the civil dimension of the law would have fulfilled its purpose. It too was never meant to be permanent.

A believer, therefore, would have understood not only that the civil and liturgical dimensions of the law were applications of the moral dimension, but also that these applications constituted a temporary divine arrangement. Since they were never meant to be final they possessed no inbuilt permanence. They were in place only until the coming of the promised Messiah who would fulfil the Abrahamic promise. Then the final sacrifice would be made, the new international kingdom of God would emerge, and the law would be fulfilled in the hearts of God's people through the indwelling of the Spirit.

All this was already envisaged in the progressive revelation in the old covenant. In the meantime, the Lord was keeping his people separate from the influences of the other nations. He was guarding the womb within which his promise of a Saviour would come to fruition.[2]

On that day, things would change. Then—in Jesus' life, death, resurrection, ascension, and giving of the Spirit—these three dimensions of the law would be clearly seen for what they always were— moral prescriptions for the fallen image of God applied to both civil and religious life until the Saviour came and the final international community of the people of God was born. In this community there is no need for the old ceremonial law governing animal sacrifices. This community does not require old covenant civil law in order to function maximally—for it exists everywhere. But since this is the

[1] See Genesis 1:26-28; 12:1-3; Psalm 2:8; 110:1 (cf. Matthew 22:44-5); Isaiah 42:5-9; 49:6; 53:15; Daniel 7:13-14.

[2] Genesis 3:15. See Revelation 12:1-6 for an apocalyptic and dramatic representation of this.

community of the new humanity (those who are being recreated 'after the likeness of God'[1]), the great foundational principles of the Decalogue, reflecting God's original purposes for his image, remain in place. All this becomes clear in the way Jesus fulfilled the law by bringing out its various dimensions in the full light of the new day.

(iv) Jesus fulfilled the law by taking the penalty for our breach of it

Jesus fulfilled the *moral dimensions of the law* by living in perfect obedience to it, by revealing its depths,[2] but also by paying the penalty for our breach of it. He was born under the law to redeem us from its curse—which he received so that we might receive the blessing.[3] The *law-maker* became the *law-keeper*, but then took our place and condemnation as though he were the *law-breaker*. Now the requirements of the law have been fulfilled in him, its prescriptions fully obeyed, its penalties finally paid. All that remains is for this to be imputed to us in justification and imparted in us in sanctification through the ministry of the Holy Spirit.

By his death and resurrection Christ also fulfilled the *ceremonial dimension of the law*. He became our High Priest, offering himself as the real sacrifice that would take away sins once for all. His resurrection was the divine proof that the sacrifice had been accepted.[4] The inherent logic of his atonement is that the inbuilt repetitiveness of the sacrificial system has been brought to an end. For his sacrifice for sin was made once for all.

The ceremonial system, like the original tabernacle, was a collapsible structure. When the temple curtain was torn in two from the top to the bottom God was de-consecrating the temple and its liturgy. They were no longer needed—full and final propitiation had

---

[1] Ephesians 4:24; cf. Colossians 3:10.
[2] As he does in Matthew 5:21-48.
[3] Galatians 4:1; 3:13.
[4] Romans 4:23-25.

been made for sin.[1] Jesus Christ has folded up the entire collapsible temporary arrangement and carried it away.

By his death, resurrection, ascension, and the giving of the Spirit at Pentecost Jesus also fulfilled the *civil dimensions of the law*. His kingdom is not limited by either geography or a distinct ethnicity. All authority in heaven and earth is now his. He sends the gospel to all the nations. The church he builds is an international community. We no longer live in one land, nor are we confined to one ethnic group. Doubtless we can still learn important principles from the way in which the Decalogue was applied in the sphere of civil law, but we are no longer ethnic Israel. The laws that governed her as a specific nation have fulfilled their purpose.[2]

(v) Jesus fulfils the law in us through the Spirit

Although Moses ascended into the presence of God and brought down the Ten Commandments, he could not give the people power to obey them. But Jesus could. When he ascended into the presence of God he sent down his own Holy Spirit to enable us to obey the law. Paul gives us the classic statement of this:

> God has done what the law, weakened by the flesh, could not do. By sending his own Son in the likeness of sinful flesh and for sin, he condemned sin in the flesh, in order that the righteous requirement of the law might be fulfilled in us, who walk not according to the flesh but according to the Spirit.[3]

When he wrote these words Paul was not criticizing God's law. Only a few verses earlier he had said that 'the law is holy, and the commandment is holy and righteous and good'.[4] The problem lies

[1] Matthew 27:31.

[2] This point is well expressed by the *Westminster Confession of Faith*, XIX. 3 and 4 which speaks of the ceremonial law being 'abrogated' and the judicial laws having now 'expired together with the state of that people, not obliging any other now, further than the general equity thereof may require'.

[3] Romans 8:3-4.

[4] Romans 7:13. Notice that Paul speaks here in the *present* tense.

not with the law but with those to whom it has been given. It was 'weakened by the flesh'. But now—although, as we have seen, there is still conflict in our lives between the flesh and the Spirit—the Lord progressively fulfils his will in us by the Spirit's power.

In fact the Old Testament itself predicted that this day would dawn. In detailing what is 'new' about the coming 'new covenant' God had said:

> I will make a new covenant ... not like the covenant I made with their fathers when I took them by the hand to bring them out of the house of Egypt ... this is the covenant that I will make ... *I will put my law within them, and I will write it on their hearts* ... and I will be their God and they shall be my people ... I will forgive their iniquity, and I will remember their sin no more.[1]

These words help us understand the role of the law of God in our sanctification. For while it is the new covenant that is being described here, *at its heart still stands the writing of God's law.* But this time it is not written by the finger of God on stone but by the Spirit of God on our hearts.

There is no contrast therefore, and certainly no conflict, between the Spirit and the law. They appear as friends. What is written in our hearts by the Spirit is nothing less than the law of God! Jeremiah's words (and Hebrews' double endorsement of them[2]) makes it clear that the law of God still has a role to play in the life of the child of God. We are, after all, being transformed into the likeness of God's Son—who loved the law. We experience the Spirit of sonship, calling God 'Abba! Father!' and therefore we want to reflect his character as children being restored in his image through the Spirit. This, it should now be obvious, means that God's law is both internalised and empowered in our lives.

[1] Jeremiah 31:31-34.
[2] In Hebrews 8:8-12 and 10:16-17.

The New Covenant difference

In the light of all this we can begin to see *the difference the new covenant makes*. The law has not been changed—it still shows us how God's image bearers have always been meant to live. But there is a difference. For now we receive the law from the hands of the one who fulfilled it for us and has given us his Spirit to fulfil it in us. Matthew's presentation of the Sermon on the Mount thus makes clear that Jesus is the Prophet promised by Moses, the new Moses to whom we need to listen.[1]

There is a marvellous diversity in our experience of conversion to Christ. Think of Peter and Zacchaeus, of Saul of Tarsus and Timothy, of Onesimus and the Philippian Jailer. Some of us had dramatic experiences, others may have been led to Christ so gently and imperceptibly that we trusted him before we were fully conscious that we did.

At the same time there are features all conversions have in common. While sin takes a distinct shape and expresses itself uniquely in each of our lives, all of us sought and trusted the Saviour because we were conscious in one way or another of our need for him.

Some become conscious of their sinfulness, and in response try harder to be better, and endeavour to keep God's law more faithfully. But then they fail. God's law, which they aspired to obey, seems to beat them down. But then they come to Christ. What is the result? The law that had formerly been a burden they felt unable to carry now seems transformed. Instead of feeling it pressing down heavily on their shoulders as they tried their best to keep it, the burden has been lifted—almost as though the law itself is carrying them, and not the other way round. What was their burden has become their pleasure.

[1] Deuteronomy 18:18-19. Cf. Acts 3:17-26.

Has the law changed, or perhaps been diluted to make it possible for them to keep it? Not at all. Rather Christ has come down to us in the power of the Spirit and written the law in our hearts.

This is the difference the gospel makes. Jesus' words in the Sermon on the Mount no longer seem like unmitigated demands, but become holy counsels for our lives. Now we know the meaning of the 'righteousness that exceeds that of the scribes and Pharisees'! The Spirit of the law-obeying Jesus has now come to indwell us. We have entered a new creation; the old has passed away and the new has come.[1] Spirit-given affections and desires on the one hand, and God's revelation of his will on the other, have, at last, become friends in us.[2] Now we have received the law from the hands of Jesus.

Jesus makes all the difference to everything, including our love for the law!

A litmus test

Jesus says that our reaction to the law is an indication of our response to his kingdom—and also the measure of how we will be regarded in it.[3]

What is his logic? How are our reaction to God's law and our reaction to God's Son so intimately related to each other?

The Spirit of Jesus writes the law in the hearts of those who belong to him. The Spirit of Christ in us and the word of God to us exist in total harmony. Thus our response to the commandments of God reveals the nature of our response to the Son of God. This is why, despite the often assumed antithesis between law and love,

[1] 2 Corinthians 5:17.
[2] The role of the fourth commandment which has proved to be a subject of difficulty and controversy for Christians throughout the centuries is briefly discussed in Appendix 3.
[3] Matthew 5:19.

John 'the apostle of love' was so impressed by his Saviour's teaching, 'If you *love* me, you will keep my *commandments*.'[1]

So the work of the Spirit conforms us to Jesus Christ by writing the law of God in our hearts, and giving us energy to obey it. Herein lies the beautiful harmony between God's law and our love.

Loving your in-law

The apostle Paul expressed this new relationship to God's law in a memorable way (although our Bible translations struggle to express his meaning):

> To the Jews I became as a Jew, in order to win Jews. To those under the law I became as one under the law (though not myself being under the law) to win those under the law. To those outside the law I became as one outside the law (not being outside the law of God but under the law of Christ).[2]

Christians are not *under the law*. Yet we are not *outside the law*. Rather we are *under the law of Christ*. Not *under* but not *outside* the law, and yet *under the law of Christ*—what kind of riddle is this?

There is a similar riddle in Romans 8:

> We have died to the law through the body of Christ

so that now we

> belong to another, to him who has been raised from the dead, in order that we may bear fruit for God ... now we are released from the law, having died to that which held us captive, so that we serve not under the old written code but in the new life of the Spirit.[3]

Yet a few breaths later on, Paul will say that the Father has given his Son for us and his Spirit to us—

---

[1] John 14:15. The powerful impact of these words on John emerges in 1 John 2:3-6; 7-8; 3:7, 10, 22-24; 5:2-3.

[2] 1 Corinthians 9:20-21.

[3] Romans 7:4, 6.

in order that the righteous requirement of the law might be fulfilled in us, who walk not according to the flesh but according to the Spirit.[1]

How can it be that although we are not *under* the law, yet its requirements are fulfilled in us? On the one hand we seem no longer to be related to it; and then on the other we are related to it!

Paul solves the riddle by saying that he is not *hupo nomon* ('under the law'), yet nor is he *anomos Theou* ('outside the law of God') but he is *ennomos Christou* ('in law of Christ'). What is his solution?

- The Christian is not under the law.

- Yet the Christian is not an outlaw with respect to the law—a lawbreaker.

- Rather the Christian becomes an 'in-law' of the law.

How does someone become your 'in-law'? Not by your marriage to that person directly, but by your marriage to their relation.

In the same way the Christian's relationship to the law is not direct—we are no longer married to the law but to Christ.[2] But he is the one who both loved the law and embodied it. Marry him and we become connected to all that is his—including the law given by his Father! Thus the new covenant believer's relationship to the law comes through marriage to Christ. It is a faith relationship. Furthermore we now share one Spirit with our husband Jesus Christ and he enables us to love what our husband loved—a love expressed in Old Testament words applied to the Lord Jesus in the New Testament:

> Then I said, 'Behold I have come;
>   in the scroll of the book it is written of me:
> I delight to do your will, O my God;
>   your law is written within my heart.'[3]

---

[1] Romans 8:4.
[2] As Paul explains in Romans 7:1-4.
[3] Psalm 40:7 cited in Hebrews 10:7.

We love the law because we love our husband! Yes, there are times when our in-law may not be best pleased with our husband's bride, but since the law is an in-law and not itself our husband it has no authority to condemn us; so long as we are loved by our husband it cannot break up our marriage. And so long as we enjoy a loving union with our husband we will grow in love for the law, because it is our 'in-law'. Indeed we will begin to want to please our in-law because we love everything about our husband!

A young woman loves her fiancé and looks forward to becoming his wife. But she is understandably nervous about her relationship with her prospective mother-in-law. She has a reputation as a perfectionist! Yet, perhaps gradually, the girl comes to love her because she loves her husband. She comes to see her mother-in-law wants only her best. Her 'perfectionism' is actually her goodness.

It is the same with God's law. We are related to it through our husband Jesus Christ. And for his sake we come to know and love the law and realise that its commands are for our best. It does not come to Christian believers in naked condemning power. But in the hands of him who has died under its condemnation, was raised for our justification, and has given us his Holy Spirit, it provides wisdom and direction for our lives. Our husband loves us; he wants us to love him. But he also wants us to love our in-law—and he gives us the Spirit who inspired his own love for the law to empower us to keep it.

Empowered by the Spirit to track with the law

In my childhood there was a television programme imported to the United Kingdom from the USA. It was about a railroad engine driver called Casey Jones. The theme song to the series went like this:

> Casey Jones, steamin' an' a rollin',
> Casey Jones, you never have to guess;
> When you hear the tootin' of the whistle
> It's Casey at the throttle of the Cannonball Express.

As the Cannonball Express kept rolling, coal was piled onto the fire that heated the boiler that gave the steam-engine its power to thrust the train forwards as Casey operated the throttle. But Casey Jones's train needed more than steam—it needed the track to run on, to give direction to its driving energy.

The relationship between the Spirit of God and the law of God in the life of the believer is like that. Without the power of the Spirit we would lack the love for God that energizes us to keep his law. But without the law of God our love for him would lack direction. Thus we discover that the way of Christ leads us more and more into obedience to God's law.

As Ralph Erskine quaintly expressed it in his *Gospel Sonnets*:

> When I the gospel-truth believe
>   Obedience to the law I give.
> And when I don't the law observe,
>   I from the gospel-method swerve
>
> Thus gospel-grace and law-commands
>   Both bind and loose each other's hands.
> They can't agree on any terms,
>   Yet hug each other in their arms.
>
> To run to work, the law commands;
>   The gospel gives me feet and hands:
> The one requires that I obey;
>   The other does the pow'r convey.
>
> A rigid master was the law
>   Demanding brick, denying straw;
> But when with gospel tongue it sings,
>   It bids me fly, and gives me wings.[1]

---

[1] Ralph Erskine (1685–1752) was one of the earliest ministers in the Associate Presbytery, a secession from the national Church of Scotland founded under the leadership of his older brother Ebenezer. He maintained a correspondence with Jonathan Edwards. His way of 'winding down' after he had preached at the Sunday worship services was to try to turn the themes of his messages into poetry, some of which was published in his *Gospel Sonnets*. Involved in the famous Marrow Controversy

This is what Jesus means when he says that he has come to *fulfil* the law.[1] It is what Paul means when he says that faith *establishes* the law.[2] It is the reason the New Testament is full of exhortations and reflections on the law of God.

We trust and love him who said 'If you love me, you will keep my commandments.'[3] Why then would we find obeying the law—written in the heart at creation, then inscribed on tablets of stone at Sinai, then written in the heart of Jesus, and finally rewritten in our hearts by the Holy Spirit—a strange or unpalatable thing? Surely the truth is—as our spiritual fathers well understood when they wrote the great catechisms of the church[4]—the biblical application of the commandments of God provides a guide for the whole of life and produces in us deep instincts that cause us to live as those who are devoted to God and seek his glory.[5]

---

at the heart of which stood issues related to the law and the gospel, Erskine penned many lines in the above vein describing the inter-relationship of the two.

[1] Matthew 5:17-20.

[2] Romans 3:31.

[3] John 14:15.

[4] *The Larger Catechism* (Qs. 91-152) and *The Shorter Catechism* (Qs. 39-84)—as significantly, Jesus did in his Sermon on the Mount—show the genius of the Ten Commandments in their comprehensive instruction for the whole of life and their relevance in helping to answer the 'What should I do?' questions in life.

[5] For a fine, readable, practical guide to the role of the law in the life of the Christian, see Alistair Begg, *Pathway to Freedom* (Chicago: Moody Press, 2003).

9

Keep Going

My first boss when I was a very young minister trumpeted from the high pulpit: 'Few great men finish well.' I remember, sitting below him in 'the assistant's chair' thinking, 'O, no! Please, no!' He was referring specifically to men in the Bible, but he clearly intended his words as a warning to all of us, great or small. At the time it seemed one of the saddest things I had ever heard about the Christian life. Yet the mini-biographies in Scripture abound with examples of people who began well, but whose progress slowed down and whose spiritual energy seemed to dry up. My boss added an illustration of his own: 'The Christian life is like riding a bicycle; if you don't keep peddling you will eventually fall off.'[1]

The story has been repeated all too often. It is always one of the hidden sadnesses in pastoral ministry—the number of people in whom ministers invest themselves but who no longer walk beside them. No doubt this was why the anonymous author of Hebrews made perseverance a major theme of his 'word of exhortation'.[2]

---

[1] In the interests of full disclosure, at the time I thought the illustration rather unimaginative. But it passed the most important test of any illustration: four decades later I still remember both the illustration and (the real test of any illustration), the point it was intended to illustrate. Having repented of my youthful rush to judgment and revised my estimation of my boss's illustration I am now passing it on!

[2] Hebrews 13:22.

Towards the climax of his letter he writes about keeping going as one of the hallmarks of genuine faith that was vividly illustrated in his portrait gallery of the heroes of the Old Testament.[1] His description of them leads to the appeal that follows:

> Therefore, since we are surrounded by so great a cloud of witnesses, let us also lay aside every weight, and sin which clings so closely, and let us run with endurance the race that is set before us, looking to Jesus, the founder and perfecter of our faith, who for the joy that was set before him endured the cross, despising the shame, and is seated at the right hand of the throne of God.
>
> Consider him who endured from sinners such hostility against himself, so that you may not grow weary or fainthearted. In your struggle against sin you have not yet resisted to the point of shedding your blood. And have you forgotten the exhortation that addresses you as sons?
>
> > 'My son, do not regard lightly the discipline of the Lord, nor be weary when reproved by him. For the Lord disciplines the one he loves, and chastises every son whom he receives.'
>
> It is for discipline that you have to endure. God is treating you as sons. For what son is there whom his father does not discipline? If you are left without discipline, in which all have participated, then you are illegitimate children and not sons. Besides this, we have had earthly fathers who disciplined us and we respected them. Shall we not much more be subject to the Father of spirits and live? For they disciplined us for a short time as it seemed best to them, but he disciplines us for our good, that we may share his holiness. For the moment all discipline seems painful rather than pleasant, but later it yields the peaceful fruit of righteousness to those who have been trained by it.
>
> Therefore lift your drooping hands and strengthen your weak knees, and make straight paths for your feet, so that what is lame may not be put out of joint but rather be healed. Strive for peace with everyone, and for the holiness without which no one will see the Lord.[2]

[1] Hebrews 11:1ff.
[2] Hebrews 12:1-14.

Hebrews is all about persevering in sanctification. Without holiness, writes the author, 'no one will see the Lord.' We must therefore 'strive' for it.[1] He uses vigorous language. His verb (*diōkō*, strive) appears regularly in the New Testament with the sense of 'persecute'.[2] Such strong language was needed here because these Christians were facing hardship and opposition. They therefore needed to pay careful attention to the gospel, to digest what they had heard, so that they would not drift away.[3]

What do you need to do to slow down and go backwards in the Christian life? Hebrews' answer is: 'Nothing.' Drifting is the easiest thing in the world. It is swimming against the tide that requires effort. And the Christian life is against the tide all the way. Spiritual weariness, being 'sluggish',[4] is one of our great enemies. The author is all-too-familiar with its tell-tale signs.

Christians then, as now, were confronted by many pressures. Some of them had suffered deeply for their testimony to Jesus Christ.[5] We might think that anyone who has withstood trials would be in no danger of failing to persevere. But the battle to be holy is fierce, the conflict is long, the opposition is strong, and the obstacles are many. Even those who have won great victories in the past can become weary. Spiritual lethargy can set in, and we begin to drift. We constantly need to be encouraged to keep going.

All this is illustrated in the early chapters of Hebrews by the Exodus. The people of God left Egypt and were led through the desert towards the land of Canaan. But the desert can be a dangerous place. It is full of tests and temptations, not least to grumble and to want to return to the old ways of Egypt.[6]

---

[1] Hebrews 12:14.

[2] Most frequently in connection with Saul's conversion in Acts 9:2-5; 22:4, 7, 8; 26:11, 14, 15. More generally the verb means 'to hurry, to run'.

[3] Hebrews 2:1.

[4] Hebrews 6:12. The term *nōthros* was used of a workman who was careless.

[5] Hebrews 10:32-34.

[6] Hebrews 3:7-19; 4:2.

Sometimes pilgrimage can seem a lot harder than bondage. The Exodus generation had experienced the power of God and tasted his blessing.[1] But there were cucumbers and melons in Egypt;[2] in the wilderness there were only manna and quails.

The reaction of the Israelites may seem to us almost inconceivable.

Imagine you had witnessed the plagues of Egypt. You had hidden indoors as the Angel swept through the land bringing death to the first-born in all the families. Imagine the frequent glances at you that night if you were the first-born in your family. Would you not have been tempted to go outside, just to make sure one more time that blood had been daubed on the door post and the lintels?[3]

But you were spared.

Imagine further that you had seen the sea open up and had passed through it with your family—then looking back you saw your pursuers being drowned. Think of what it must have been like to witness these and the other mighty works that God did through Moses. Surely you would say to yourself, 'No one could witness the power of God as I have and then drift away.' Yet experience would eventually lead you to say, 'How wrong could I be?' The author of Hebrews is simply exegeting Scripture when he tells us that it is possible to see such things and yet fail to persevere in the life of faith.

No wonder the author was so anxious to encourage these believers to press on. As he comes to the beginning of a series of powerful exhortations he urges them:

> Therefore do not throw away your confidence, which has a great reward. For you have need of endurance, so that when you have done the will of God you may receive what is promised.

---

[1] As in Hebrews 6:4-6 blessings may be tasted which—as the author makes clear in 6:9—are not definitive of salvation. He believes his readers have experienced 'better things—things that belong to salvation'.

[2] Numbers 11:5.

[3] Exodus 12:7, 13

And he adds:

> But we are not of those who shrink back and are destroyed, but of those who have faith and preserve their souls.[1]

This then becomes a key theme in his homily. True believers do not shrink back. They believe and persevere. They press on into the future and arrive at the fullness of salvation—just like the great heroes of the faith in the past.

A central element in the faith of these men and women was its future orientation. They looked forward to possessing what they had not yet fully experienced. Real faith always has this characteristic. And since we are surrounded by a great cloud of witnesses to this kind of faith, the author urges us to keep running.

He places emphasis on three elements in this perseverance in holiness.

1. 'Hindrances strew all the way'[2]

Hebrews famously compares the Christian life to a race—like a long-distance steeplechase. We face various hindrances and obstacles. How do we overcome them? We are to 'lay aside every weight, and sin which clings so closely'.[3]

These two expressions complement each other. The first ('weight') is metaphorical, the second ('sin') is not.

What is not quite so clear is whether the author is using the figure of speech known as hendiadys (describing one reality in two different but related ways) so that the 'weight' *is* the 'sin which clings'.

Or is he reflecting on two distinguishable aspects of the hindrances to our growth in holiness: 'weights' that hinder which are

---

[1] Hebrews 10:35-36, 39.
[2] From the hymn 'Thou hidden Love of God' by Gerhard Tersteegen (1697–1769), translated by John Wesley (1703–91).
[3] Hebrews 12:1.

not necessarily sinful in themselves on the one hand, and, on the other, things that are in themselves sinful?[1]

The 'sin which clings so closely' would then be deep-dyed indwelling sin, shaped to and by our own lives and contexts, becoming indistinguishable from our personalities—thus clinging 'so closely'.

Some such distinction seems likely.

Excess baggage?

Excess weight is never a good thing. But its effects may not be immediately apparent—until we begin to run. Then it becomes a hindrance. Similarly in the Christian race. So, says the author of Hebrews, let us get rid of everything that weighs us down, keeps us back, or hinders us from a swift obedience to Christ.

If these hindrances are to be distinguished from 'sin which clings so closely' the point is fairly obvious. Wearing a fine suit can make an individual look distinguished; a well-tailored coat may be a delight for a woman to wear; a strong suitcase is useful for a long-haul flight. But you do not run the steeplechase in the Olympic Games wearing a suit, or the five thousand metres wearing a coat, and you would not think of running in either while carrying a suitcase! Serious athletes appear at the starting line as highly disciplined individuals. Training, diet, proper rest, even a sports psychologist will all have played a part in the preparations. And in addition a team of scientists will have been involved in the background, perfecting their running gear.

---

[1] Perhaps the relationship is even closer than that, as Calvin seems to have thought. In this case the 'weight' refers to 'all kinds of burdens which delay and impede our spiritual race, such as the love of this present life, the pleasures of the world, the desires of the flesh, earthly cares, riches and honours, and everything else of this kind.' He thinks of 'sin which clings so closely' as 'the heaviest burden ... the fount of sin itself, that is the lust which so possesses all of us that we feel we are held by its snares on every side.' John Calvin, *The Epistle of Paul the Apostle to the Hebrews and The First and Second Epistles of St Peter*, tr. William B. Johnston, eds., David W. Torrance, Thomas F. Torrance (Edinburgh: Oliver and Boyd, 1961), 187-8.

The point is that many things that are appropriate and legitimate can become hindrances if you are planning to run a race. If so they should be put aside.[1]

Paul makes the same point by means of a military metaphor: 'No soldier gets entangled in civilian pursuits, since his aim is to please the one who enlisted him.'[2] Why? Because such distractions might compromise the soldier's focus and usefulness. Military life is not the same as civilian life. Likewise, the Christian life is different. If we are going to persevere we need to have a spirit of athletic and military self-discipline, and self-denial. What is essential and central must be given priority. Not only the bad, but even the good needs to be subordinated to the best. Everything is subordinate to the goal of winning and the fulfilment of the mission.

Jesus addressed a similar issue in his Parable of the Soils. He warned that 'desires for other things' can destroy the influence of the seed of God's word.[3]

Paul gives us further instruction in the context of his dialogue with the Corinthians. Some of them seem to have been insisting on their freedom to develop their own life-patterns and habits by saying: 'There is nothing *wrong* with a Christian doing ____' or 'There is nothing *against* a Christian spending his or her time doing ____ ... we are free in Christ.' In response Paul calls the church to think and act with greater maturity. He argues that the key issue is not merely legitimacy but spiritual profitability.

The question we need to be asking is not:

• Is it alright for me to do this as a Christian?

But rather these questions:

[1] On this (as on much else) John Newton gives spiritually sane and wise counsel, *Letters of John Newton*, ed. Josiah Bull (1869; repr. Edinburgh: Banner of Truth Trust, 2007), 106-17; also found in John Newton, *Works* (1839; repr. Edinburgh: Banner of Truth Trust, 2015 ed.) vol. 1, 396-402.

[2] 2 Timothy 2:4.

[3] Mark 4:19.

- Is this going to build up?

- Is this going to strengthen the fellowship of God's people?

- Is this going to advance my goal of running towards Jesus Christ and glory?

- Is this something that laying to one side will better enable me to serve Christ?

So mature Christians develop an instinct to ask 'Will this bring most glory to God?' 'Is this wise?'

If indeed the 'weight' Hebrews mentions refers to such diversions, what it represents will, no doubt, vary from one person to another. But whatever specific form the 'weight' may take it will have a tendency to divert us from, or drain us of energy for, serving the Lord Jesus Christ. And the litmus test of all things is whether they draw us beyond themselves to more love for Christ, or whether, like weights, they hold us back.

Detachment

Like Paul, then, the author of Hebrews[1] teaches us that in our pursuit of holiness we must commit ourselves to live in this world and indeed enjoy this world as those who do not belong to it. We need to cultivate a right spirit of detachment. Paul gives very specific illustrations:

> This is what I mean, brothers: the appointed time has grown very short. From now on, let those who have wives live as though they had none, and those who mourn as though they were not mourning, and those who rejoice as though they were not rejoicing, and

[1] Since Hebrews was written anonymously we cannot identify the author with any authority. The attraction of attributing it to Paul, as was done in the early centuries, is that his authorship eased the path for the church to recognize Hebrews as part of the divinely given canon of the New Testament—on the basis that apostolic authorship essentially guaranteed canonicity. But Hebrews 2:3 does not read like the words of the same man who wrote Galatians 1:12, 17; 2:7-9.

those who buy as those who had no goods, and those who deal with
the world as though they had no dealings with it. For the present
form of this world is passing away,[1]

Holiness, as we saw at the beginning, is unreserved devotion to
the Lord. It means belonging entirely to him. This inevitably produces a certain detachment from the world. It no longer clings to us
with its this-worldly superglue.

Paul's words may strike contemporary Christians as far too
world-denying. But the extent to which they do so may be an indication that we ourselves are carrying excess baggage. We may not
have noticed it until we encountered these penetrating words or
met a Christian whose life mirrors them. Yet we may even have sung
similar sentiments without realising it. Perhaps these words:

> Turn your eyes upon Jesus
>> Look full in his wonderful face
> And the things of earth will grow strangely dim
>> In the light of his glory and grace.[2]

Or these:

> My will is not my own
>> Till thou hast made it thine.[3]

Whatever we have we must hold with an open palm.

We are brought back here to the foundational gospel principle:
putting off must never be separated from putting on Christ. If we
hold resolutely to Christ our grip on his gifts in creation will have
only secondary strength. And, in addition, since we are involved in
an ongoing struggle to grow in holiness we will also be resolutely
avoiding anything that will weigh us down and hold us back in the
race—even if there is 'nothing wrong with them'. 'I discipline my

---

[1] 1 Corinthians 7:29-31.
[2] The refrain to the hymn 'O soul, are you weary and troubled' by Helen H.
Lemmel (1863–1961).
[3] From the hymn by George Matheson (1842–1906) 'Make me a captive Lord.'

body and keep it under control', writes Paul, 'lest after preaching to others I should be disqualified.'[1] Our spiritual gifts, no matter how great, do not in themselves guarantee perseverance.

In this godly detachment lies our freedom to run the race. But in addition we need to deal with 'sin that clings so closely'.

2. Entangled?

Is this simply a general statement meaning that we must be quit with sin and put it aside in every shape or form? Or does it refer to the specific ways in which sin folds itself around and manifests itself in our individual lives? Sin has a way of knitting itself into the very fabric of our being, into our character and personality, into our propensities and our weaknesses and, yes, even into our strengths—sometimes *especially* into our strengths. It becomes my distinctive sin.

Indwelling corruption has the potential to express itself in any and every form of sin. Yet, as Augustine argued, sin is not an objective, quantifiable 'something' which attaches itself to us. Rather it is the distortion of our persons. Sin is not 'it' but 'I'! It takes a particular shape in each of us, and comes to expression in our individual character—which is already fallen and twisted against the Lord. We will not run far in the Christian race before we realise this and discover the ways in which sin trips us up—or, more precisely, trips us down.

The Greek philosophers employed the axiom 'know thyself'. It was inscribed in the forecourt of the temple of Apollo at Delphi. It occurs frequently in the writings of Plato; it is found regularly on the lips of Socrates. It would eventually take on a deeply secular meaning, well expressed in Alexander Pope's Enlightenment couplet, which opens his poem 'An Essay on Man':

> Know then thyself, presume not God to scan.
> The proper study of mankind is Man.

---

[1] 1 Corinthians 9:27.

Christians have a significantly different form of the maxim: 'Know thy *sinful* self.' Know the ways in which Satan trips you up. Know what your sinful weaknesses are. Know your particular temptations. Only then will you learn to employ the appropriate and specific antidote provided in Christ to enable you to overcome indwelling sin, to persevere and to grow. For only then will you be able to name the particular manifestation sin takes in your own life.

At the same time there is another dimension to our self-knowledge. We have already seen it in different connections. It is 'know your *Christian* self!'—be conscious not only of what you are by nature, but of who and what you have become in Christ. For we must never lose sight of what we are in Christ when we are reflecting on what we are in ourselves.

The shock of self-discovery

It is always a shock to our pride when we discover that we are sinners—and not merely people who occasionally sin. By nature we excuse our sins as infrequent aberrations when in fact they are revelations of our deepest nature. Sin is not superficial to us, a mere flesh wound. It is a deep distortion, a twisted hostility towards God and his reign over us. And although believers now belong to the new creation in Christ, we still live in the old one, and in the same body. So long as that is true, sin remains and entangles us, and needs to be unmasked, untangled, and thrown off.

Simul justus et peccator

This is not something we discover only once in our lives. Luther was right, the Christian is always *simul iustus et peccator*—at one and the same time righteous in Christ and yet a sinner in himself. True we are no longer what we once were; but neither are we what one day we shall be. Until then the earthquake of conversion continues to issue its aftershocks. As the mirror of God's word[1] is put into our hands, we will frequently discover ourselves saying, 'Lord, is that what I am really like? Then help me to disengage from that pattern of sin and deal with its root cause.'

This is, at least in part, Paul's concern in Romans 7:14-25. The entire chapter is an extended reflection on the significance of God's law in the life of the Christian. In Christ we have died to the law that condemned us; we are no longer married to it, but have been raised with Christ and are now united or 'married' to him. Yet when we look at ourselves in the light of God's law—which remains 'holy and righteous and good' and 'spiritual'[2]—we are dismayed by what we see as its light penetrates our souls. We share Paul's cry: 'Wretched man that I am! Who will deliver me from this body of death?'[3] He already knows the only possible answer: Jesus Christ can!

Paul found one particular commandment 'got under his skin'.[4] The same may be true for us. Read them out loud—is there one commandment in particular that causes your voice to change a little, or makes you hesitate as you come to it, or even makes you read it more quickly? Or which one requires more effort to read calmly, guarding yourself against Jesus' interpretation of it in the Sermon on the Mount?[5] If you were a preacher or Sunday School teacher, or can imagine yourself as one ... which commandment would cause you most inner tension when you were explaining it and how we can conform to it? Or as you pray through all ten commandments, do you hesitate at any point to say, 'Lord, enable me to be this without reservation or deviation today'?

---

[1] See James 1:23.

[2] Romans 7:12, 14.

[3] Romans 7:24.

[4] For an extended discussion of why the tenth commandment in particular may have functioned in Paul's experience of conversion see below, Appendix 3.

[5] See Matthew 5:17-48.

Sin 'clings' to us. Our translations offer several suggestions for the unusual compound adjective used here by the author of Hebrews (*euperistatos*). Its root is the verb 'to stand' prefixed by 'well' (*eu*) and 'around' (*peri*). Hence the renderings 'clings so closely' (RSV, ESV); 'so easily entangles' (NIV); 'clings so easily' (JB); 'dogs our feet' (J. B. Phillips); 'sin with its clinging folds' (Moffatt, clearly playing on the idea of the long flowing garments worn in antiquity).

Parents who play sports with their children always remember the day when their son or daughter first beat them. Before then we felt we always had reserves we could draw on at will in order to maintain our superiority. And then the day comes when we are like Samson shorn of his locks.

I still remember such a day. I was playing golf with one of our sons, and found myself several holes 'down' to him. It had happened before; I knew I could put my foot on my golfing accelerator, focus on playing better, draw level, and then pull away for the accustomed paternal victory. But not this time! What I did not realise was that he had developed greater engine power since we had last played. That day he kept winning. And since that day until this, I have never beaten him again!

We make the same mistake with sin. It is 'our' sin, and therefore we can decide the moment when we will throw it off and defeat it. Or so we think. But John Bunyan was right—

> Sin, rather than 'twill out of action be,
> Will pray to stay, though but a while with thee;
> One night, one hour, one moment, will it cry,
> Embrace me in thy bosom, else I die:
> Time to repent [saith it] I will allow,
> And help, if to repent thou know'st not how.
> *But if you give it entrance at the door,*
> *It will come in, and may go out no more.*[1]

---

[1] John Bunyan, from a broadsheet, *A Caution to stir up to watch against sin*, (1684).

Sin may have lost its dominion over us, but it retains its power in us. It is sin still. The price of victory is constant vigilance. Yes, there is grace to cover all our sin; but that grace leads us to mortify it, not to tolerate it.

Evangelical teaching today stresses God's grace. But true grace is nothing more or less than Jesus Christ come to save us—not only to *forgive* us but to *save* us—that is to set us free from sin, and to transform our lives and make us holy. 'This is the will of God,' says Paul, 'your sanctification.'[1] He spells this out:

> For the grace of God has appeared, bringing salvation for all people, training us to renounce ungodliness and worldly passions, and to live self-controlled, upright, and godly lives in the present age, waiting for our blessed hope, the appearing of the glory of our great God and Saviour Jesus Christ, who gave himself for us to redeem us from all lawlessness and to purify to himself a people for his own possession who are zealous for good works.[2]

Those who experience the grace of God in justification want to experience his grace in sanctification too. That involves strenuous activity on our part. Scores of New Testament imperatives make this clear. For without holiness we will never see the Lord.[3] Never!

In this connection our spiritual forefathers spoke about '*acting* faith'. They meant 'acting' not in the sense of 'pretending' but of vigorous action, spiritual focus on the promises and commands of God's word, and a resolute commitment to trust and obey him in everything.

This, in summary form, is what Hebrews tells us to do. We are to bring to bear on indwelling sin all the force of the word of God; we are to let affectionate love for the Lord expel affection for sin.

Sin always has a tendency to complicate our lives—creating confusion in our thinking, double-mindedness in our willing, and

[1] 1 Thessalonians 4:3.
[2] Titus 2:11-14.
[3] Hebrews 12:14.

distortion in our affections. In contrast the gospel simplifies our lives. Simply put:

> Trust and obey,
> For there's no other way
> To be happy in Jesus,
> But to trust and obey.[1]

Encouragements for the race

There are obstacles; but it is not enough to know only about them. Indeed it could be spiritually hazardous for us to become so fixated on the problems that face us in sanctification that we end up losing sight of the encouragements. So having alerted us to two obstacles, the author of Hebrews provides two major encouragements.

Eagle-eyed readers will perhaps have noticed that in the discussion above we have reversed the author's order by highlighting the challenges we face. But the author of Hebrews first highlights the encouragements and the motives we have for dealing with them. Either way the typical New Testament logical sequence we have seen before is still embedded in his words here: Since A is true, make B true too:

- Since A is true: *we are surrounded by so great a cloud of witnesses,*

- Therefore make B true: *let us also lay aside every weight and sin … and let us run.*

The author is simply drawing on the basic logic of the gospel, and indeed of the whole of Scripture: know your sin, but know also the power of God's grace. Not the obstacles in our way but the cloud of witnesses surrounding us, and the presence of our Saviour watching us and waiting for us are to fill our horizon. Not even sin and its strength should be allowed to loom so large in our thinking or feeling that it covers up the sight of Christ and his people.

[1] From the hymn by John H. Sammis (1846–1919), 'When we walk with the Lord in the light of his word.'

The great cloud of witnesses

The author of Hebrews does not leave us in any doubt about the identity of the great cloud of witnesses. He had listed them in the preceding verses. How are we to think of them? Probably not merely as spectators watching us but as fellow participants who have run before us. Hebrews is not saying: Imagine yourself running in this Christian race and you see Moses and Elijah in the stands cheering you on. Rather he is saying that even although these saints 'did not receive what was promised', they persevered in faith and are examples to us of what it means to live by faith. They believed God's promises, they kept running towards Christ, and they sought to deal with their sin. They were witnesses to the reality and nature of persevering faith that is 'the assurance of things hoped for, the conviction of things to come'.[1] They trusted God's promises, and pressed on towards the goal—the appearing of the Lord Jesus Christ himself— even although none of them ever reached it. Like Abraham they did not know exactly where their race would finish; like the prophets 'they searched and inquired carefully, inquiring what person or time the Spirit of Christ in them was indicating when he predicted the sufferings of Christ and the subsequent glories'.[2] They kept running. Their witness to the nature of persevering faith should be a major encouragement to us

But our eyes are not fixed on the great cloud of witnesses. We are surrounded by them, but not focused on them. No, our eyes are to be fixed on Jesus. Having emphasised this towards the beginning of his letter,[3] the author repeats it now towards the end.

---

[1] Hebrews 11:1.
[2] 1 Peter 1:11.
[3] Hebrews 3:1.

Jesus the author and perfecter of our faith

'Fix your eyes upon Jesus.' Do so because he is your Saviour; but also because you realise he is the *founder* of your faith.

The word 'founder' (*archēgos*) is used on only four occasions in the New Testament, and always of Jesus himself.[1] Translated as 'author', or 'founder' (in the ESV) it denotes a person whose actions create a new situation for those who belong to him. By accomplishing a particular feat he guarantees that they will share in its results.

Imagine a military commander leading his men on a rescue mission. Their pathway must go through uncharted jungle, and there is a deadline for their special operation. Unexpectedly they find themselves confronted with a ravine. If they cannot cross it their detour will mean they cannot make the deadline. Their mission will fail. There is no other way for them to fulfil their task but to cross the ravine. The situation is a terrible stalemate. But it so happens that the commander is also the world long jump champion. He takes a rope, makes a run towards the ravine … his men hold their breath … he leaps … and lands on the other side. A rope bridge is then constructed and all of his men pass over safely to the other side. He alone accomplished the leap; his whole company benefit. Jesus Christ is such a commander.

Jesus is the *object* of the faith of the saints of the Old Testament—they looked to his coming. But he is also the one who perfectly exercised and exemplified persevering faith. He is both pioneer and perfecter. He encourages us but he also sustains us. He persevered to the end. He is well able to help us to persevere to the end. But we must keep our eyes fixed on him. Otherwise we will grow weary and lose heart. Our endurance depends on his endurance. For he endured all that we have to endure and more. He despised the shame of the cross in the light of his future glory.

[1] Hebrews 12:2, Acts 3:15; 5:31; Hebrews 2:10.

He experienced implacable opposition from sinful men. He stayed the course longer, faced more difficult conditions, and tasted more ferocious opposition than we ever do.[1] Yes, Jesus is the Saviour. But he is also the forerunner, the pioneer of faith, the reconnaissance officer who has gone through all the struggles and overcome all the obstacles that faith can ever meet. Never lose sight of him. He is well able to keep you going.

Are we ready for such a race?

Before we start there are certain issues we need to settle.

Important decisions

There were times during Jesus' early ministry when vast crowds followed him. At one crucial point he emphasized that discipleship is costly (the muddle-headed notion that it offers 'health, wealth, and happiness' is a diameter removed from our Lord's teaching). He stressed the importance of counting this cost: 'any one of you who does not renounce all that he has cannot be my disciple'.[2]

The author of Hebrews learned from Jesus. His homily contains a checklist of issues Christians need to settle. He wants us to have a clear understanding of what sanctification involves over the long haul. These issues are key—and we need to think seriously about them before we go any further. We can narrow them down to three crucial questions.

First: *Am I willing to resist sin to the point of shedding my blood?*

Some of the first readers of Hebrews seem to have been on the brink of throwing in the towel. Opposition has a way of wearing us down and exhausting our resistance. 'Look,' the author writes, 'you need to develop a simple resolution: be willing to resist sin to the point where you would shed your blood rather than sin. Jesus did

[1] Hebrews 12:2.
[2] Luke 14:33.

that, and you belong to him. You do it too.' Jonathan Edwards-like we need to learn to inscribe in our journals:

Resolved: I will shed my blood rather than live a life of sin.

Is being a Christian as serious as that? Yes it is. Are we expected to resist sin to the point of shedding our blood? Yes, we are. Following Christ has always been a life and death matter:

Some were tortured, refusing to accept release, so that they might rise again to a better life. Others suffered mocking and flogging, and even chains and imprisonment. They were stoned, they were sawn in two, they were killed with the sword. They went about in skins of sheep and goats, destitute, afflicted, mistreated—of whom the world was not worthy—wandering about in deserts and mountains, and in dens and caves of the earth.[1]

It was as serious as this for the great cloud of Old Testament witnesses. It was as serious as this for Jesus. Think of it this way: if he had not resisted sin to the point of shedding his blood, we would have no Saviour. But he sanctified himself, consecrating himself to die for our sin.[2] If this is so, then let us echo the words of the blunt-speaking C. T. Studd, 'If Jesus Christ be God and died for me, then no sacrifice can be too great for me to make for him.'[3]

If Jesus had failed to resist sin to the point of shedding his blood, he would have died because of his own sins. His ability to save us, and therefore our salvation, depended on him being willing to die rather than sin. We live in a day when such seriousness is a virtue feared rather than pursued. It should not be so with the Christian.

---

[1] Hebrews 11:35-38.

[2] John 17: 19.

[3] C. T. Studd (1860–1931). Born into privilege and educated at Eton and Trinity College, Cambridge, Studd played cricket for England against Australia in the 1882 Test Match for which 'The Ashes' were named. Later he became a missionary with Hudson Taylor's China Inland Mission (CIM), and then served in India and Africa, becoming founder of the Worldwide Evangelisation Crusade (WEC).

The author of Hebrews is saying, 'Since Jesus is the author and finisher of your faith, be serious.' We must not trifle.

Remember the thought that would come to Charles Simeon, when he glanced at the portrait he kept of his late younger friend Henry Martyn:

> Mr Simeon used to observe of Martyn's picture, whilst looking up at it with affectionate earnestness, as it hung over his fire-place, 'There!—see that blessed man! What an expression of countenance. No one looks at me as he does—he never takes his eyes off me; and seems always to be saying. Be serious—Be in earnest—Don't trifle—don't trifle.' Then smiling at the picture and gently bowing, he added: 'And I won't trifle—I won't trifle.'[1]

That is exactly the issue. Am I willing to resist sin to the point of shedding my blood? Am I resisting sin? Or am I trifling?

Second: *Am I remembering the encouragements Scripture gives me?*

It is important to live a balanced Christian life. But that is not quite the same thing as seeking a golden mean between two extremes. That could be little more than a form of Christian stoicism—a kind of stiff upper lip, keeping the emotions well in check. But that is not the biblical model. By contrast the gospel keeps us balanced not by limiting our emotional range but by stretching it.

On the one hand, there is a radical call to be willing to resist sin even if it means shedding our life-blood. That stretches our emotions to the limit.

On the other hand there is an equally stretching word of encouragement:

> Do not regard lightly the discipline of the Lord, nor be weary when reproved by him. For the Lord disciplines the one he loves, and chastises every son whom he receives.[2]

---

[1] William Carus, ed., *Memoirs of the Life of the Rev. Charles Simeon M.A. With a Selection from his Writings and Correspondence* (London: J. Hatchard & Son, 3rd edition 1868), 276 fn.

[2] Hebrews 12:5-6. The words are cited from Proverbs 3:11-12.

Everything that takes place in the life of the Christian is an element in the heavenly Father's programme of child-training.[1] Every moment of pain has a purpose. Every hurt is employed by him to draw me closer to Christ and to make me more like him. Every hardship is therefore an evidence of my spiritual legitimacy.

Here the author of Hebrews appeals to and applies a basic human principle. The father who truly cares about his son disciplines him. Failure to discipline is not a mark of love but of indifference. Indeed the author goes so far as to say that *not* to be disciplined raises questions about legitimacy. We respect human fathers only when they take their responsibility seriously—how much more should we respect and submit to the Father of our spirits?

The teaching is virtually self-explanatory.

Third: *Am I convinced that without holiness I will never see the Lord?*[2]

What is God doing in his long-term project in our lives? We need to remind ourselves frequently of this, and to learn to see the short term in the light of it. The answer? He is disciplining us, training us for our good so that we may 'share his holiness'.[3]

God is a single-minded God. He is absolutely determined to make me holy. What possesses me to think that I can be indifferent to—or worse refuse and resist—his good purpose? And if the all-wise and all-loving One has set his heart on this, why would I want anything different for myself? How foolish I would be to resist when he means to employ every means at his disposal (which, after all, is *everything*) to bring me to the goal of holiness?

Holiness is *that important*. Are you therefore striving for it? See to it that you do! This is the message of Hebrews.

---

[1] The word translated 'discipline' in Hebrews 12:7-11 is *paideia*, child-training.
[2] Hebrews 12:14.
[3] Hebrews 12:10.

Specific directions

Along the route of its teaching on our perseverance in holiness, Hebrews positions a variety of signposts to help us. In drawing this chapter to a close we should pause beside five of them.

(1) It is still true that 'The heart is deceitful above all things, and desperately sick; who can understand it?'[1] It therefore also remains true that we must learn to guard our hearts against the deceitfulness of sin[2] and against the disobedience of unbelief.[3] This summons us to a conscious awareness of our calling to be holy and to a well-developed sensitivity to the subtle ways in which sin entangles us.

(2) While we are called to be holy as individuals the author of Hebrews unites with Paul in teaching us never to lose sight of the important role that fellowship plays in encouraging perseverance.[4] There is a communal dimension to biblical exhortations. We are to seek harmony with others; we are to guard fellowship with one another.[5] We are to 'See to it that no one fails to obtain the grace of God; that no "root of bitterness" springs up and causes trouble, and by it many become defiled.'[6] Those who rebel against God seek to justify themselves on the grounds that others share their sin.[7] Conversion therefore entails that those who are growing in genuine holiness want others to walk the way of holiness with them. Holiness in this respect has a dynamic that is the antithesis of sinfulness which seeks to drag others down with it.

(3) Memory plays a more strategic role in our progress in holiness than we often think. Its importance is pervasive in Scripture. From early days God's people are urged, negatively, not to forget,

---

[1] Jeremiah 17:9.
[2] Hebrews 3:13.
[3] Hebrews 3:1; 3:14; 4:2; 12:14-17.
[4] Hebrews 10:24; 3:13.
[5] Hebrews 12:14.
[6] Hebrews 12:15.
[7] See Romans 1:28-32.

and positively, to remember what God has done for them, who they are as a result, and what God has called them to be. So here in Hebrews believers are urged to be strengthened by the memory of God's persevering grace in the past.[1]

The ministry of the word of God, the visual sermons of baptism and the Lord's Supper are each in its own way an *aide-memoire* to help us on the way. Our memories are frail—and become even more so as the years pass. The growing Christian will therefore work hard at developing a well-stored memory. This is all the more important since we have become accustomed to using technological memory to the extent we do (many mobile or cell phone users now cannot remember any number other than their own—and often not even that!). Studies of human behaviour patterns are increasingly confirming what we already know from experience: our powers of memory are being weakened by lack of exercise. Christians are not immune, and are wise to reflect on the spiritual implications of forgetting. Without ever envisaging the challenges of the twenty-first century the Scriptures urge us to develop well-stocked memories.

(4) Without extensively discussing the role of the mind as such,[2] the author places the same premium on its use as we saw Paul doing. In particular he emphasizes the importance of our minds being focussed on the Lord Jesus. For one thing his whole sermon is Christ-centred and Christ-full. For another we are specifically exhorted to 'consider Jesus'[3] and to understand his high priestly ministry;[4] both of which involve us in 'looking to Jesus'.[5] Thus we are encouraged to fix our minds on him as the author and finisher of our faith, and as the one

[1] Hebrews 10:32. Deuteronomy 8:1-20 illustrates this principle with its powerful call to 'remember' on the one hand and not 'forget' on the other.

[2] The references to the mind in Hebrews 8: 10 and 10:16 (both quotations of Jeremiah 31:33) are an exception. Nevertheless a variety of other statements reflect on the use of the mind.

[3] Hebrews 3:1.

[4] Hebrews 2:17; 4:14.

[5] Hebrews 12:2.

who endured—as the Model, Pioneer, and Author of all persevering faith, both his and ours.

(5) We are to receive the ministry of those who are called to take care of us spiritually and to shepherd us. Hebrews describes their ministry very specifically as 'keeping watch' over us.[1] Spiritual health involves a willingness to obey and submit to those who lead us. Independent-mindedness and isolationist tendencies are inappropriate for the Christian who is conscious of the continuing influence of indwelling sin. Growth in holiness, we have seen, is set within the community life of the church family. We are not to neglect fellowship in worship, ministry, and discipline. We are to encourage one another.[2]

This raises an important question: In my pursuit of holiness am I exercising a genuine pastoral concern for my fellow believers? Am I really concerned, not only to grow myself but that others will grow with me, go with me, and arrive at the destination with me? Or is my pursuit of holiness little more than a quest for self-development rather than a concern for the glory of God and increased love for, and Christ-like service of, his people? Any form of holiness that is concerned only about itself cannot be authentic.

So we must make sure that these two things are held together— on the one hand our own pursuit of Jesus Christ and on the other our desire to see others running with us. When they are we will find ourselves surrounded not only by a great cloud of witnesses from Scripture whose examples urge us on, but by the strength of the fellowship to which we belong on earth. Then we will have all the more reason to throw off every weight and the sin that can entangle us.

For this too is part of what it means to be devoted to God.

---

[1] Hebrews 13:17.
[2] Hebrews 10:23-25.

10

The Ultimate Goal

From beginning to end being a Christian and being holy are virtually synonymous. We are, after all, 'called [to be] saints'.[1] The gospel calls us to a new and transformed life in Christ. It makes it possible for us to resist being squeezed into the mould of the present age and conformed to its patterns. Instead, we are transformed through the renewing of our minds.

A major element in this renewal is the paradox which we first saw captured in Paul's exhortation in Romans 12:1-2 and then illustrated in various ways throughout his letters. He speaks in the *imperative mood*—we are exhorted to *consecrate ourselves to God*; but the transformation that results is expressed in the *passive voice*. We are to commit ourselves to being *acted upon by God*.

Yet clearly the New Testament does not mean by this that we divide the field of sanctification up into sections and say, 'This here is my part, and that over there is God's part'—as though we were each responsible for, say, fifty per cent of the task (or perhaps seventy-five per cent seen as God's work and twenty-five per cent ours, or the like). No! Rather *we are to work out* our salvation into our lives because *the Spirit is working* 'to will and to work for his good pleasure'.[2]

---

[1] Romans 1:7; 1 Corinthians 1:2; cf. Philippians 1:1; Colossians 1:1
[2] Philippians 2:12-13.

We have explored what this means. But now one final question remains to be settled: What is the Spirit's purpose as he works salvation in, and our goal as we work it out into our lives? Yes, we are being transformed—but *into what?*

We have already had hints of the answer; now we must spell it out, as Paul does clearly and simply:

> For those whom he foreknew he also predestined to be conformed to the image of his Son, in order that he might be the firstborn among many brothers.[1]

The marvellous ultimate truth of the gospel is that God and man are to share the same goal, or end. In this sense we might be bold enough to revise the *Shorter Catechism* and preface its first question with an even more fundamental one:

Question 1: What is the chief end of God?

Answer: God's chief end is for the Father, the Son, and the Spirit to glorify God in each person and as one God, and to enjoy being that God forever.

Question 2: What is the chief end of man?

Answer: Man's chief end is to glorify God, and to enjoy him for ever.

God does everything for his own glory.[2] That is both his desire and his delight. Amazingly he has created us to do the same. However as Augustine noted,

> You stir man to take pleasure in praising you, because you have made us for yourself, and our heart is restless until it rests in you.[3]

But how can this be accomplished so that his happiness and ours coincide? And how can this still be possible since we are fallen creatures and by nature hostile to his will and glory?

[1] Romans 8:29.
[2] Romans 11:36.
[3] Augustine, *Confessions*, 1.1.

Sanctification and Christlikeness

God means to do this first of all by taking us again fully into his possession and then by a progressive process of sanctification in which we become de-conformed to this age and also transformed with a view to being finally re-conformed to the image of Jesus Christ—God's Son in our flesh. This explains the big picture of our redemption: we were created to be God's sons mirroring him in miniature form, living out his family likeness. We are restored to this by regeneration and adoption, and one day will be fully conformed to it. Ultimately this means Christlikeness—fully reflecting the image of Jesus Christ our elder brother. God's designing of our destiny predates history; its fulfilment will come about when history reaches its climax, its *telos*, its *eschaton* in the glorification of Christ in his people and throughout the cosmos.

The goal therefore has a personal quality. Yes, it involves knowledge and understanding.[1] But ultimately sanctification is not merely cerebral—knowing the plan of salvation, understanding the truth, and the way to everlasting life. It is *personal.* It involves our persons and characters. It means knowing and becoming like the one who said '*I am* the way, the truth, and the life.'[2] There is no way or truth or life that is somehow abstractable from the Lord Jesus himself. He does not show us a way that is separable from his person, or a series of propositions we can call 'the truth' if we think about them apart from him; nor do we possess life in ourselves but only in him.

Family likeness

The mantra 'Christianity is Christ' is heard less frequently today than it used to be. Sometimes it was misconstrued, setting experience of Christ in opposition to understanding, implying that it is everything whereas doctrine is confusing, merely intellectual, speculative,

[1] Ephesians 4:24; Colossians 3:10.
[2] John 14:6.

even divisive. Yet we cannot know Christ without knowing about Christ. Thus properly understood, since the whole Bible is about Christ, Christianity is Christ after all.

Within this context sanctification, seen as the reproduction in us of the family likeness of Christ, means that every believer within his or her own personality and character becomes a 'reminiscence of Jesus'. While the various New Testament writers employ their own distinct concepts and language to explain what holiness is, they share this feature in common. The image of God that has been marred is being restored.

But it is especially in Paul that we see this perspective worked out in full.

For Paul the 'big picture' of God's purposes is expressed in terms of the parallels and contrasts he sees between Adam and Christ. In our fallen condition, for all our individuality, each of us bears the image of Adam. So when we are brought into Christ the Spirit weaves Christlikeness into each unique Christian life. Thus he creates a family whose members share similar characteristics, instincts and dispositions. They have the same approach to life, the same kinds of responses to similar situations, the same love and admiration for, and growing likeness to, their Elder Brother Jesus Christ. This is the world-wide experience of all who are being sanctified. We recognise in each other what, apparently, the world cannot see. Our true lives are 'hidden in Christ with God',[1] but family members are 'insiders' and we recognise the family love in one another.

The principle that Christ's character is reproduced in believers was so deeply embedded in Paul's thinking that on occasion he illustrated it instinctively, perhaps without realising he was doing it.

He provides a beautiful example of this in the context of urging the Philippians (and us) to work out the salvation that the

---

[1] Colossians 3:3. Cf. 1 John 3:1-2.

Spirit works into us. It follows closely on the heels of his wonderful description of 'the mind of Christ':

> Do nothing from rivalry or conceit, but in humility count others more significant than yourselves. Let each of you look not only to his own interests, but also to the interests of others. Have this mind among yourselves, which is yours in Christ Jesus, who though he was in the form of God, did not count equality with God a thing to be grasped, but made himself nothing, taking the form of a servant, being born in the likeness of men. And being found in human form, he humbled himself by becoming obedient to death, even death on a cross …[1]

These much admired words feed into Paul's exhortation to work out salvation into our lives and into Christian fellowship. But we need to read on. What follows a few verses later? Paul refers to Timothy and Epaphroditus.

About Timothy he says:

> I have no one like him, who will be genuinely concerned for your welfare. They all seek their own interests … But you know Timothy's proven worth, how as a son with a father he has served with me in the gospel.[2]

On Epaphroditus he comments:

> I have thought it necessary to send to you Epaphroditus … your messenger and minister to my need … he has been longing for you all and has been distressed because you heard that he was ill. Indeed he was ill, near to death … he nearly died for the work of Christ, risking his life to complete what was lacking in your service to me.

We should not miss the thread here: what was first seen in Christ—the self-forgetfulness, the servant spirit, the considering others more important than himself—has been 'worked out' into the lives of Paul's two associates. Of course both of them had probably

---

[1] Philippians 2:3-8.
[2] Philippians 2:20-22. Cf. John 5:19.

first seen the same features in Paul himself.[1] So here are three completely different men, with very different personalities; but in each there was a beautiful reminiscence of the Lord Jesus. This is what sanctification looks like in flesh and blood terms. It always resembles Jesus. This is the process the Spirit inaugurates in regeneration and will finally consummate in glorification.

Ultimate destiny

Everything that happens in the Christian life takes place under the sovereign superintendence of our heavenly Father. He 'works all things according to the counsel of his will'.[2] Thus everything works together for our good.[3]

But what is the 'good'? That has been a perennial question for the philosophers, and had already been much discussed by Paul's day. What marks his thinking out as distinctive, and consistent with the whole of Scripture, is that he defines 'good' in terms of God, and here more specifically in terms of Jesus Christ. For Paul goes on to say that the ultimate 'good' towards which all things work together is our conformity to Christ. This is the goal God has in view and in accomplishing it he causes even what is evil to 'work together' for the 'good' of his children. Through friction and affliction he polishes graces and transforms character to reflect again the image of God fully and perfectly revealed in Jesus Christ. Ultimately, for Paul this includes and involves the resurrection-transformation.[4]

From beginning to end the Spirit is the agent in this transformation: 'We all, with unveiled face, beholding the glory of the Lord, are being transformed into the same image from one degree of glory into another. For this comes from the Lord who is the Spirit.'[5]

[1] Philippians 3:17.
[2] Ephesians 1:11.
[3] Romans 8:28.
[4] Philippians 3:20-21. Cf. 1 Corinthians 15:48-49.
[5] 2 Corinthians 3:18.

This creates a demarcation line between Christians and non-Christians. For the non-Christian the future at first seems long and the past short. Slowly that perspective changes. Eventually the past seems to have been all too short. And now the future seems short too.

What is the difference for the Christian? It is this: the Christian lives *from the future into the past.* He or she sees time in the light of eternity and therefore views affliction through lenses tinted with glory. Nor is the relationship between the two merely chronological—suffering now, glory then; it is causal: 'This light momentary affliction *is preparing for us* an eternal weight of glory beyond all comparison.'[1] It is as though struggles, suffering, trials, are, in the Spirit's hands, the raw materials out of which he creates glory in us. So we learn to live our lives, and to see the sometimes painful process of being made holy, in the light of the final glory we will share with Christ. For this is where the whole process is heading.

Knowing this helps us to understand why it can be such a painful process. By nature we are not very auspicious candidates for the production of glory! But our lives are in the hands of a very determined heavenly Father. He knows that without holiness we will not have the capacity to see the Lord.[2] For only those who are like him will be able to see him as he is.[3]

Grasp this and it sheds light on our path. Is my life more rather than less challenging now that I have become a Christian? Am I puzzled by what the Lord seems to be doing in the circumstances of my life? Do I face trials and experience affliction, even forms of persecution I never expected? Am I discovering more sin in my heart than I ever imagined before I became a Christian? Then he is sanctifying me. And this is a much bigger, wider, longer, deeper work than I

[1] 2 Corinthians 4:17.
[2] Hebrews 12:14.
[3] 1 John 3:2.

first realised when I became a Christian. God is not interested in short-term results but long-term, permanent (everlasting!) changes.

Jesus promised that when he sent the Spirit he would come to make believers a home for the Father and the Son.[1] This is not a matter of rearranging furniture, or even building an extension, although it may include both. It involves demolition and major reconstruction. Much needs to be put off; much needs to be put on. To apply Paul's building metaphor, God is not using wood and hay and stubble but fire-tested, refined metals and precious stones.[2] He means his building to last for all eternity. He knows that only what is Christ-like can survive in his presence.

This perspective impacts everything. It provides a new focus. Things that once seemed important to us now appear to be trivial. We assess everything now in the context of the great 'will it last forever?' question. This does not mean that we demean the God-given rhythms of work and rest. Nor does it mean that we do only those things that seem to be 'most spiritual'. That could easily lead to the kind of false spirituality that Paul occasionally had to counter. Holiness is not a process of becoming either more or less than truly human. But God's ultimate goal provides a touchstone by which we regulate our lives. Nothing now is seen as an end in itself; the end of everything we do becomes glorifying God in the knowledge that we will enjoy him both now and for ever.

In addition we come to see that suffering is not an obstacle to God's purpose but a means to achieving it. What makes no sense otherwise may begin to make sense when set within the frame of God's artistry.

As individuals and, alas, as churches, we are easily taken up with, and spend so much time and energy on what will last only for a day and then be gone. But our personal sanctification and being part of

---

[1] John 14:16-23.
[2] 1 Corinthians 3:12-13.

the 'holy catholic church' means that we must always ask: 'Will this pattern, pursuit, or programme enhance our likeness to Christ? In what way will it serve eternal ends?' For if the only things that last for eternity in God's presence reflect the glory of his Son, why would we pursue anything less?

But there is a further dimension to this transformation which will bring it to a comprehensive climax.

The body of holiness

We saw earlier that the Spirit's transforming work already has an impact on our physical or bodily existence. It is 'in our mortal body' that we must no longer allow sin to reign;[1] it is our bodily members that we are to offer not as slaves to sin but as slaves to righteousness.[2] It is our bodies that we are to present to God as living sacrifices.[3] The body is for the Lord, and the Lord is for the body.[4] Our bodies are temples of the Holy Spirit.[5] We are to glorify God in our bodies.[6]

In this connection Paul asked the Corinthians two important questions: 'Do you not know:

(1) 'that your bodies are members of Christ?'

(2) 'that your body is a temple of the Holy Spirit?'[7]

We are expected to know these things.

But do we? And if we do know them is our knowledge merely informational? Or is it transformational—the kind of mind-and-heart-and-will-and-affections understanding that determines how we live? The key lies in Paul's words, 'you are not your own, for you were bought with a price'.[8] In this statement lies the gulf between

[1] Romans 6:12.
[2] Romans 6:18.
[3] Romans 12:1.
[4] 1 Corinthians 6:13.
[5] 1 Corinthians 6:19.
[6] 1 Corinthians 6:20.
[7] 1 Corinthians 6:15-19.
[8] 1 Corinthians 6:20.

the mould of the present age and the mould of the gospel. The issue is not only '*Who* am I?' but '*Whose* am I?' The answer to the latter question will determine the answer to the former. This is ground zero in our sanctification—we have yielded up our insistence on self-determination; we are entirely the Lord's. That includes our bodies; indeed it applies especially to our bodies because we are our bodies!

This is our reasonable service or worship.

Notice once again the internal gospel logic at work here. If God's determined desire and purpose for us is the final sanctifying of our bodies in resurrection, it follows that this shapes his work in us and should determine our living for him. Indeed this is one reason Christians stress the resurrection of the body in which, by the power of the Spirit, Christ will transform our lowly bodies to be like his body of glory.[1] Then will come to completion what the *Westminster Confession* describes as the 'sanctification [that] is throughout in the whole man'.[2] Then the divine benediction will be fulfilled:

> May the God of peace himself sanctify you completely, and may your whole spirit and soul and body be kept blameless at the coming of our Lord Jesus Christ.[3]

We have seen that the Bible as a whole knows nothing about a human spirituality that is detached from bodily existence any more than it knows of a future that shows no interest in the resurrection of the flesh.[4] The Scriptures know nothing of a sanctification that is 'spiritual' but makes no impact on us physically. We sin through

[1] Philippians 3:21.

[2] *Westminster Confession of Faith*, XIII.2.

[3] 1 Thessalonians 5:23-24.

[4] It should scarcely need saying here that the final vision of the Bible does not anticipate disembodied souls existing in a rarefied heaven, but a renewed world, a new heavens and new earth in which righteousness dwells. This is why Paul does not want to be 'unclothed' in death, but further clothed with a heavenly body. 2 Corinthians 5:1-5.

our eyes and ears, our tongues, our hands and our feet. They are put to different and better use in the Christian life, and marvellously in glory they will serve the Lord without sin. If that is to be their destiny *then*, it will have a knock-on effect (or more accurately a knock-back effect) on our Christian lives *now*. Daily we will learn to sing:

> Take my *life* and let it be,
> Consecrated, Lord, to thee ...
>
> Take my *hands* ...
>
> Take my *feet* ...
>
> Take my *voice* ...
>
> Take my *intellect* ...
>
> Take my *will* ...
>
> Take my *heart* ...
>
> Take my *love* ...
>
> Take *myself* ...[1]

Why does this knowledge of the future make such an impact on our lifestyle in the present? Because this gospel perspective—the hope of the resurrection of the body, the prospect of being finally delivered from the influence of sin so that we will find it 'natural', even 'easy' to love, serve, obey, worship, and delight in the Lord—alone makes sense of the long, sometimes hard process of sanctification. And if we want to be wholly the Lord's *then*, we will want to be wholly his *now* as well as *then*.

Recall Paul's experience in which he felt himself transported into heavenly realms where he 'heard things that cannot be told, which man may not utter'.[2] Clearly, although he never revealed what he

[1] From the hymn by Frances Ridley Havergal (1836–79), 'Take my life, and let it be.'

[2] 2 Corinthians 12:4.

saw, this experience left a permanent mark on him.[1] But however unique that experience was, every Christian is given a taste of it. For

> What no eye has seen, nor ear heard,
>   nor the heart of man imagined,
> what God has prepared for those who love him—
> *these things God has revealed to us through the Spirit.*[2]

In this sense we have already been given a glimpse of the Promised Land:

> The men of grace have found,
>   Glory begun below.
> Celestial fruits on earthly ground
>   From faith and hope may grow.
>
> The hill of Zion yields
>   A thousand sacred sweets
> Before we reach the heav'nly fields,
>   Or walk the golden streets.[3]

Who does the working together?

A translation issue confronts us in Romans 8:28. It is not possible to be dogmatic about the subject of the verb 'work together'.

Older translations like the Authorised (King James) Version and the Revised Standard Version assumed that God himself is the subject (He works everything together for the good ...'). More recent translations (NIV, ESV) have tended to adopt the view that the subject is 'all things' ('for those who love God all things work together for good'). Meanwhile other scholars have argued that the *most natural*

---

[1] We best interpret its uniqueness when we remember the degree to which he experienced suffering for Christ. Special callings will always receive special provisions.

[2] 1 Corinthians 2:9-10. Contrary to the way these words are sometimes read we should notice that they have been revealed *now*.

[3] From the hymn by Isaac Watts (1674–1748), 'Come we that love the Lord.'

subject is in fact the Holy Spirit. He, after all, is the dominant subject in the immediately preceding verses.[1]

Whether or not this is true grammatically,[2] it is true theologically. The Spirit's role is always that of the executive of the Trinity. His task is to employ every instrument to transform Christ's younger brothers into his family likeness. Even if this is not explicitly stated in Romans 8:29 it is spelled out in 2 Corinthians 3:18: we are all being changed through the Spirit's multi-faceted ministry; we are all undergoing a divine metamorphosis into the likeness of Jesus Christ, from one degree of glory into another.

The question, then, is this: How is this to be accomplished in us? What happens in our lives that produces such likeness to Jesus?

We have already seen various aspects of the New Testament's answer to this question. We must now draw our thinking to a conclusion by considering two further elements: the role occupied in our sanctification by (1) the believer's imitation of the example of Christ and (2) the believer's participation in the sufferings of Christ.

1. Imitation

The Spirit transforms us into the likeness of Jesus Christ. He does this in us but he also does it through us. There is, we have seen,

---

[1] Romans 8:26-27. In technical grammatical terms the translation problem lies in the words *panta sunergei eis agathon*. Does this mean 'all things [*panta*] work for the good …' or that 'he' works all things for good? If the latter then God himself is the worker, perhaps more specifically the Holy Spirit whose ministry Paul has been particularly expounding in the preceding verses. In favour of some form of the latter is that strictly speaking it is not true that 'all things work together for good' in and of themselves. Paul must therefore have implicitly viewed the Father or the Spirit as the subject of the 'working-things-together for good'.

[2] If the strongest argument *in favour* of understanding the Spirit as the subject is the fact that he is the named subject in the previous two verses (he is mentioned four times in Romans 8:26-7), the most obvious argument *against* is that the subject of the immediately following sentence is clearly the Father ('he … predestined to be conformed to the image of his Son'). The reference to *his* Son implies that the antecedent is a reference to the Father.

a kind of synergism in our sanctification—we work out what the Spirit works in. This includes his ministry of stimulating in us a desire to imitate Jesus Christ.

Jesus taught his first disciples to do this. Having washed their feet in the Upper Room, he exhorted them to follow his example.[1] The role of the Spirit is now to stimulate in us a desire to imitate Jesus and become like him in humble-minded service.[2]

Think of the situation of the Christians in Rome when Paul dictated his letter to them. There were considerable tensions between Jewish and Gentile believers. Earlier in the church's life Jewish believers had probably been forced to leave Rome because of conflict between Jews in the Roman synagogues and the Christians. But now they had returned—to a church that was dominated by Gentiles.[3] Tensions had escalated. The fellowship of the church was

---

[1] While some Christian traditions have built this into a formal rite in the life of the church (the *Pedilavium*) it seems clear that this was not how the apostles understood Jesus' words. For one thing, unlike baptism and the Lord's Supper, we find no re-enactment of it in the New Testament. In addition the one context in which washing the feet of disciples is mentioned it is used in a metaphorical sense. It is one of the qualifications listed for enrolment in the 'order of widows' in the churches in Ephesus (1 Timothy 5:10). But if having 'washed the feet of the saints' was a ritual or 'sacrament' in the church it could hardly be used to distinguish one member from another, any more than saying 'must have received the Lord's Supper' distinguishes one church member from another.

[2] In this sense John 13:1-17 is a dramatic expression of the truth Paul expresses in a Christological fashion in Philippians 2:1-14.

[3] While not explicitly stated, this seems the natural way to piece together Paul's encounter in Corinth with the Jew Aquila and his wife Priscilla. They had left Rome under the decree of the Emperor Claudius (Acts 18:2). The Roman author Suetonius records that Claudius (Emperor from AD 41–54) expelled Jews from Rome because of rioting instigated by 'Chrestus'—probably Christ. This may well suggest that the antagonism that erupted against the preaching of Christ in synagogues in more remote parts of the Empire manifested itself also in Rome and was dealt with in this radical way—but to the disadvantage of the Jews rather than Gentile Christians—some of whom were Roman citizens. It is not difficult to imagine then that when Jewish believers returned to Rome they found that the churches had taken on a decisively Gentile flavour in which there was no longer any recognition of the Old Testament laws governing 'kosher' food and the religious observance of certain

in danger of fragmentation. Its members had come to Christ from different backgrounds, Jewish and Gentile. As a result their consciences reacted differently to such issues as the dietary and calendar laws of the Old Testament. They reached different conclusions about the food they could eat and the days they should observe as special. All parties seem to have felt equally strongly that they were right! They could not avoid the conclusion that others were wrong.[1]

When fellow Christians are at loggerheads and the unity of the church family is threatened, how do we act in a way that is Spirit-led and genuinely sanctified? How are we to cope?

Paul takes us back to first principles in order to answer:

Principle of action: You must not act simply to please yourself.

Reason for the principle: Jesus never acted simply to please himself.[2]

Jesus himself is the litmus test for all of our attitudes. His example is to be the driving force in our devotion. He *never* sought to please himself. If we are his we too are called to live in the same way.

Simon Peter echoes this when he says that Jesus left us an example that we should follow in his steps.[3] The term he employs (*hupogrammos*) denotes the copperplate writing of a teacher which a school pupil would then try to copy.

That was how youngsters in my generation learned cursive script—by copying what the teacher did. Sometimes she would sit down beside us and write in our jotters so that we could carefully

---

days as 'holy'. Given the feelings that have arisen in churches today over styles of worship, and for example the disappearance of older hymns, not to mention older forms of musical accompaniment, it is not difficult to imagine the tensions that emerged in the churches in Rome.

[1] Exactly how many different groupings there may have been in the churches in Rome has been a matter of debate, but it does not materially affect the central issue Paul is discussing. See Romans 14:1-15:13.

[2] Romans 15:1-3.

[3] 1 Peter 2:21.

follow her example and make our own copy. My teacher must often have thought, 'He would do better at following my example if I could get inside him and help him!' What makes copying Jesus' example possible is that he has given us his Spirit to enable us to do it. The Spirit is the one who takes what belongs to Jesus and shows it to us.[1] But he also comes to indwell us, to empower us from within.

Are you familiar with the way the Lord Jesus wrote the story of his life? Then with the Spirit's help, imitate him—write those same characteristics into your life too.

This imitation of Christ is accompanied by our participation in him.

2. Participation

We have already seen different aspects of what it means to be 'in Christ'. We have come by faith to share in all he is and has done for us. As we have seen, in Christ we have died, been buried, and have now been raised into the life of the new humanity.

But the New Testament paints this participation on a broad canvas. We not only share inwardly and spiritually in Christ's death and resurrection; we also share in his sufferings in order that we may share in his glory.[2]

Paul was conscious that here, as elsewhere, God had made him a kind of larger-than-ordinary-life-size working model of a profound spiritual principle.[3] He bears the marks of a true apostle in

---

[1] John 16:14-15.

[2] See Romans 8:17. We are heirs of God and co-heirs with Christ; we will therefore both co-suffer and be co-glorified with him. Only if we are '*Sunpashcites*' (sufferers with Christ) will we become '*Sundoxites*' (glorified with Christ); only those who suffer with him are glorified with him. Or, stated otherwise, if we are '*Sunpaschites*' it is certain that we will be '*Sundoxites*'. All who are in Christ receptively participate in all he has done for them.

[3] In 1 Corinthians 4:9 he sees himself and his fellow apostles as coming at the end of the line, exposed for all to see rather than hidden in the crowd, 'like men sentenced to death, a spectacle to the world, to angels, and to men.' Cf. 1 Timothy 1:16.

distinction from the 'super-apostles' who were influencing the Corinthians. In fact, he argues, the demeaning he experienced, the sufferings to which he had been exposed, were the marks of a true apostle because they were the evidence of his deep union with and participation in the death and resurrection of Christ.[1]

The force of what Paul says may be clearer if we consider three passages in 2 Corinthians. It may help to do so in reverse order.

2 Corinthians 13:4

Paul was criticized by 'super-apostles'[2] who regarded their own impressiveness as a hallmark of true Christian ministry—not least in comparison with his unimpressive appearance and the lack of rhetorical flourishes in his preaching.[3] He responded by saying that in fact weakness is much more of an authentic apostolic mark than the kind of 'power' of which the super-apostles boasted. At least this was true of Jesus—

> For he was crucified in weakness, but lives by the power of God. For we also are weak in him, but in dealing with you we will live with him by the power of God.[4]

We can too easily let our eyes slide over these words on the assumption that we know what Paul is saying here. If so we should pause and read them carefully. For he is not saying here what he says elsewhere namely that although he is weak in himself he can do all things in Christ.[5]

That sentiment is true, but it is not the principle Paul is enunciating to the Corinthians.

Look again at his words: 'we also are weak *in him*'. Paul is not saying he is weak in himself but strong in Christ, true though that

---

[1] A point he had made earlier to the Galatian Christians, Galatians 6:17.
[2] 2 Corinthians 11:5; 12:11.
[3] 2 Corinthians 11:6; 12:10.
[4] 2 Corinthians 13:4.
[5] Philippians 4:12-13.

is. Rather here he is saying that it is in Christ—not in himself—that he is weak!

What does he mean? Union with Christ means that we come to participate not only in his death but also in his weakness. This weakness is not something *from which* union with Christ *delivers* us, but *into which* union with Christ *brings* us. Union with Christ does not protect us from suffering but commits us to suffering. Because of the closeness of our fellowship with our Lord we find ourselves sharing in weakness, suffering, persecution, trials, and shame like that experienced by Jesus himself.

At least Paul thought so. In fact he believed there were still deeper dimensions of participation in Christ's sufferings he was yet to experience.[1] Indeed he wanted to have fellowship (*koinōnia*) in them. This is expressed by him in words of great power:

> All I care for is to know Christ, to experience the power of his resurrection, and to share his sufferings, in growing conformity with his death, if only I may arrive at the resurrection from the dead.[2]

Christ's death and resurrection were inseparable realities. In Christ these two dimensions always go together: death and resurrection; weakness and strength; shame and glory. They were symbiotic in him; they will be symbiotic in us. We must not deny the weakness in affirming the strength, or deny the death in affirming the resurrection; or deny the shame in affirming the glory—either in him or in ourselves.

The whole of the Christian life is born out of this womb of our union with Christ in his death and resurrection, sufferings and glory. This is the DNA of the child of God who is being transformed into the likeness of the Elder Brother. I am weak in Christ. I share in his

---

[1] Colossians 1:24.

[2] Philippians 3:10, *The New English Bible* (Oxford and Cambridge: Oxford University Press, Cambridge University Press, 1961).

sufferings. I share in his persecution. I share in his trials. But I am also strong in Christ and I overcome sin and I am faithful in trials and I grow in grace through suffering.

Earlier in the letter we find Paul speaking of this in greater detail:

2 Corinthians 4:10-12

> [We are] always carrying in the body the death of Jesus [literally, the *dying*[1]] of Jesus, so that the life of Jesus may also be manifested in our bodies. For we who live are always being given over to death for Jesus' sake, so that the life of Jesus may also be manifested in our mortal flesh [body]. So death is at work in us, but life in you.[2]

This passage contains several remarkable features. One is Paul's unusual use of the name 'Jesus' without the addition of any descriptive titles ('Christ' or 'Lord'). Ordinarily he employs at least one of these. Here he omits them probably to highlight the human dimension of our Lord's experience and to underline that what God was doing in Jesus' humanity is related to what he plans to do in ours. It was through death and weakness that Jesus entered into strength and glory; it will also be thus for us in union with him. So real and close is this union that Paul can say: 'We always carry around in our body the *dying* of Jesus.'

This was physically true for Paul. He had experienced:

> Far more imprisonments, with countless beatings, and often near death. Five times I received at the hands of the Jews the forty lashes less one. Three times I was beaten with rods. Once I was stoned. Three times I was shipwrecked; a night and a day I was adrift at sea; on frequent journeys, in danger from rivers, danger from robbers, danger from my own people, danger from Gentiles, danger in the city, danger in the wilderness, danger at sea, danger from false

---

[1] Paul uses two different words in verses 10 and 11 both translated 'death' in ESV: *nekrōsis* which denotes the process, the putting to death ('dying') and *thanatos* which denotes the state.

[2] 2 Corinthians 4:10-12.

brothers; in toil and hardship, through many a sleepless night, in hunger and thirst, often without food, in cold and exposure.[1]

He bore in his body the marks of Jesus.[2]

No doubt the *magnitude* of Paul's suffering was related to his special role in the purposes of God. But the suffering itself was intended to create in him a reflection of the Lord Jesus for others to see.

The result? He tells us:

> So death is at work in us, but life in you.

Here is another point at which we can detect the fingerprints of Stephen's witness in the development of Paul's theology of the Christian life.[3] For the immediate context of his conversion was when 'death worked in' Stephen and as a result 'life worked in' Saul. This is why their lives are linked together in Luke's narrative of the early church in Jerusalem. The life of Jesus was never more clearly manifested in Stephen that when he 'carried in his body the dying of Jesus', with the result that the life of Jesus was revealed to Saul of Tarsus. What else could explain Saul's rage? As the Lord himself explained, the persecution of Stephen was rooted in Stephen's union with Jesus. Persecuting Stephen (and others who were united to Christ) was persecuting Christ himself.[4] This became for Paul a fundamental principle, a substructure of his understanding of the Christian life, embedded within his own experience, and applicable to the experience of every believer.

---

[1] 2 Corinthians 11:24-27.

[2] Galatians 6:17.

[3] This is not to imply that the Spirit was absent from the shaping of Paul's thinking, but the 'inspiration' of Scripture was an organic reality and engaged the experience and personalities of the human authors. As B. B. Warfield put it, 'If God wished to give His people a series of letters like Paul's, He prepared a Paul to write them, and the Paul He brought to the task was a Paul who spontaneously would write just such letters.' B. B. Warfield, *Revelation and Inspiration,* in *The Works of B. B. Warfield* (New York: Oxford University Press, 1927), 1, 101.

[4] Acts 9:4. Cf. Matthew 25:40, 45.

Paul expresses a further dimension of this same principle at the very outset of his letter:

2 Corinthians 1:5

For as we share abundantly in Christ's sufferings, so through Christ we share abundantly in comfort too.[1]

In the Old Testament an aromatic oil with its own distinct formula and fragrance was used for priestly anointing.[2] Ultimately it was symbolic of the anointing of Jesus with the Holy Spirit for his ministry as our High Priest. But on closer examination we discover the oil of his anointing contained unique ingredients too—suffering and glory.

Psalm 133 uses the picture of the sacred priestly anointing to describe and explain the covenant union and communion that the people of God share in common:

> Behold how good and pleasant it is
>   when brothers dwell together in unity.
> It is like the precious oil on the head
>   running down on the beard,
> on the beard of Aaron,
>   running down on the collar of his robes![3]

The oil with which Aaron was anointed flowed over his head onto his beard and then down over his garments. On those garments were symbolic representations of the whole people of God.[4] They were to share in the anointing of their High Priest. What he experienced 'flowed over' into the whole community.

In the same way, the Spirit's anointing of the Lord Jesus contained the ingredients of death and resurrection, suffering and glory.

[1] 2 Corinthians 1:5.
[2] Exodus 30:22-33.
[3] Psalm 133:1-2.
[4] Exodus 28:6-30.

Paul seems then to envisage that anointing now flowing from the head of Christ to the members of his body. So we come to share in the overflow of his death, his sorrow, his suffering, and his shame.[1] Thankfully we also share in the power of his resurrection, his joy, his victory and his glory.

The balance here is important. It is created by our sharing in both death and resurrection, never one without the other. Yes, there will be diversity in the way in which, and in the degree to which, each of us will experience the outworking of this union with the crucified and risen one. Paul clearly experienced it in large measure. But in this world all those who are in Christ will share in his suffering. But so too will they experience the comfort of the resurrection. There is, as Calvin explains, a dual dimension to our union with Christ, both an inward and an outward mortification and vivification.[2] In the world we experience tribulation; but he has overcome the world, and in him so shall we.[3]

Calvin well describes this reality when he writes:

> The government of the Church of Christ has been so divinely constituted from the beginning that the Cross has been the way to victory, death the way to life … There is, therefore, no reason why afflictions should unreasonably depress us, although we were miserable under them, since the Spirit of God declares us blessed.[4]

Since this is what the Spirit did in Jesus' humanity in bringing him through suffering to glory, it is the model he employs permanently in bringing us to glory too.

It is in this comprehensive sense that God the Father has destined us to be conformed to the image of his Son that he might be the

---

[1] Colossians 1:24.

[2] See *Institutes*, III.8-10.

[3] John 16:33.

[4] John Calvin, *The Epistle of Paul to the Hebrews, The Epistles of Peter*, tr. W. B. Johnston, eds., D. W. Torrance and T. F. Torrance (Edinburgh: Oliver and Boyd, 1963), 240.

firstborn of *many brothers*. This is our *final* destiny. It is both individual and corporate. It is the climactic ingredient in the blueprints Scripture has drawn for our ongoing Christian experience. It is the epicentre of all God's work in us. It belongs to the essence of the process of sanctification and the holiness which is its end product. Likeness to Christ is the ultimate goal of sanctification.[1] It *is* holiness. It is therefore also the ultimate fruit of being *devoted to God.*

[1] 2 Corinthians 3:18.

APPENDIX 1

The Trinity
in the New Testament

The classical doctrine of the Trinity teaches us that there is one God who exists in three distinct persons, the Father, the Son, and the Holy Spirit. Typically this is stated as God having his existence in *one substance and three persons.*

There is mystery here. But it is the mystery in the light of which clarity is brought to all of our thinking about God, creation, providence, and redemption. Like the light of the sun we cannot gaze into it without danger; and yet it is the light in which we are able to see everything else more clearly. As Augustine wrote: 'In no other subject is error more dangerous, or inquiry more laborious, or the discovery of truth more profitable.'[1]

The purpose of this appendix is not to provide an exposition or defence of the classical doctrine of the Trinity but the more modest one of underlining the extent to which the joint work of the Father, the Son, and the Holy Spirit undergirds and permeates the teaching of the New Testament.

What follows then simply collates a number of New Testament passages under various headings to demonstrate how deeply into the warp and woof of the gospel the presence of the Trinity is woven,

---

[1] *On the Holy Trinity*, trans. A. W. Haddon, revised and annotated by W. G. T. Shedd: *The Works of St Augustine, Nicene and Post Nicene Fathers*, ed. Philip Schaff (reprinted Grand Rapids: Eerdmans, 1978), III.19.

in frequent references to the joint work in the believer of two or all three persons in the Trinity.

In classical orthodox Christianity the language of 'substance' and 'persons' has been used. This is not itself biblical language but the church has never seriously managed to improve on it. The point in this appendix is not to expound, explain, or defend this particular language but to show that only when we read the New Testament through trinitarian lenses can we make sense of its message. And since our fellowship in the Spirit is with the Father and the Son (1 John 1:3) it is tremendously important for our growth in sanctification that we learn to live, serve, and worship in a Trinity-conscious way.

1. Statements reflecting on the relationship of the Father and the Son

- The Son dwells at the Father's side, or in his bosom (John 1:18).

- The Father knows the Son and the Son knows the Father (Matthew 11:27).

- The Father loves the Son and shows him all he does (John 5:20).

- The one who is from God (the Son)—only he has seen the Father (John 6:46).

- The Son loves and abides in the Father, just as the Father abides in the Son (John 10:38, 30; 14:10; 15:9-10).

- The Father and the Son share all things (John 16:15).

- The glory of the Father and the Son is experienced in common (John 17:5).

2. Statements reflecting on the Father's and the Son's relationship with the Spirit

- The Spirit goes out from the Father in their divine communion with one another (John 15:26).

- The Spirit searches the deep things of God and knows his thoughts (1 Corinthians 2:10-11).

- The Father knows the mind of the Spirit (Romans 8:27).

- The Spirit 'of God' is the Spirit 'of Christ' (Romans 8:9).

3. Statements reflecting the foundational and pervasive nature of God in his trinitarian interaction with his creation.

- The Trinity engages in creation and its sustaining (John 1:1ff; Colossians 1:15-17; Hebrews 1:2; 2:10).

- The Trinity is engaged in the work of incarnation (John 3:16; Hebrews 2:11-14; Luke 1:35).

- The Trinity is present in Jesus'

   (i) Baptism (Luke 3:21).

   (ii) Temptations (Luke 4:1-12).

   (iii) Ministry (Matthew 12:25-28).

   (iv) Crucifixion (Romans 8:32; Hebrews 9:14).

   (v) Resurrection (Romans 1:3ff; 1 Peter 3:18).

   (vi) Ascension and Pentecost (John 14:15-17; 15:26).

4. The Trinity is seen as essential to the accomplishing of redemption and to its application:

- The summary of all the blessings of our redemption is expressed in trinitarian terms (Ephesians 2:18).

- The whole of the Christian life is marked by the reception of the name of, and involves personal fellowship with, the Trinity in baptism (Matthew 28:18-20).

- The plan and privileges of salvation are provided by the Trinity (Ephesians 1:4ff; 2 Thessalonians 2:13-14).

- The accomplishing of salvation is done by the Trinity (Romans 8:34; Titus 3:4-6; 1 Peter 1:2).

- The revelation in the gospel comes to us from the Trinity (1 Corinthians 2:1-10; 1 Thessalonians 1:4-6).

- The nature of fellowship with God is seen in trinitarian terms (2 Corinthians 13:14).

- The Christian life as kingdom-life is trinitarian (Romans 14:17-18).

- The Christian life as a life of sonship is the fruit of the work of the Trinity (Romans 8:9-17; Galatians 4:6).

- The Christian life as life in the Spirit is viewed within a trinitarian matrix (Ephesians 5:18-20).

- Sanctification involves the work of the Trinity (1 Corinthians 6:17-20).

- Ongoing faith depends on the Trinity (Jude 20-21).

- True worship is always trinitarian (Philippians 3:3).

- The unity and diversity of the church is grounded in the Trinity (1 Corinthians 12:3-6, 12-13).

- Worldwide evangelism is a trinitarian mission (Matthew 28:18-20).

- The consummation of all things will be the work of the Trinity (1 Corinthians 15:22-28; Philippians 3:21).

APPENDIX 2

'We Died to Sin
... He Died to Sin'

In Romans chapter 6 Paul states that by definition Christians have 'died to sin'.[1]

He speaks of Christ in similar terms: 'For the death he died he died to sin, once for all' (6:10).[2]

The meaning of the expression 'died to sin' is clearly an important key to interpreting this entire chapter. But what that meaning is has been much disputed throughout the history of the church.

As was noted in chapter 4 the challenge of understanding Paul's words is well illustrated by the comment of Dr D. Martyn Lloyd-Jones when he was asked when he would be willing to preach through Paul's letter to the Romans: 'When I have really understood chapter 6', he replied.[3] It was not until eleven years later that he preached two sermons on Romans 6. The following year he commenced his decade-long expositions of the whole epistle (from 7 October 1957 to 1 March 1968). There is little doubt that the turning point was his understanding of Paul's expression 'died to sin'.

A glance at various commentaries will show that Dr Lloyd-Jones' difficulties with Romans 6 were by no means unique. Over the

---

[1] Romans 6:2.

[2] All parenthetical references in this appendix are to Romans chapter 6 unless otherwise stated.

[3] D. M. Lloyd-Jones, *The New Man* (Edinburgh: Banner of Truth Trust, 1972), xi.

centuries Paul's teaching has challenged even the ablest and most careful exegetes.

'Died to sin'—the fact

The expressions 'died to sin' (6:2, 10) and 'dead to sin' (6:11) are found in Paul's writings *only* in Romans 6. Thus following the basic rule of interpretation that we should compare 'other places that speak more clearly'[1] on a subject has limited usefulness. It is doubtful, for example, whether Peter's apparently similar statement that 'Christ bore our sins in his own body on the tree *so that we might die to sins …*' (1 Pet. 2:24) sheds much light on what Paul means. For (1) Peter is speaking about something *we do* as a result of Christ's death; Paul is speaking about what *has been accomplished* once-for-all in and through Christ's death; and (2) Paul uses the singular 'sin' whereas Peter is speaking about multiple specific acts (sins).

Three things however should be noted:

(1) Paul uses the same expression ('died to sin') of both Christ and believers. Christ 'died to sin' (verse 10); and we also 'died to sin' (6:2). In the light of this, we must consider ourselves now to be 'dead to sin' (6:11).

(2) It is a general principle for interpreting Scripture that the same expression used in the same context ordinarily carries the same meaning, or at least a clearly analogous meaning.[2]

(3) There are contextual reasons for applying this principle in Romans 6:1-14. The driving logic of Paul's teaching here is: Whatever is said of believers is true of them because of their union with Christ

---

[1] The principle of interpreting difficult or unclear passages of Scripture recommended in *The Westminster Confession of Faith*, I.ix.

[2] Not all commentators adopt this principle in interpreting Romans 6. Thus for example C. E. B. Cranfield comments 'The expression … used in v. 2 … is now used in a quite different sense.' C. E. B. Cranfield, *A Critical and Exegetical Commentary on The Epistle to the Romans* (Edinburgh: T. & T. Clark Limited, 1975) 1, 314. This however is an arbitrary statement.

in what he has done. To express this the other way round, what was first true of Christ ('he died to sin, once for all' 6:10) will also be true of those united to him ('we … died to sin' 6:2). The identity resides in the fact that the only death to sin we have died is the death to sin we died in Christ's death to sin.

Paul's logic can therefore be expressed in a simple syllogism:

Major premise: We are united to Christ (6:3-5, 8).

Minor Premise: The Christ to whom we are united died to sin (6:10).

Conclusion: We died to sin in Christ's death to sin (6:2).

Our death to sin is, therefore, dependent on, intimately related to, and defined by Christ's death to sin. Paul unpacks this in the following way:

We died to sin (6:2-3) because we are united to Christ (6:5).

We therefore died with Christ in the death he died (6:8).

The death he died he died to sin (6:10).

Therefore as those united to him we are to think of ourselves as dead to sin and alive to God (6:10-11).

This integration of Christ's death and ours indicates that 'died to sin' has one basic meaning in both cases. Indeed, the only death to sin we have died is the one we have died in union with Christ in his death to sin.

'Died to sin'—in what sense?

Paul asks the Christians in Rome, 'Has your faith never grasped what your baptism proclaimed to it, namely that in union with Christ believers died to sin and therefore cannot live in it any longer?' But what does he mean?

Of the several interpretations of the expression 'died to sin' that have been held we will focus on three.[1]

---

[1] Cranfield characteristically provides a carefully articulated list, but as will be seen it is by no means exhaustive. He suggests that the possible interpretations

(1) The first is the view that 'died to sin' suggests the idea of immunity from sin, and that therefore, in some sense, Paul held a 'perfectionist' or idealist view of Christians in Christ. This view was expressed in the older standard scholarly commentary on the Greek text of Romans by W. Sanday and A. C. Headlam.[1] A few have adopted it, perhaps most notably in the twentieth century J. B. Phillips who rendered Paul's explanatory words 'one who has died has been set free from sin'[2] as: 'a dead man can safely be said to be immune to the power of sin'.[3] The vast majority of commentators reject this and similar interpretations, and for good reason. For the fact is that this can never 'safely be said' about the Christian. Not a few who have understood Paul in this way have tied themselves in spiritual knots trying to believe that it is true.

(2) An alternative exegesis, with a long history of support from noted New Testament interpreters, takes 'died to sin' as an essentially forensic statement: we are 'legally dead' to sin in the sense that our guilt has been dealt with. The expression therefore refers to our 'personal standing before God' not to any existential 'deliverance from sin'. Thus justification motivates sanctification.

---

would seem to be: (i) They died to sin in God's sight when Christ died; (ii) They died to sin in their baptism; (iii) They have been called and empowered to die to sin; (iv) They will die to sin finally when they die. In the present writer's view his delineation does not adequately include the interpretation which is adopted here.

[1] W. Sanday and A. C. Headlam, *A Critical and Exegetical Commentary on The Epistle to the Romans* (Edinburgh: T. & T. Clark, 1895), 155 where they 'interpret' Paul's words: 'In like manner do you Christians regard yourselves as dead, inert and motionless as a corpse, in all that related to sin'. Earlier they note: 'If more sin only means more grace, shall we go on sinning? Impossible. The baptized Christian cannot sin ... the Christian, united with Christ in his baptism, has done once for all with sin, and lives henceforth a reformed life dedicated to God.' They add: '[This at least is the ideal, whatever may be the reality.]' *ibid.*, 153. This hardly does justice either to the meaning of Paul's words or to his reliability as a teacher of the gospel.

[2] Romans 6:7.

[3] J. B. Phillips, *The New Testament in Modern English* (London: Geoffrey Bles, 1960), 319-320. J. B. Phillips' paraphrase was justly known for his wonderful ability to draw out the nuances of Paul's Greek, but this is one place where even Homer nods, possibly in this case under the influence of Sanday and Headlam.

In this sense Paul's argument would seem to be: Since you have been justified it would be inconsistent for you to live in sin. The death in view then is to sin's guilt, not to sin as power. Thus to say that 'Christ died *to sin*' is essentially synonymous with 'Christ died *for our sins*' and in that death we died to their guilt and condemnation.

The classic exposition of this position is found in Robert Haldane's commentary on Romans:

> The meaning of this expression ['died to sin'] is very generally misunderstood, and extended to include death to the *power* of sin, to which it has not the smallest reference. It exclusively indicates the justification of believers, and their freedom from the guilt of sin, having no allusion to their sanctification, which, however, as the Apostle immediately proceeds to prove, necessarily follows … Their justification he expresses by the term *dead to sin* …

A determining element for interpreters who hold this view tends to be that this is the only sense in which Paul could say that Christ 'died to sin' (6:10); i.e. that he died *for* sin. The sense in which we 'died to sin' must therefore be that we died in Christ's death for our sin. Thus when he comes to interpret the same phrase used of Christ later in the passage, Haldane writes:

> Our Lord never felt the power of sin, and therefore could not die to it. But He died to the *guilt* of sin—to the guilt of His people's sins, which he had taken upon Him; and they, dying with Him, as is above declared, die to sin precisely in the same sense in which he died to it. This declaration, then, that Christ *died to sin*, explains in the clearest manner the meaning of the expression 'dead to sin,' verse 2, proving that it signifies exclusively dying to the guilt of sin; for in no other sense could our Lord Jesus Christ die to sin.[1]

A similar view was later expounded by Haldane's gifted fellow countryman, the nineteenth-century biblical theologian George Smeaton. He argued for it on similar grounds that

[1] Robert Haldane, *Commentary on Romans* (1835; repr. London: Banner of Truth Trust, 1958), 251.

the only sense in which the Sinless One can be regarded as dying to sin, is that of dying to its guilt, or to the condemning power which goes along with sin ... He died to the guilt or criminality of sin, when it was laid on Him.[1]

Haldane has also been followed by Charles Hodge, and perhaps most vigorously in the modern era by John R. W. Stott.[2] He discusses Paul's words 'died to sin' at length and echoes the principle enunciated by Haldane and Smeaton:

There is only one sense in which it may be said that Jesus 'died to sin', and that is that he bore its penalty ... We too have died to sin, not in the sense that we have personally paid its penalty ... but in the sense that we have shared in the benefit of his death ... we are free from the awful burden of guilt and condemnation.[3]

(3) There is however a third view which merits consideration. It holds that while Christ did die *for* sins, he also died in a certain sense '*to* sin' that is to the power of sin or, better put, 'to Sin as a Power'. This is the view adopted without lengthy defence in chapter 4 on the basis that it is most consistent with the entire flow of Paul's thought at this point in Romans.

This view can be supported both negatively and positively. It is rooted in the Pauline understanding that the death of Christ should be regarded as multi-valent. He died *for* sins. But in that death he also died *to* the dominion of sin. In him therefore we have also died *to sin's reign* as well as its guilt, and are now set free from its dominion.

Two considerations, negative and positive, are important here:

---

[1] George Smeaton, *The Apostles' Doctrine of the Atonement* (1870; repr. Edinburgh: Banner of Truth Trust, 1991), 163.

[2] See his extensive discussion in J. R. W. Stott, *Romans—God's Good News for the World* (Downers Grove: InterVarsity Press, 1994), 169-174. Dr Stott originally articulated this same view in his influential *Men Made New, An Exposition of Romans 5-8* (London: Inter-Varsity Fellowship, 1966). 37-52.

[3] *The Cross of Christ* (Leicester: Inter-Varsity Press, 1986), 277.

(i) The second view above somewhat arbitrarily assumes that 'died to sin' must mean 'died for our guilt', 'bore its penalty' on the grounds that this is the only sense in which we can speak of Christ dying 'to' sin. Christ could not have died to sin in the sense of 'power' simply because he never came under its power.

The undergirding motivation in this argument is the (admirable) concern to avoid any suggestion that Christ himself sinned (the assumption being how else would he have come under sin's power?).

But against this view—

(*a*) If this is the case, why did Paul not employ his customary phraseology (*for sins*) to designate his customary theology? Why choose language that he uses nowhere else? It is more natural and logical to think that he *used* this startlingly different expression because he *meant* something different.

(*b*) In this context interpreters like Haldane and Smeaton assume that there cannot be any sense in which Christ came under the power of sin. But this does not take account of the fact that if Christ died he came under the power of death. He must therefore in some sense also have come under the power of sin, since 'sin reigned in death' (5:21). In addition Paul goes on to say that 'death *no longer* has dominion' over Christ (6:9), which seems to imply that it once did (however briefly). If so, then in an integrated sense sin must also have reigned in the dominion of death. The Innocent One was treated as guilty in order to bring pardon. The Author of Life came under the dominion of death to bring resurrection from it. The one in whom righteousness reigned entered the dominion of sin in death although it had no rights over him, and by his death to sin[1] he vanquished its authority. Now neither death nor sin has any dominion over him (6:9).

(ii) The second major consideration is that to understand 'Christ died to sin' and that in him we have also 'died to sin' in the sense

---

[1] Christ's death 'to sin' (*hē hamartia*) is a dative of disadvantage.

of dying to sin's reign or dominion, and not only for the guilt of sins, coheres with the flow of Paul's argument from Romans 5:12 onwards.

(*a*) Paul's concern in Romans 6 is with the believer's deliverance from sin, not from sins (plural) as guilt.[1] His focus is on deliverance from the dominion of sin:

> We are no longer *slaves* to sin (6:6, 17-18).
> Sin is no longer our *master* (6:14).
> We are *freed* from sin (6:18, 22, cf. 6:7[2]).

This language (slaves, master, freed) indicates that Paul's universe of discourse now is the slave market and not the law court. Or in theological terms he is dealing with freedom from the reign of sin, from our slavery to sin as a master, and not justification from the guilt of our sins—with deliverance, not with motivation only.

(*b*) This is further underlined by his personification of 'sin'. This usage is pervasive in the broader context of Romans 5:12-8:4. Sin (1) reigns as a king (*basileuein* to reign, 5:21; 6:12); (2) is a general in whose hands our various bodily members are weapons (*hopla*, instruments or weapons, 6:13); (3) exercises the dominion of a tyrant (*kurieuein*, to lord it over, dominate, dictate terms to, have dominion over, 6:14); (4) treats its subjects as a slave-master would

---

[1] Apart from other considerations Paul had already dealt with sins as guilt in 3:21-4:24 and the blessings of justification in 5:1-11.

[2] In 6:7 Paul's verb is *dikaioō*, usually associated with justification. But here it almost certainly carries the nuance of being delivered from a claim. Later in the passage he employs the standard verb for deliverance from bondage, *eleutheroō* in relation to sin (6:.18, 22), and the general context suggests that in verses 7, 18, and 22 parallel, if not identical, ideas are in view. David Brown employs the suggestive illustration of the use of the term 'justify' in Old Scots. Thus those judicially 'executed' at a certain spot in Edinburgh were said to be "justified at the Grassmarket'" (the place of public execution). D. Brown, *The Epistle to the Romans* (Edinburgh: T. & T. Clark, n.d.), 63. In view was not a declaration of their righteousness but that now that their debt had been paid they were delivered from all further claims on them. In 6:7, then, as John Murray and others suggest, 'the thought is, no doubt, that of being "quit" with sin' and expresses the 'decisive breach with the reigning power of sin'. *The Epistle to the Romans* (Grand Rapids: Eerdmans, 1960), i, 222.

(6:16, 17, 20); (5) is an employer whose wages are death (6:23); (6) and continues to be a lodger who has not been finally evicted (7:20).

In fact, in the course of chapter 6, Paul uses the word 'sin' preceded by the definite article (*hē hamartia*) more than a dozen times. While too much should not be made of this, yet when it is coupled with the variety of personifications he uses in the chapter, a case could be made out for highlighting his emphasis by translating 'The Sin' as though it were a multi-personalitied monster—which indeed is how Paul presents it.

The fact that Paul uses such unusual and striking phraseology here cannot be accidental. Given its uniqueness we should not therefore assume that the statement 'Christ died to sin' is synonymous with 'Christ died for our sins' or 'gave himself for our sins' (*huper tōn hamartiōn hēmōn*, 1 Cor. 15:3; Gal. 1:4). The prepositions are different; and in one instance the noun is consistently singular and in the other plural. The governing expressions are different ('*for* sins' and '*to* sin'). These are distinct but inseparable realities.

Of course, sins always bring guilt, but it is axiomatic in biblical teaching that individual sins are the result of bondage to sin.[1] That bondage cannot be dealt with by justification alone. If Paul was referring here only to justification his argument would be not that we have been 'set free from sin' (6:18, where *eleutheroō,* freedom in the ordinary sense of liberation from captivity is used), but that because we have been justified we are set free from the *guilt* of sins and therefore ought to set ourselves free from its *power* by relying on the Holy Spirit.

Paul goes to some length to unravel what happened when in Christ we 'died to sin'. Involved in this is the crucifixion of the old self with Christ (6:6). This statement also suggests that something additional to and distinct from, yet never separated from, justification takes place in union with Christ.

[1] John 8:34.

Death to sin and the dominion of sin

The Innocent One came under condemnation; the one who has life in himself voluntarily came under the dominion of death; and at the same time the Sinless One came under the dominion of sin. Sin's guilt, sin's dominion, and sin's penalty are inextricably linked. Christ cannot have died without allowing himself to come under sin's guilt, sin's reign, and sin's penalty. Having done all of this for us he is able to 'save to the uttermost those who draw near to God through him'.[1]

It would seem then that we ought to take Paul's expression 'died to sin' as teaching that Christ came under sin's dominion in order to destroy its reign. Here the famous axiom of Gregory Nazianzus is applicable, 'that which he has not assumed he has not healed'.[2] Only what has been accomplished in Christ is available to us. If Christ did not die to the dominion of sin then he cannot have provided resources to free us from its dominion, only from its guilt. This would provide motivation but not deliverance. But if indeed Christ died to the reign or dominion of sin, then so have those who are in Christ. They are no longer under sin's dominion—a point Paul makes explicitly (Rom. 6:14). Yes, we are no longer under the guilt of our sins because he died for them and rose for our justification. But we are also no longer under the bondage of sin because he died to it and rose again for our liberation.

There is then in the death of Christ 'the double cure' of which Augustus Montague Toplady taught the church to sing—from both 'its guilt and power'.[3]

---

[1] Hebrews 7:25.

[2] *Select Letters of Saint Gregory Nazianzus, Nicene and Post-Nicene Fathers*, eds., Philip Schaff and Henry Wace, second series, 7:51. The original context in Gregory is his critique of the Christology of Apollinarius.

[3] From the hymn by Augustus Montague Toplady (1740–78), 'Rock of Ages.' There has been long discussion as to the precise sense in which Toplady meant these words. I take them here in the sense of the reformed tradition to which he belonged rather than in the Wesleyan 'second blessing' sense.

This, however, does not mean we are already set free from its presence. We must continue to battle against it, just as Paul urges us to do in Romans 6:11-14. We need not fear that this teaching on dying to the dominion of sin leads to any kind of unrealistic quietism.[1]

We have already noted in the interests of fairness that highly respected commentators have held that Paul teaches that Christ died only to the guilt of sin. But equally in the interests of fairness we should note that the view adopted here (that in his death Christ came under the dominion of sin) is far from being a novelty, or in any sense idiosyncratic, as a catena of witnesses can testify. It is an interpretation with a substantial pedigree:

(i) James Fraser of Alness (1700–69) noted in the course of his remarkable exposition of Romans:

> Christ died unto sin, that is, he became free from the reign of sin. This implies, that our blessed Lord had been under the reign of sin ... sin exercises its reign in giving death. Now, Christ having put himself in the vice[2] of sinners, and bearing our sins in his own body on the tree, he was there, and then, under the reign of sin ... sin finding him in the vice, or place of sinners, and bearing their guilt, it reigned over him unto death ... he became free from the reign of sin, so that sin cannot, and death by virtue of sin cannot, any more reign, or have dominion over him.[3]

(ii) John Murray gives especially vigorous expression to this same view in his handling of Romans 6:2, 10. He argues first that it would

[1] Quietism views believers as *passive* rather than *vigorously active* in sanctification.
[2] That is, 'in the place of', from the Latin *in vice*.
[3] James Fraser, *A Treatise on Sanctification* (Edinburgh, 1774; repr. 1897), 70-71. The family history of Fraser (1700–69) breathes the spirit of the Scottish Covenanters. His father was imprisoned in Dunottar Castle, and then essentially given to George Scot (of Pitlochie) and then shipped by him to New Jersey. Set free, Fraser's parents then moved to New England and returned to Scotland following the Revolutionary Settlement in 1688. His *Treatise on Sanctification* was his response to John Locke's view of Romans 5 and 6, and contains a remarkable exposition of Romans 6-8.

be arbitrary to interpret Paul's use of the expression 'died to sin' (and the similar expression 'dead to sin' 6:2, 10, 11) in two different ways. He then notes that,

> as applied to believers in verses 2 and 11 the thought is that they died to the power of sin.

He goes on to explain the sense in which this may also be said of our Lord:

> May the same be said of Christ? It cannot be said of Christ that sin exercised its power over him in the same sense in which it ruled over us. We were the bond-slaves of sin in its defilement and power; sin did not thus rule over him. Nevertheless, Christ was identified in such a way with the sin which he vicariously bore that he dealt not only with its guilt but also with its power. Death ruled over him until he broke its power (vs. 9). So sin may be said to have ruled over him in that his humiliation state was conditioned by the sin with which he was vicariously identified. He was made sin (II Cor. 5:21), and sin as power must be taken into account in this relationship. It was by his own dying that he destroyed the power of sin, and in his resurrection he entered upon a state that was not conditioned by sin. There is good reason to believe that it is this victory over sin as power that the apostle has in view when he says that Christ died to sin once. And it is because Christ triumphed over the power of sin in his death that those united to him in his death die to the power of sin and become dead to sin (vss. 2, 11).[1]

Professor Murray was sufficiently convinced of the theological soundness of his view to reject the exegesis exemplified by Haldane and others. Thus the view that Paul refers

> exclusively to [Christ's] dying to the guilt of sin fails to take account of the leading thought of vss. 1-11. And it also misses an all-important aspect of our Lord's vicarious identification with sin and of the efficacy accruing to us from his victory over sin's power.[2]

[1] John Murray, *The Epistle to the Romans* (Grand Rapids: Eerdmans, 1960), 1, 225.
[2] *Ibid.*, 224-225, fn. 14.

(iii) Herman Ridderbos also gives support to this view:

Here again the thought is not that Christ died once 'for the sake of' or 'for the atonement of' sin (in the sense of justification or reconciliation) but that he once died to sin (considered as an authority that exercises power, asserts its claims), freed himself from it and escaped it by his death.[1]

(iv) D. Martyn Lloyd-Jones, to whom reference has already been made, gives expression to a general form of the view that 'sin' in Romans 6 refers to sin-as-power when he notes that the term 'died to sin'

means exactly what it means in verse 2, in verse 6, and in verse 7 … 'died to the realm and to the rule and to the reign of sin' … He [Christ] died to that whole relationship to sin into which He once put Himself voluntarily for our salvation. He has died unto it as a power, as something that reigns . . .[2]

(v) Douglas Moo similarly notes:

That other ruling power of the old age, sin, could be said to have had authority over Christ … he was subject to the power of sin.[3]

Objections

In perhaps the most sustained exposition of the view that Paul refers *only to the guilt of sin*, John Stott argues that to interpret 'died to sin' as a reference to freedom from the dominion of sin,[4]

---

[1] Herman Ridderbos, *Paul*, tr. J. R. de Witt (Grand Rapids: Eerdmans 1975) [Dutch, 1966], 208.

[2] *Op. cit.*, 103.

[3] Douglas Moo, *Romans* (Grand Rapids: Eerdmans, 1996), 379.

[4] Dr Stott focussed on this issue in at least three of his works over a period of some thirty years, first in his *Men Made New* (1966), and briefly in *The Cross of Christ* (1986), and more fully in *The Message of Romans* (1994). Although his views on Romans 7 underwent a significant development, the development in the exposition of chapter 6 seems to be limited to the recognition that there are other alternatives to his own view than the 'Higher Life' approach which clearly (and rightly) concerned him in *Men Made New*. This little book had a significance far greater

(*a*) does not seem to be the natural way to explain the link between sin and death in the expression 'died to sin'; and

(*b*) Does not cohere with the passage as a whole, since he notes:

> Nor in fact do Christian people seem to be altogether beyond the reign of sin, since we still need to be urged not to let it reign over us (12).[1]

In response, however, it may be said that, with respect to

(*a*) To understand Christ dying *for* sins as the only sense in which he may be said to have died *to* sin strikes us as a very *unnatural* way to explain Paul's two different expressions. Furthermore, while it would be appropriate to say that Christ died for our sins, nowhere does Paul suggest that as Christ died for our sins so we also died for our sins. In addition this criticism reverses Paul's concern here. He is not attempting to explain 'the link between sin and death' in general but the specific relation between Christ's death (and ours in him) and sin. And with respect to

(*b*) Since 'Don't steal!' does not necessarily imply that the person being addressed is stealing, it is just as appropriate for Paul to say 'Don't let sin reign' to the person over whom sin no longer reigns. To return to the illustration used in chapter 4: it is altogether appropriate to say to a person with new citizenship who has received 'call-up' papers from the government of his native land, 'Don't let them reign over you anymore!' Thus the command to refuse the reign of sin does not imply that the individual addressed is under its reign, but that it is his or her calling to resist its attempts to exercise that reign.

It is, of course, possible to quibble over which of the alternative expressions—'reign', 'power', 'rule', 'authority', 'dominion'—

---

than its one hundred pages of exposition might suggest to a casual reader. Its origin lay in the 'Bible Readings' or systematic expositions at the Keswick Convention in 1965. These are often viewed as marking the death-knell of any 'Higher Life Message' in the British Keswick movement.

[1] *The Message of Romans*, 172, fn. 111.

best expresses Paul's nuance in stating this position. But the verbs employed in Romans 5:12-6:14 (*basileuō* [5:21; 6:12] rule, reign over; *kurieuō* [6:14], lord it over, exercise dominion over, dictate terms to) suggest that the basic notion is the exercise of authority and dominion. Christ died to the dominion of sin under which he came in death. In Christ we participate in all that this means. If this participation brings us deliverance from the dominion of sin, that can only be true for us because it was first true of our sinless Lord. To express it in the bold words of Professor Murray: 'sin may be said to have ruled over him [Christ]'.[1] But he broke its dominion, and because we are united to him he has thereby broken its dominion over us.

Implications

What are the implications of this interpretation?

(1) The first is *Christological*. While this is not the main focus of the present study, it should not pass unnoticed. Growth in sanctification will always include a deepening appreciation of the person and work of the Lord Jesus Christ.

Our Lord Jesus Christ saw the cross as the hour when darkness reigned.[2] It was the time when to a deeper level he seems to have entered into the sphere in which sin and death ruled. This correlates with the appalling horror the passion proved to be to the sinless Son of God. It explains in part why the Gospel writers employ vivid and emotive language to describe our Saviour's experience: he 'began to be deeply distressed and troubled' and why his soul was 'overwhelmed with sorrow to the point of death'.[3] He was about to taste death not just as physical disintegration, but as the sphere of sin's reign. This gives substance to Luther's statement that 'No one ever feared death so much as this Man.'[4]

[1] *Op cit.*, 1, 225.

[2] Luke 22:53.

[3] Mark 14:33-34.

[4] Cited by C. E. B. Cranfield, *The Gospel according to St Mark* (Cambridge: Cambridge University Press, 1959), 431.

(2) The second implication is *soteriological*, and is drawn out by Paul in Romans 6. If, in union with Christ in his once-for-all death to the dominion of sin, we have died to sin's dominion, we are now free from its reign.

Only when we realize the proportions of this deliverance will Paul's imperatives strike home with their full force.[1] If sin's reign over us is ended, then we must not—indeed *cannot*—go on living as though we were still its subjects.[2] It now becomes irrational to use the body as if it were still the body in which sin reigned.[3] Since grace now reigns; sin shall not be our master![4]

If, then, for our sake, the Lord Jesus Christ died to the dominion of sin, the depth of the love displayed *by him* and the grace bestowed *through him*, as well as the resources provided *in him* for the deliverance of those who are under the dominion of sin, become immensely significant for us. This is why the meaning of his dying to sin ought not to be diluted simply because it may be in danger of being misunderstood.

We have noted that great and godly names can be cited in support of a different interpretation. We are called to develop the disposition of the Bereans who examined the Scriptures for themselves.[5] But perhaps enough has been said here to provide a solid exegetical and theological foundation for the view that in his death our Lord died to sin in the sense that he came under its dominion, and broke the power of that dominion in order that it might be broken in our lives. This view leads us into a fuller appreciation of the wonder of the grace which is ours in union with Christ, as chapter 4 seeks to show.

---

[1] Romans 6:11-14
[2] Romans 6:12
[3] Romans 6:13.
[4] Romans 6:14.
[5] Acts 17:11.

APPENDIX 3

The Conversion of Saul of Tarsus

Paul states that he would not have known sin had it not been for the law (Romans 7:7a). In his case it seems that the tenth commandment in particular had a role to play in his conversion to Christ ('You shall not covet'; Romans 7:7b).

Interpreters who hold that Paul is speaking of his own experience at this point in Romans 7 sometimes suggest that the reason this particular commandment had such a powerful effect on him was its distinctive *inwardness*—other commandments could be observed externally, but in its very nature the tenth commandment deals with internal desires. This, however, raises an important question: Would someone like Paul, schooled in the Old Testament, think of the other commandments as *merely external*? Was this the issue with both Paul and the Rich Young Ruler in the Gospels (Matthew 19:16-22)? Perhaps. But any reasonable reading of the Old Testament makes clear that the commandments of God were meant to reach to the heart, to the desires and motivations. Externalism in religion is just as sinful in the Old Testament as it is in the New.

A more nuanced answer is to be found in Paul's life. For the experience he describes here integrates well with Luke's narrative in Acts 6 and 7, and 8 and 9. It appears in the way he interweaves the lives of Stephen (whose presence dominates Acts 6, 7) and Saul (Paul) of Tarsus (whose presence dominates 8:1-3 and 9:1-31).

Saul of Tarsus was the outstanding young Jew in his circle of young Pharisees in Jerusalem. He tells us that he had advanced in Judaism 'beyond many of my own age among my people … extremely zealous was I for the traditions of my fathers' (Galatians 1:14). Here 'beyond many' is probably a euphemism for 'beyond everybody'. He viewed himself, after all, 'as to righteousness under the law, blameless' (Philippians 3:6).

The picture we are given here is of a young man who with respect to religious and spiritual development had no peer whose ability and giftedness he felt any need to covet. That is *until he encountered Stephen*.

We know nothing of Stephen's pre-history. He was one of the seven men chosen to deal with the tensions that arose between 'the Hellenists' and 'the Hebrews' in the Jerusalem church. All seven chosen to resolve the issue in connection with the distribution of mercy ministry have Greek names. They were 'Hellenists'. They were highly respected men ('of good repute, full of the Holy Spirit and of wisdom' Acts 6:3) apparently from the groups in which the complaints had first emerged (itself an interesting pastoral tactic!).

Stephen was one of these men. Indeed he stood out among them: 'full of grace and power, [he] was doing great wonders and signs among the people' (Acts 6:8).

A group from (probably) one particular synagogue 'rose up and disputed' with him:

> Then some of those who belonged to the synagogue of the Freed-men (as it was called), and of the Cyrenians, and of the Alexandrians, and of those from Cilicia and Asia, rose up and disputed with Stephen (Acts 6:9).

Just as in our large cities immigrant Christians often form ethnic churches, the same sociological pattern seems to have been true in the Jerusalem synagogues. The intriguing element in this narrative is that *this particular synagogue was probably the one with which Saul of Tarsus had associated.* It included 'those of Cilicia' (where Tarsus was located). The fact that Luke provides us with uniquely detailed membership information is surely not accidental. It is a clue to what follows. He tells us that 'they could not withstand the wisdom and the Spirit with which he [Stephen] was speaking' (Acts 6:10). What is Luke's agenda here? Even before he mentions Saul of Tarsus, Luke is introducing the first man in his peer group who was in every sense his superior.

Here was a man whose gifts and graces might evoke a deep, implacable envy in the young Pharisee! Despite being 'on the opposite side' Stephen was a man who had something Saul lacked but was worth coveting: grace, faith, wisdom, *and* the presence and power of the Spirit of the ancient prophets (Acts 6:5, 8, 10).

Here then is a clue to 'the goads' against which Saul kicked (Acts 26:14). Now, at last, the law was under his skin; irritation, aggravation, covetousness, opposition, and eventually persecution were all stimulated within. 'Sin came alive'—Saul died (Romans 7:9). It is a pattern that has been repeated many times in the long story of those who have been brought to faith in Christ. It is also an indication to us not to despair when we see someone becoming inexplicably hostile to the gospel or to Christians; God still uses a variety of 'goads' in order to awaken and then subdue. Quiet, faithful, humble, gracious Christian lives are among those 'goads'. What happened on the road to Damascus, and in the house in Straight Street, Damascus, had a significant pre-narrative.

APPENDIX 4

The Fourth Commandment

In almost any discussion of the role of the law in sanctification there is one commandment that causes considerable debate—the commandment on the Sabbath day (Exodus 20:8-11). It is certainly the commandment that seems to give evangelical Christians the greatest difficulty. Many, while holding that the other nine commandments remain in place, believe that the fourth commandment has ceased to have an obligatory role to play in the Christian life.

Here, more than anywhere else, any suggestion that there might be a *moral* commandment related to the way we use Sunday as a Christian Sabbath is likely to be described as 'legalism'.[1]

The debate here is both sensitive and important. On the one hand if we observe what God has not commanded us to do, we are at the very least in Paul's category of 'the weaker brother'.[2] And on the other hand if we *insist* that other Christians observe what God has not commanded, we are in danger of a form of legalism.

---

[1] In some ways this is the least helpful of criticisms because of the undifferentiated use of the term 'legalism'—what is meant by it in this context? And why would obedience to this commandment constitute 'legalism' whereas in the case of the other nine it would be commendable? If keeping the Sabbath day is 'legalism' this needs to be demonstrated theologically not simply announced arbitrarily.

[2] See his extended discussion in Romans 14:1–15:7. Notice the paradox in this context: those who would say they had a 'strong conscience' about observing days and not eating meat are described by Paul as 'weaker' Christians. The paradox is that such usually regard themselves as 'strong', not weak.

While we cannot in a brief appendix settle a dispute that has been extended through centuries, it may be helpful to some readers to note the following:

The biblical considerations appealed to in favour of dismantling the fourth commandment are several:

1. The New Testament sees the Sabbath commandment as a type of our rest in Christ. It is part of the law that has found its fulfilment in him. This is indicated by Paul's teaching in Romans 14:5 and hinted at in Colossians 2:16.

2. While the other nine commandments appear to be quoted or alluded to in one way or another in the New Testament, the fourth commandment is conspicuous by its absence.

3. While the other nine commandments are clearly of a moral nature, the Sabbath commandment is a ceremonial ordinance given to the old covenant people. Like all liturgical and ceremonial laws that were part of the Mosaic ordinances it is no longer applicable to the new covenant people.

To these considerations the following responses may be made:

1. What Paul refers to in Romans 14:5 and Colossians 2:16 is not the weekly Sabbath as such but the *application* of the *Sabbath principle*—i.e. the additional 'Sabbaths' or holy days in the Levitical law. While he regards these as no longer binding on Christians he does not regard their observance by Jewish Christians (and perhaps by others influenced by them) as a wholesale denial of the gospel— although he does see it as the sign of a 'weak brother' whose conscience has not been fully liberated by all the implications of the gospel.[1]

2. An argument can be made on the basis of the flow of 1 Timothy 1:8-11 that Paul includes the fourth commandment in his general thinking about the law of God:

[1] See, for example, the brief discussion in John Murray, *The Epistle to the Romans* (Grand Rapids: Eerdmans, 1959, 1965), 2, 257-259.

The law is laid down for the lawless and disobedient, for the ungodly and sinners, for:

> The unholy and profane
> Those who strike fathers and mothers (commandment 5)
> Murderers (commandment 6)
> Sexually immoral (commandment 7)
> Enslavers (commandment 8)
> Liars, perjurers (commandment 9)
> Whatever else is contrary to sound doctrine

Here there is clear and ordered reference to commandments five to nine. It is certainly arguable therefore that the reference to those who are 'unholy' and 'profane' has in view the breach of the fourth commandment since the Sabbath day was 'holy'.[1]

3. The fulfilment of this commandment in Christ does not mean that the law is now a dead letter. After all he fulfils not only the fourth commandment, but all of the commandments.

4. The fourth commandment summoned Israel to 'remember' the Sabbath day. It is natural to understand this as a reference back to a reality already in place (and rooted in Genesis 2:2-3) rather than referring to something altogether new in Moses' day.

5. The Exodus and the giving of the Law to govern new life in the Promised Land suggest a return to Eden. New creation echoes and restores original creation. In this latter context God made man as his image and gave him a Garden-Temple to expand to the ends of the earth.

The Cosmic Gardener worked for six days and rested on the seventh in order to provide a pattern for the Earth Gardener. So 'God ... *rested* on the seventh day ... So God *blessed* the seventh day and made it *holy*, because on it God rested from all his work that he had done in creation.'

---

[1] Cf. George W. Knight III, *The Pastoral Epistles—A Commentary on the Greek Text* (Grand Rapids: Eerdmans, 1992), 83-85, especially 84. Cf. Gen. 2:3.

This explains why the Exodus people knew of Sabbath days before the law was given.[1]

Thus, Sabbath is not, first of all, a redemptive ordinance but a creation ordinance that is shaped in Scripture to each major stage in biblical history (Adam to Moses; Moses to Christ; Christ to the end of history). As such it may now be 'de-Mosaicised' in certain respects, but it continues to be an integral part of God's pattern for his image, in creation, in typological redemption in the Mosaic ordinances, and in the fulfilment of his promise to give rest in Jesus Christ.

6. A further consideration here is rarely recognised. If there is no Sabbath, is the seven-day week simply an accident of history? Is there no divinely-planned rhythm to life? Often in this debate it is forgotten that the fourth commandment regulates not merely one day in the week but seven. It is actually a commandment about *work* as well as rest!

Should Christians have not only acquiesced but positively encouraged the proposal during the days of the French Revolution to move to a ten-day week? But if the concept of the week is an element in the structure of creation, we are bound to recognise the significance of the day of rest—and then to understand that the resurrection of Christ changed the day from the end of the week to the beginning and on this day the Lord's people sought to meet together. Many of them were not at liberty to choose which if any day in the week they might use for their own rest and refreshment since they were slaves. This advises us *both* that we should not under-read the significance of the Sabbath-Lord's Day, nor perhaps should we over-read how it was used by the earliest Christians.

---

[1] Exodus 16:22-26. It may be responded that there is no reference to the Sabbath day between Adam and Moses. There is nothing particularly surprising about this. The New Testament tells us that the early Christians met on the first day of the week, but this fact is almost entirely absent from the greater part of the New Testament. What happens regularly often goes without mention precisely for that reason.

7. There is a further general consideration here that rarely seems to enter the debate about the Decalogue, although it is important to it. Twice in his 'word of exhortation' the author of Hebrews cites Jeremiah 31:33:

> For this is the covenant that I will make with them
> after those days, declares the Lord:
> I will put my laws on their hearts,
> and write them on their minds.[1]

In the context of our discussion the question arises, '*which laws* does God put on the hearts of the people and write on their minds'? Presumably the author of Hebrews did not think this included the ceremonial and civil aspects of the law, since he is teaching believers outside the Promised Land that the ceremonies were all fulfilled in Christ.

Is this then merely a broad metaphor for the idea of obedience? To his first readers and hearers the most natural way to interpret his words was as a reference to the Decalogue. Was he therefore crossing his fingers behind his back hoping that they would all understand he meant that only nine of the laws would be written on their hearts?

Application

If the fourth commandment continues to be God's word for our blessing and for the shape of the Christian life, how is this relevant to our ongoing sanctification?

The Sabbath was not inaugurated at Mount Sinai but in the Garden of Eden. The giving of the Ten Commandments contained a deliberate echo of the pattern that God had given to Adam and Eve. He had worked for six days in bringing creation into being. They were his image—and therefore he made provision for them to imitate him. So he therefore 'blessed' the seventh day and set it apart from the other days (Gen. 2:1-3). It was not only the seventh day, it

[1] Cited in Hebrews 8:10; 10:16.

was the rest day—a day free from work; a day to bless and call holy, just as God himself had done—a day to reflect on and enjoy the wonders of God and to worship him for them.

The significance of this should not be missed. The gift of the Sabbath provided a wonderful way of regulating the whole of life. It provided an inbuilt weekly time-and-motion study to help us to live well.[1]

When the fourth commandment was given it was set within the context of the Exodus. It had, as at creation, a weekly application. But the seven-fold rhythm was extended further and applied to the whole of life in the regulation of the Sabbath years and every fifty years in the Sabbath-Sabbath Year of Jubilee. So there was a basic application of the commandment each week, and an extended application of it every seven years, and then in a major way every fifty years. Not only weeks but years were governed by this principle of working and looking forward to the time of rest.

But when Moses received the commandment at Sinai it was also a reminder that the people had been redeemed from their bondage in Egypt. Now it was a reminder of both creation and redemption. Yet something remained—whether in Eden or at Sinai the time of

---

[1] When Christians ask: 'Is it ok for me to do X on Sundays?' the first response should normally be not 'yes' or 'no' but 'Why would you be doing it?' The most common answer to that question is probably 'Because I don't have time for it in the rest of the week.' This highlights the importance of understanding the whole of the fourth commandment. The problem here is not how we spend Sunday; it is how we are using Monday to Saturday. We are living the week the wrong way round, as if there had been no resurrection! Use Sunday as a day of rest, worship, fellowship first and we will almost inevitably begin to discipline our use of time in the other six days of the week. Grasp this and the Sabbath principle becomes one of the simplest and most helpful of all God's gifts. The burden-free day at the beginning of the week both regulates the days that follow and refreshes us for them.

The Old Testament (perhaps to our surprise) tells us very little about how believers actually kept the Sabbath day. Its regulations were few and simple and focused on the twin principles of resting from work and delighting in the Lord. By either neglecting God's gift, or by going beyond Scripture in the way we regulate it, we may forfeit both rest and delight.

rest lay at the end of the week, and at the end of six years, and at the end of forty-nine years.

This was what the resurrection changed.

Although no commandment is given to this effect, and indeed the New Testament provides us with no extended explanation, it is a very remarkable phenomenon that Christians seem to have begun almost immediately to live life according to a different weekly rhythm. They met on the first day of the week, not the last day;[1] they called that day 'The Lord's day'. It was the day on which the Lord had risen, and the day on which he had gathered with them. What creation had looked forward to—the new creation in Christ; what the Exodus had pre-figured—the exodus that Jesus would accomplish in Jerusalem (Luke 9:31)—had now been realized. Now the new creation had been inaugurated—and it had a different calendar from the old. The Lord of the Sabbath had come; he had entered into his rest from his atoning labours; now he fulfilled his promise to give rest to the weary and heavy-laden who trusted in him.

Old covenant believers lived by faith looking forward to the dawning of the new age of restoration; new covenant believers live in the light of its dawning (1 Cor. 10:11), and in the power of the Spirit. So there is discontinuity; but there is also deep-seated continuity. We can put the big picture in the following way:

Creation covenant believers (Adam and Eve) had God's law clearly written in their hearts. In addition they were given a further commandment related not so much to God's character as to his activity in creation which they were to image: six days of work followed by one day of rest.

So they received God's law directly from God's hands.

---

[1] The reference to 'the first day of the week' in 1 Corinthians 16:2 is not because offerings should be calculated on Sundays *per se* but because this was the day Christians gathered. The offering in view here was the special collection Paul discusses in 2 Corinthians 8-9, not what churches today call 'the offering'.

Old (Sinaitic) covenant believers were sinners. Their understanding and their instincts were now distorted. In order for them to know God's will for his image-bearers they now needed to have his law given to them in writing. Further, they needed it to be expressed in a way that was appropriate for sinners ('You shall not …'). In addition, since for the time, until the coming of Christ, they were a single people group in a specific land, it was shaped to their particular national experience. They received the law in an appropriate way through Moses.

This leads us to the third stage. In the new covenant in Christ, with the promise of the Spirit at its centre, the law is now written in our hearts again by the Holy Spirit. In this sense, while Adam received the law from the hands of the Creator, and Israel received it from the hands of Moses, we now receive it from the hands of Jesus. The rhythm of our obedience is transformed. Unlike old covenant believers we are not waiting for the day of fulfilment—it has already come in Christ. Our Sabbath day is therefore changed from the last day to the first day (since we live the whole week in the light of the resurrection and in the presence of the risen Christ who has given us rest).

But if the day of fulfilment has come why would we need a Sabbath day? Because the day of fulfilment is not yet the day of final consummation. Yes, we have been raised with Christ, but he has not yet returned. Yes, we have died to sin, but sin has not yet died in us. Yes, we have been set free from bondage to the evil one, but we still live in the world he influences, deceives, and blinds. The Christian life is therefore marked by a new setting in time between the 'already' (Christ's death, resurrection, and Pentecost) and the 'not yet' (his return and our glorification with him). Using the first day of the week well, like using the other six days well, involves discipline and, yes, self-denial. That is written into the gospel we believe.

The Pharisees who entered into controversy with Jesus got all this disastrously wrong not only in relation to the fourth commandment but in relation to all of the commandments. Our Lord's teaching makes this crystal clear. They were not, and are not, to be trusted. We do not receive the law from the hands of the Pharisees but from the hands of the Lord Jesus. Because we are not yet set free from the presence of sin we will still find that our sinful wills can both twist and resist the commandments. In our fallen nature we often fail to keep them fully even while overall we find them our delight. It should no more surprise us that this is true of the fourth commandment than it is, say, of the commandment not to covet, or of Jesus' insistence that the seventh commandment has got to do with our eyes and our inner thoughts and desires and not only with outward actions.

Perhaps a simple if personal illustration will help here. I was brought up by devoted parents who—although they did not attend church until after I became a Christian in my early teens—made sure I 'kept the Sabbath day'. No work was done in the house; the idea that I would be allowed to go out to play was as remote as my flying to school! And so the Sabbath day was a day of prolonged misery; a real burden; a day of 'not doing'; not a day to which I looked forward.

I can still sense the transformation that took place in my experience of Sunday when I became a Christian. It was now no more of a burden than a bird's wings. Rather than crush me it seemed to sustain me. Boredom was gone. It became the best day of the week. And yet it was still Sunday; it was still the first day of the week. But the sense of duty in going to the church services which I had attended and the Bible reading which I had been doing for several years, believing that doing these things might make me a Christian—these seemed overnight to be transformed into a delight.

What was the explanation? Simple: we need to come to Christ to find true Sabbath rest. For then God writes his law into our hearts by the Holy Spirit. Then at last we receive the law from the hands of the one who came to bring us forgiveness and power, and no longer from the hands of the Pharisees. Then we can 'call the Sabbath a delight' (Isaiah 58:13).

APPENDIX 5

The 'Blueprint Passages'

---

(1) *1 Peter 1: 1-25*

Peter, an apostle of Jesus Christ,

To those who are elect exiles of the Dispersion in Pontus, Galatia, Cappadocia, Asia, and Bithynia, according to the foreknowledge of God the Father, in the sanctification of the Spirit, for obedience to Jesus Christ and for sprinkling with his blood:

May grace and peace be multiplied to you.

Blessed be the God and Father of our Lord Jesus Christ! According to his great mercy, he has caused us to be born again to a living hope through the resurrection of Jesus Christ from the dead, to an inheritance that is imperishable, undefiled, and unfading, kept in heaven for you, who by God's power are being guarded through faith for a salvation ready to be revealed in the last time. In this you rejoice, though now for a little while, if necessary, you have been grieved by various trials, so that the tested genuineness of your faith—more precious than gold that perishes though it is tested by fire—may be found to result in praise and glory and honor at the revelation of Jesus Christ. Though you have not seen him, you love him. Though you do not now see him, you believe in him and rejoice with joy that is inexpressible and filled with glory, obtaining the outcome of your faith, the salvation of your souls.

Concerning this salvation, the prophets who prophesied about the grace that was to be yours searched and inquired carefully, inquiring what person or time the Spirit of Christ in them was indicating when he predicted the sufferings of Christ and the subsequent glories. It was revealed to them that they were serving not themselves but you, in the things that have now been announced to you through those who preached the good news to you by the Holy Spirit sent from heaven, things into which angels long to look.

Therefore, preparing your minds for action, and being sober-minded, set your hope fully on the grace that will be brought to you at the revelation of Jesus Christ. As obedient children, do not be conformed to the passions of your former ignorance, but as he who called you is holy, you also be holy in all your conduct, since it is written, "You shall be holy, for I am holy." And if you call on him as Father who judges impartially according to each one's deeds, conduct yourselves with fear throughout the time of your exile, knowing that you were ransomed from the futile ways inherited from your forefathers, not with perishable things such as silver or gold, but with the precious blood of Christ, like that of a lamb without blemish or spot. He was foreknown before the foundation of the world but was made manifest in the last times for the sake of you who through him are believers in God, who raised him from the dead and gave him glory, so that your faith and hope are in God.

Having purified your souls by your obedience to the truth for a sincere brotherly love, love one another earnestly from a pure heart, since you have been born again, not of perishable seed but of imperishable, through the living and abiding word of God; for

> 'All flesh is like grass
> and all its glory like the flower of grass.
> The grass withers,
> and the flower falls,
> but the word of the Lord remains forever.'

And this word is the good news that was preached to you.

(2) *Romans 12:1-2*

I appeal to you therefore, brothers, by the mercies of God, to present your bodies as a living sacrifice, holy and acceptable to God, which is your spiritual worship. Do not be conformed to this world, but be transformed by the renewal of your mind, that by testing you may discern what is the will of God, what is good and acceptable and perfect.

(3) *Galatians 2:20*

I have been crucified with Christ. It is no longer I who live, but Christ who lives in me. And the life I now live in the flesh I live by faith in the Son of God, who loved me and gave himself for me.

(4) *Romans 6:1-14*

What shall we say then? Are we to continue in sin that grace may abound? By no means! How can we who died to sin still live in it? Do you not know that all of us who have been baptized into Christ Jesus were baptized into his death? We were buried therefore with him by baptism into death, in order that, just as Christ was raised from the dead by the glory of the Father, we too might walk in newness of life. For if we have been united with him in a death like his, we shall certainly be united with him in a resurrection like his. We know that our old self was crucified with him in order that the body of sin might be brought to nothing, so that we would no longer be enslaved to sin. For one who has died has been set free from sin. Now if we have died with Christ, we believe that we will also live with him. We know that Christ, being raised from the dead, will never die again; death no longer has dominion over him. For the death he died he died to sin, once for all, but the life he lives he lives to God. So you also must consider yourselves dead to sin and alive to God in Christ Jesus.

Let not sin therefore reign in your mortal body, to make you obey its passions. Do not present your members to sin as instruments for unrighteousness, but present yourselves to God as those who have been brought from death to life, and your members to God as instruments for righteousness. For sin will have no dominion over you, since you are not under law but under grace.

(5) *Galatians 5:16-17*

But I say, walk by the Spirit, and you will not gratify the desires of the flesh. For the desires of the flesh are against the Spirit, and the desires of the Spirit are against the flesh, for these are opposed to each other, to keep you from doing the things you want to do.

(6) *Colossians 3:1-17*

If then you have been raised with Christ, seek the things that are above, where Christ is, seated at the right hand of God. Set your minds on things that are above, not on things that are on earth. For you have died, and your life is hidden with Christ in God. When Christ who is your life appears, then you also will appear with him in glory.

Put to death therefore what is earthly in you: sexual immorality, impurity, passion, evil desire, and covetousness, which is idolatry. On account of these the wrath of God is coming. In these you too once walked, when you were living in them. But now you must put them all away: anger, wrath, malice, slander, and obscene talk from your mouth. Do not lie to one another, seeing that you have put off the old self with its practices and have put on the new self, which is being renewed in knowledge after the image of its creator. Here there is not Greek and Jew, circumcised and uncircumcised, barbarian, Scythian, slave, free; but Christ is all, and in all.

Put on then, as God's chosen ones, holy and beloved, compassionate hearts, kindness, humility, meekness, and patience, bearing with one another and, if one has a complaint against another, forgiving each other; as the Lord has forgiven you, so you also must forgive. And above all these put on love, which binds everything together in perfect harmony. And let the peace of Christ rule in your hearts, to which indeed you were called in one body. And be thankful. Let the word of Christ dwell in you richly, teaching and admonishing one another in all wisdom, singing psalms and hymns and spiritual songs, with thankfulness in your hearts to God. And whatever you do, in word or deed, do everything in the name of the Lord Jesus, giving thanks to God the Father through him.

(7) *Romans 8:13*

For if you live according to the flesh you will die, but if by the Spirit you put to death the deeds of the body, you will live.

(8) *Matthew 5:17-20*

Do not think that I have come to abolish the Law or the Prophets; I have not come to abolish them but to fulfill them. For truly, I say to you, until heaven and earth pass away, not an iota, not a dot, will pass from the Law until all is accomplished. Therefore whoever relaxes one of the least of these commandments and teaches others to do the same will be called least in the kingdom of heaven, but whoever does them and teaches them will be called great in the kingdom of heaven. For I tell you, unless your righteousness exceeds that of the scribes and Pharisees, you will never enter the kingdom of heaven.

(9) *Hebrews 12:1-14*

Therefore, since we are surrounded by so great a cloud of witnesses, let us also lay aside every weight, and sin which clings so closely, and let us run with endurance the race that is set before us, looking to Jesus, the founder and perfecter of our faith, who for the joy that was set before him endured the cross, despising the shame, and is seated at the right hand of the throne of God.

Consider him who endured from sinners such hostility against himself, so that you may not grow weary or fainthearted. In your struggle against sin you have not yet resisted to the point of shedding your blood. And have you forgotten the exhortation that addresses you as sons?

> My son, do not regard lightly the discipline of the Lord,
>   nor be weary when reproved by him.
> For the Lord disciplines the one he loves,
>   and chastises every son whom he receives.

It is for discipline that you have to endure. God is treating you as sons. For what son is there whom his father does not discipline? If you are left without discipline, in which all have participated, then you are illegitimate children and not sons. Besides this, we have had earthly fathers who disciplined us and we respected them. Shall we not much more be subject to the Father of spirits and live? For they disciplined us for a short time as it seemed best to them, but he disciplines us for our good, that we may share his holiness. For the moment all discipline seems painful rather than pleasant, but later it yields the peaceful fruit of righteousness to those who have been trained by it.

Therefore lift your drooping hands and strengthen your weak knees, and make straight paths for your feet, so that what is lame may not be put out of joint but rather be healed. Strive for peace with everyone, and for the holiness without which no one will see the Lord. See to it that no one fails to obtain the grace of God; that no 'root of bitterness' springs up and causes trouble, and by it many become defiled; that no one is sexually immoral or unholy like Esau, who sold his birth right for a single meal. For you know that afterward, when he desired to inherit the blessing, he was rejected, for he found no chance to repent, though he sought it with tears.

(10) *Romans 8:29*

For those whom he foreknew he also predestined to be conformed to the image of his Son, in order that he might be the firstborn among many brothers.

Books by Sinclair B. Ferguson published by the Trust

A Heart for God

Child in the Manger: The True Meaning of Christmas

Children of the Living God

Deserted by God?

Discovering God's Will

From the Mouth of God: Trusting, Reading, and Applying the Bible

Grow in Grace

Healthy Christian Growth

Heroes of the Faith

Icthus: Jesus Christ, God's Son, the Saviour (co-author Derek Thomas)

John Owen on the Christian Life

Let's Study Ephesians

Let's Study Mark

Let's Study Philippians

Man Overboard! The Story of Jonah

Read Any Good Books?

Sermon on the Mount

The Christian Life: A Doctrinal Introduction

The Pundit's Folly: Chronicles of an Empty Life

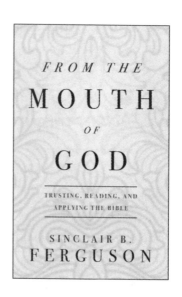

From the Mouth of God
Trusting, Reading, and Applying the Bible

Sinclair B. Ferguson

THE BIBLE—

Why should we believe—as Jesus did—that it is 'the mouth of God'?

When did it come into existence?

Is it inerrant?

What do we need to learn in order to understand it better?

How does its teaching change our lives?

In *From the Mouth of God*, Sinclair B. Ferguson answers these and other important questions about trusting, reading, and applying the Bible.

For me, I'm still living off the first two pages of the introduction, where Sinclair briefly expanded upon his choice of title, From the Mouth of God. *The Bible is the mouth of God. Pause. Pause longer. Repeat. The Bible is the mouth of God. That totally changes the way I open it, read it, and hear it. I hope it will do the same for you.*
—Dr David Murray

ISBN 978 1 84871 242 3 | 224 pp. | paperback

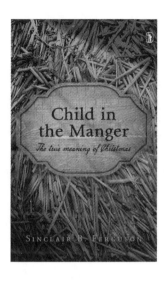

Child in the Manger
The True Meaning of Christmas
Sinclair B. Ferguson

What is Christmas really all about? Does it actually have any 'meaning'?
Child in the Manger—The True Meaning of Christmas sets out to explore
that question. When we find the answer we realise that it isn't only for
Christmas time. These pages are an invitation to explore
what that meaning is.

This small book would make an excellent gift.

ISBN 978 1 84871 655 1 | 216 pp. | small clothbound

About the Publisher

The Banner of Truth Trust originated in 1957 in London. The founders believed that much of the best literature of historic Christianity had been allowed to fall into oblivion and that, under God, its recovery could well lead not only to a strengthening of the church, but to true revival.

Inter-denominational in vision, this publishing work is now international, and our lists include a number of contemporary authors along with classics from the past. The translation of these books into many languages is encouraged.

A monthly magazine, *The Banner of Truth*, is also published and further information will be gladly supplied by either of the offices below or from our website.

THE BANNER OF TRUTH TRUST

3 Murrayfield Road
Edinburgh, EH12 6EL
UK

PO Box 621, Carlisle
Pennsylvania, 17013
USA

www.banneroftruth.org